Christopher Knight worked i ... thirty years, specializing in co ... His writing career began almo ... years conducting research into ... he has written four books on the subject co-authored with Robert Lomas. His first book, *The Hiram Key* was published in 1996 and it immediately went into the UK top ten bestseller list and remained in the list for eight consecutive weeks. It has since been translated into 37 languages and sold over a million copies worldwide, becoming a bestseller in several countries. He now divides his time between marketing consultancy and historical research for writing books.

Alan Butler qualified as an engineer, but was always fascinated by history, and made himself into something of an expert in astrology and astronomy. Since 1990 he has been researching ancient cultures, pagan beliefs and comparative religion and has published several successful books on such topics as the Knights Templar and the Grail legend. He is also a published playwright and a successful radio dramatist.

Christopher Knight and Alan Butler have written two successful books together, *Civilization One* and *Who Built the Moon?*

By the same authors

Previous books by Christopher Knight
(co-authored with Robert Lomas)
The Hiram Key
The Second Messiah
Uriel's Machine
The Book of Hiram

Previous books by Alan Butler
The Bronze Age Computer Disc
The Warriors and the Bankers
The Templar Continuum
The Goddess, the Grail and the Lodge
The Virgin and the Pentacle
Sheep

By Christopher Knight and Alan Butler
Civilization One
Who Built the Moon?

THE
HIRAM KEY
REVISITED

FREEMASONRY: A PLAN FOR A NEW WORLD ORDER

CHRISTOPHER KNIGHT & ALAN BUTLER

WATKINS PUBLISHING
LONDON

First published in hardback as Solomon's Power Brokers
in the UK and USA 2007 by
Watkins Publishing, Sixth Floor, Castle House,
75–76 Wells Street, London W1T 3QH

This edition published 2010

1 3 5 7 9 10 8 6 4 2

Designed and typeset by Jerry Goldie

Printed and bound by Imago in China

British Library Cataloguing-in-Publication Data Available

Library of Congress Cataloging-in-Publication Data Available

ISBN: 978-1-907486-13-5

www.watkinspublishing.co.uk

Distributed in the USA and Canada by Sterling Publishing Co., Inc.
387 Park Avenue South, New York, NY 10016-8810

For information about custom editions, special sales, premium and
corporate purchases, please contact Sterling Special Sales
Department at 800-805-5489 or specialsales@sterlingpub.com

*This Book is dedicated to the memory of Earl William Sinclair,
builder of Rosslyn Chapel and creator of Freemasonry.*

ACKNOWLEDGEMENTS

Directly and indirectly many people have assisted us in the creation of this book and we thank them all. However we'd like to offer specific thanks to the following:

- Our partners, Caroline Knight and Kate Butler, for their patience and forebearance, and Kate for her efforts with the Index.
- Our publisher Michael Mann, who guides and advises but never cajoles.
- Peter Bently, whose incredible editing of this book has taken him well above and beyond the call of duty.
- John Ritchie, both for his permission to employ written material on Rosslyn Chapel and the excellent photographs he also allowed us to use.
- We would also like to offer thanks to Prof. Philip Davies, Dr Jack Millar and Prof. James Charlesworth.

Contents

TEXT ILLUSTRATIONS

All illustrations have been created, photographed or, where it is a generic heraldic design, manipulated by the authors unless otherwise stated.

PLATES

Plate 1. Clairvaux Abbey, Champagne, the headquarters of St Bernard of Clairvaux – Alan Butler.

Plate 2. Rosslyn Chapel as it appeared in 1917 – courtesy of Peter Stubbs, Edinburgh.

Plate 3. The ruins of the former St Matthew's Chapel, now standing in a cemetery close to the present Rosslyn Chapel – courtesy of John Ritchie.

Plate 4. Contemporary picture of St Bernard of Clairvaux, now to be seen in the treasury of Troyes Cathedral, together with relics of St Bernard's skeleton – Alan Butler.

Plate 5. Troyes Cathedral in Champagne, France. Troyes was the headquarters of the Star Families from the 11th to the 14th century – Alan Butler.

Plate 6. The East Window of Rosslyn Chapel with the light box clearly shown in the point of the arch – courtesy of John Ritchie.

Plate 7. The interior of the Rosslyn light box is highly reflective, as is demonstrated here when a high-powered torch was shone into the aperture – courtesy of John Ritchie.

Plate 8. A five-pointed star or pentacle, carved into the fabric of a church in Yorkshire, England. This 15th-century example proves conclusively that the pentacle was often used as a Christian symbol – Alan Butler.

Plate 9. Is this a representation in stone of the Holy Shekinah in her guise as an angel? – courtesy of John Ritchie.

Plate 10. This carving from Rosslyn Chapel is said to depict a Masonic-style initiation, at a time before Freemasonry even existed! – courtesy of John Ritchie.

Plate 11. Examples of botanical carving within Rosslyn Chapel. Depicted here is some form of aloe or cactus – courtesy of John Ritchie.

Plate 12. The South Porch of Rosslyn Chapel – courtesy of John Ritchie.

Plate 13. A very rare carving from Rosslyn – this one depicting a Green Woman – courtesy of John Ritchie.

Introduction

What had just happened to me, I asked myself? The evening had started entirely normally but then I had been stripped of my clothes and dressed in virtual rags. My valuables had been taken and I was then hustled forward by men on either side, each with a tight hold on my upper arm.

As soon as I had stepped into the room I had been blind – the darkness was near total. Yet I could sense the large group of people around me – the odd creak of a chair, a small cough, the occasional shuffle of feet. My guides walked me for quite a distance from point to point with questions being fired at me from time to time.

Then my minders pulled me to a halt and relaxed their grip. A figure suddenly moved close in front of me. Even though my eyes had by now adjusted to the gloom I couldn't make out his face but he seemed to be very tall and he began to tell me a story – something about an ancient builder and a Temple in Jerusalem.

The words made no sense to me and I had closed my eyes for a second or two. I opened them again just in time to catch a glimpse of something moving quickly out of the darkness towards me and I felt a glancing blow crack down on my cheek. Before I could blink, hands grabbed at me – pushing me down onto one knee. I recovered my footing and quickly received a second blow and then a third hit me square in the forehead. I was pulled down before being wrapped in a sheet by many unseen hands.

At this point I definitely felt like I was in some bizarre dream, as funereal organ music filled the air and countless footsteps seemed to be circling around my prostrate body. It all stopped suddenly after a minute or so and the cloth was peeled back from my face. A man took my hand out of the shroud and tried to pull me up but I fell back as the hand slipped away. Another attempted to raise me but failed – then I felt a powerful hand take firm grip around my right wrist and I was yanked to a standing position.

Suddenly the light increased a little. Everything was in monochrome but thanks to a star-shaped beam of light above the shoulder of my attacker I could take in the dozens of faces that filled the windowless room. The man in front pointed behind me and told me to turn and look at the spot where I had been lying. There, by the light of the single star, I could just make out a small cluster of objects. At first I could not recognize them but as I stared in the half-light I could make out a human skull and some bones of some long-decomposed cadaver.

The ritual was now finished and I dressed myself once again in my black suit and tie and joined the celebrations with my brothers, for the world now had one more Master Mason. As of that moment I was a fully qualified Third Degree Freemason.

Now, at last, I was permitted to ask my fellow Masons to explain all three rituals I had endured over the preceding six months. 'This is going to be interesting,' I told myself.

That was in September 1976. Thirty years have now passed since I walked out of the Masonic Temple wearing the small leather apron of a Master Mason given to me under the authority of the United Grand Lodge of England. I was brimming over with curiosity and enthusiasm – but I had no inkling at all as to just how much the proceedings of that evening were going to change my life.

To be honest, I had joined 'the Craft' in the first place as a matter of simple nosiness. I wanted to know what these men did behind closed doors that had given rise to all kinds of rumours. I knew that Freemasonry was a secretive fraternal order found mainly in Europe and those areas of the globe where the British Empire or its offspring, the American 'empire', had ever had influence. But was it the benign organization it seemed to be or did it have a covert agenda as critics sometimes suggest?

As a young Master Mason it slowly dawned upon me that none of the importantly titled Freemasons had a clue as to what the rituals were really about. They would have a meal and plenty of beer after the evening's ritual was over and compliment each other on the 'sincerity' with which they had delivered the memorized mumbo-jumbo – but there was never any discussion about what it all meant or where it came from.

From Calcutta to Calgary and Canberra to Cape Town, men dressed in splendid – if somewhat oddball – regalia meet in windowless rooms to perform arcane rituals in word-perfect manner without understanding why. The rituals are passed on from generation to generation, word for word – but for what?

Like every candidate for the Third Degree, I was made to act out the role of Hiram Abif, the man who is said to have been the architect of King Solomon's Temple in Jerusalem nearly 3,000 years ago. The legend tells how his own workmen attacked Hiram because they wanted to extract a great secret from him. The architect refused to give them the unspecified secret and was killed by the third of three blows to the head.

I began my personal investigation into the origins of Freemasonry as soon as I realized that no answers to my various questions existed. As the years of research rolled on and I started to uncover some tantalizing facts, I began to think that a book written about it might be of interest to at least a few people. I enlisted the help of a fellow Freemason, Robert Lomas, and several years later the result was finally published under the title *The Hiram Key*.

One man who read that book was Alan Butler, and he saw immediate parallels with his own research. Alan made contact and we began a process of sharing our deepest findings into the origins of Freemasonry and the extraordinarily ancient science that we found lies behind it.

Alan and I have now been conducting research jointly for the last ten years. This is our third book together and it is the one that goes right back 3,000 years to tell the full story of a group of hereditary super-priests from Jerusalem who set out to change the world. *The Hiram Key* was the book that uncovered the ancient heritage behind Freemasonry but, inevitably, it raised far more questions than it provided answers.

The task we have set ourselves in this book is to investigate deeper and wider in order to piece together, step by step, the progress of an ancient priesthood, which according to Masonic ritual was established by King Solomon. These people were almost a cult within a cult – Jews with a secret knowledge of the movements of a blazing star they called the Shekinah. This brilliant astronomical wonder lit up the pre-dawn sky of Jerusalem at the dedication of Solomon's Temple and appeared again at propitious occasions heralding great events – including the birth of the promised Messiah a millennium later.

The mark of these secretive power brokers – whom we call 'the Star Families' – was two equilateral symbols overlaid one upon the other to form a six-pointed star, a device which, as we will explain in Chapter 1, precisely describes the latitude of Jerusalem in astronomical terms.

This symbol of the Star Families remained unseen by the outside world until the moment when the armies of Europe were induced, through Star Family influence, to march on Jerusalem and recapture from the Muslims the sacred city from which the families had been expelled centuries earlier, under Roman rule. It was then a device used by the military wing of the Star Families – the Knights Templar. Today it is an important piece of imagery for Freemasonry and it has been adopted (after much debate) by the state of Israel.

In the following chapters we will discover how Solomon's power brokers have influenced and even directed the development of the Western world by infiltrating the Roman Catholic Church and national governments. Our investigation uncovers audacious and breathtaking powerplay from the time of Solomon's Temple in Jerusalem to George W Bush's White House in Washington DC.

We start with the beginning of all Judaeo-Christian ritual and myth – the Book of Genesis. And we finish by considering the enormity of the potential end game, which appears to be very close to its dramatic conclusion.

Christopher Knight,

CHAPTER 1

In the Beginning

The biography of God is not all sweetness and light

In the beginning, according to the Book of Genesis, God created all of heaven and earth before making the seas, the land, plants and animals and eventually humans. The sequence in which he performed his acts of creation varies according to different Old Testament traditions but we do know two very important facts about God from verse 26 of Genesis, where he says, 'Let us make man in our image, after our likeness'. This tells us that, according to Genesis, God was, in appearance at least, a man – and since God uses the word 'we', so apparently were his colleagues.

Today, most Jews and Christians fully accept the scientific view that the universe is many billions of years old and that humans evolved into their present form around 115,000 years ago. It therefore follows that a truly gigantic period of time elapsed between the creation of the heavens and the earth and the making of Adam and Eve. Even after the first humans arrived it would be more than another 110,000 years before God can definitely be identified as interacting with the creatures that looked like him.

Whilst there are many references to God in the Bible suggesting that he spoke with, and directed, such Middle Eastern figures as Noah, Enoch and Abraham, it is generally accepted by biblical scholars that these were traditions concerning a variety of deities that were welded together by the people who first wrote down the Old Testament a millennium or two later.

Of these stories, the earliest account of Yahweh actually appearing on Earth was around 3,500 years ago. Here he was the tribal deity of a small clan of metalworking people who lived in the mountains of the Sinai Peninsula, that triangular region of desert that has the Mediterranean Sea to the north, the Gulf of Suez to the west and the Gulf of Aqaba to the East. It is a remote and inhospitable place with few resources other than the scattering of precious stones and minerals that had been mined there since early in the ancient Egyptian dynastic period. Life must have been hard for the clan known as the Kenites, who scoured the arid mountains and rolling sand dunes for minerals from which to extract the metals with which they so famously worked. The Old Testament speaks of their great skill in the art of working both iron and bronze for many purposes, especially the manufacture of musical instruments.

The Kenites took their name from the belief that they were descended from Kain (Cain), the son of Adam and Eve, and their god was Yahweh, who was considered to be a storm deity of the mountains of the Sinai.

Moses and the Exodus

Life must have been very quiet for the Kenites and one can only imagine that these isolated tribesmen must have been greatly surprised when they saw an endless column of people heading towards them across and around the tightly packed, jagged peaks of rock that rise more than a mile and a half above the surrounding sea. These strangers explained how they had escaped from captivity in Egypt and crossed right through the waters of the River Nile under the leadership of an 80-year-old ex-army general called Moses.[1]

However, Moses himself was no stranger to the Kenites. They knew him well because he had previously worked for them as a shepherd for no less than 40 years. This bearded wanderer had originally been a clean-shaven general in the Egyptian army and an important member of the royal court until he had committed a murder and gone on the run in the Sinai desert. Moses had married Zipporah, the daughter of Reuel, who was the

'Jethro', or high priest and leader of the Kenites. Moses and his brother Aaron had also been initiated into the priesthood of the Kenites and had begun to worship their god, Yahweh.

At some point Moses left his people and climbed up the largest mountain in the Sinai. There he had a meeting with that master of storms, Yahweh. The deity presented the old soldier with a number of instructions for life, including what we know today as the Ten Commandments. However, the relationship between God and Moses was not always an easy one. On one occasion his wife, Zipporah, had to rescue Moses (and, according to some biblical scholars, their eldest son Gershom) from an attack carried out by Yahweh who had, for reasons unknown, decided to kill him.

Moses announced that his mobile nation was to continue on its journey, taking the Kenite god with it in a specially constructed box called the 'Ark of the Covenant'. The plan was to head in a vaguely northeasterly direction in search of a land that Yahweh had promised them. The problem was that hundreds of tribes of Canaanites already occupied the land.

The box in which they carried God was entirely Egyptian in design. It was made of *shittim* wood, or acacia – the only tree that grows to any size in the arid sands of this desert region – and upon it sat two gold-covered effigies of winged sphinxes. When God had conversations with Moses the divine voice would emanate from the box between these two gilded carvings.

The band of Hebrew escapees from Egypt continued their journey with the deity, that had manufactured the entire universe, safe inside the little box, which had been constructed with four extended poles so that it could be carried over the difficult terrain that confronted the Hebrews. Yahweh effectively took over the leadership of the column, dictating the pace to his carriers by making himself impossibly heavy when he wanted them to stop, and lighter when he wished to go faster.

As the people of the Exodus travelled through the desert the Ark was carried a safe 2,000 cubits (over half a mile) ahead of the main party. And, according to ancient tradition, we are told that Yahweh would clear a safe pathway for the nation by burning snakes, scorpions and thorns with two jets of fire as though there were flamethrowers slung from the undercarriage of the gold-plated Ark.

Unfortunately for the followers of Moses their new god was prone to fits of ill temper. For example, when Moses' nephews Nadav and Avihu used a non-approved source to ignite a fire to offer a burned sacrifice to Yahweh they were immediately consumed by a bolt of flame that, according to the Old Testament, was fired by Yahweh from inside his box. Yahweh continued to be easily annoyed. Priests who cared for the Ark had to think about every move, as even looking at the box at an improper time would result in immediate immolation in a ball of flames.

A Planned Return?

In our view, the Israelites' 40-year journey to the land of Canaan was not an accidental event; rather than a spontaneous escape from Egyptian slavery, it was almost certainly a planned return to an old homeland.

It is now known that around 200 years before the Exodus, weather conditions had suddenly changed and the land of Canaan had been baked dry by soaring temperatures. Towns across the eastern inland areas had almost emptied as rapid climate change dried up water sources and withered crops before they could establish themselves. Small villages lost many of their number as people tried in vain to scratch a living from the hard-baked soil. The endless drought appeared to be a curse from the gods and the only recourse was either to travel south to the land of the life-giving River Nile and work for the Egyptians, or head north to the more temperate climate of leafy Lebanon.

A couple of centuries later, the climate changed back to normal as suddenly as it had gone awry. Over a decade or two, the summer in Canaan reverted to being simply very hot instead of a veritable furnace. Rivers began to flow and springs refilled. People started to head back to their old homeland from both the north and the south.

The group led by Moses, and later his successor Joshua (Hebrew for Saviour), headed east and north into the land of Canaan, which was once again promising to be 'a land of plenty'. Upon arrival they set about destroying every township they came across so that they could take the food and the water supply for themselves. The following extract is typical of the bloodlust that God appears to have instructed.

> And the LORD said unto me, 'Behold, I have begun to give Sihon and his land before thee: begin to possess, that thou mayest inherit his land'. Then Sihon came out against us, he and all his people, to fight at Jahaz. And the LORD our God delivered him before us; and we smote him, and his sons, and all his people. And we took all his cities at that time, and utterly destroyed the men, and the women, and the little ones, of every city, we left none to remain: Only the cattle we took for a prey unto ourselves, and the spoil of the cities which we took.[2]

Apparently on God's explicit instructions, every man, woman and child was murdered and possessions looted in towns and cities too numerous to list.

Time passed and Yahweh and his people occupied much of the 'promised land'. More than four centuries later Yahweh's chosen people came to the holy city of Jerusalem, which was eventually surrendered to David, the king of the Israelites. It is claimed that David took 30,000 men to escort the Ark and its divine contents to their new capital. To make the final journey, Yahweh's mobile home was placed on a new cart drawn by Uzzah and Ahio, the sons of Abinadab.

As the cart journeyed onwards, Uzzah accidentally invaded Yahweh's personal space in some way and died instantly in a ball of flame. David was livid with the temperamental deity and decided to go no further. However, after some time, arrangements were made to continue the journey and David tried his best to humour God by sacrificing an ox every six paces, and in traditional Canaanite style, his team danced to music around the cart as it trundled haltingly along.

A Temple for Yahweh

On arrival at Jerusalem David decided to build a temple for Yahweh and his Ark at a place above the city that was said to be the very spot where Abraham had intended to sacrifice his son Isaac, perhaps nearly 1,000 years earlier, as described in chapter 22 of Genesis.

The Israelites settled into their new capital city and then, according to the Second Book of Samuel, David fell in love with a beautiful woman called

Bathsheba, having seen her from his window while she was bathing. Bathsheba was the wife of Uriah, one of David's officers, but nevertheless the king had her brought to his chambers where he promptly had intercourse with her. This resulted in a pregnancy, and the king cunningly decided to summon Uriah back from the battlefield to relax, bathe and take time to 'visit' his wife – in the hope that the pregnancy would be attributed to Uriah.

But Uriah refused the king's offer, saying he could not 'go to my house, to eat and drink and lie with my wife' while his fellow soldiers were living in hardship in the open on the battlefield. David could not risk the wrath of a popular general so he made sure that Uriah was placed in the forefront of battle where he was soon killed.

David took Bathsheba as his wife and she subsequently gave birth to their son. But the child died, despite David's many prayers to Yahweh.

Nevertheless, Bathsheba soon bore David another son. According to 2 Samuel 12:25 he was given the name Jedidiah, meaning 'beloved of Yahweh', yet the previous verse says the child was called Solomon (Shelomoh in Hebrew). A number of scholars have suggested that his normal name was Jedidiah and that he took the throne name Solomon when David's allotted reign of 40 years came to an end. This interpretation makes perfect sense because 'Solomon' is a Canaanite name that celebrated the old god of the city. *Shelomoh* was a form of word play connected to Salem, the original name of Jerusalem – meaning the planet Venus – which in turn was associated with peace (also the root of the word *shalom* in Hebrew).

And it was King Solomon who would build what is probably the most famous temple in all of history – a temple that would become the centrepiece of Freemasonic ritual.

Solomon's elevation to the throne took place in 971BC or possibly early the following year, according to biblical scholar E R Thiele and others. This left his father, David, free to spend his time collecting materials for the building of a new temple in Jerusalem as a permanent abode for Yahweh and his earthly residence, the Ark of the Covenant.

During Solomon's own reign of 40 years he surrounded himself with all the luxuries and the external grandeur of a typical Canaanite monarch, reputedly maintaining a staggering 700 wives and 300 concubines. The building he created for his harem was, by necessity, extremely spacious – in fact it was many times the size of the planned temple to house Yahweh and the Ark. Solomon is remembered for his great wisdom and there is no doubt that his early years brought great prosperity and influence to the small Israelite kingdom.

Alongside his traditional Israelite devotion to Yahweh – the god his people had once adopted at the time of the Exodus and now kept in a gilded box – Solomon worshipped a range of other gods. Venerating a host of deities was a token of cosmopolitan kingship and, at this period, the idea that the tribal god of Israel was the only god in existence had not yet taken root. Solomon himself – unlike the later Jewish scholars who set about shaping the Bible – saw no inconsistency in his devotion to a range of deities.

Among the more unpleasant practices he embraced was the sacrifice of one's own children to the god Moloch, an ancient Canaanite solar deity. This was believed to be a necessary process for Canaanites who wanted to be true kings – appointed and empowered by the gods of heaven. It was a practice that the Israelite nation would carry on for hundreds of years before finally outlawing the procedure and inventing less grotesque techniques of establishing kingship.

It must have been very easy for Solomon to send in his guards to select a few of his hundreds of children born of concubines as sacrifices to the god Moloch. The very word Moloch is from the root word *malak*, meaning king. 'Moloch' literally means the act of becoming or being the monarch, reigning under the authority of the gods. The sacrifice to Moloch was the only way to be assured of absolute power based on an authority beyond the world of men.

According to 1 Kings 11:7 Solomon erected 'a temple' for Moloch 'on the hill over against Jerusalem'. The location of this temple where child sacrifice took place was to the southwest of the city of Jerusalem in an area called Topheth in the Valley of Hinnom, also known as the 'Valley of the Children' near to where King David's tomb is believed to be. The practice of sacrificing the king's children continued for hundreds of years until it was eventually outlawed. The 2 Kings 23 states that '... no man might make his son or his daughter to pass through the fire to Moloch'.

Whether it was due to his human sacrifices or not, Solomon and his government prospered and he entered into an alliance with Hiram I, the Phoenician king of Tyre, who greatly assisted him in his extensive building works – most particularly the great temple in which Yahweh could reside.

The Power of the Shekinah

However, the evidence suggests that, while the Ark of Yahweh was indeed kept in the Temple, when the building was first erected it was not originally dedicated to Yahweh. Solomon's polytheistic kingship required a temple that connected with the gods – a kind of 'communications centre' that gave the ruler a 'conduit to the realm of the gods in the heavens'. The key to such a building lay in an understanding of astronomy and, most particularly, the long-term movements of the planet Venus – the goddess Ashtoreth.

The worship of the goddess Ashtoreth (also variously known as Astarte, Ishtar, Anat, Ashtar, Asherat, Baalat-Gebal, and Asherah) was of central importance to Solomon. Ashtoreth was connected with fertility, sexuality, and war, and her symbols were the lion, the horse, the sphinx, the dove, and above all a star within a circle – indicating the planet Venus, which was the visible manifestation of this astral deity.

Venus lies inside Earth's orbit around the Sun and is the second in line from the Sun after Mercury. Seen from Earth, Venus is by far the brightest object in the sky after the Sun and the Moon and it appears either just before dawn as the 'morning star' or shortly after dusk as the 'evening star'. It also appears to weave a truly remarkable pattern over time when viewed from Earth.

Every eight years Venus returns to the same point in the sky, but the background stars are now different; astronomically speaking, Venus has moved one fifth of the way through the zodiac. And every 40 years Venus completes one full lap of the zodiac – ending up back where it started. This movement is accurate to a second or so and has always provided a wonderful clock and calendar for astronomer-priests. In travelling through the heavens the planet appears to describe a five-pointed star around the Sun – and this is the basis of the pentangle that has always held mystical importance for humans from all cultures.

For Solomon the cycle of Venus of precisely 40 years was of paramount importance. He, like kings before and after him, knew that every important aspect of life was governed by this divine period of 40 years, as the Old Testament records:

- Moses had led his people through the wilderness for 40 years from the age of 80 (the beginning of his third Venus cycle)

until his death at the age of 120 (the end of his third Venus cycle).
- Throughout the Old Testament God frequently allows the land to rest for 40 years.
- Israel had done evil and God gave it an enemy for 40 years.
- Eli was judge (a proto-king) of Israel for 40 years.
- Saul, the first anointed king of Israel, became king aged 40 and ruled for exactly 40 years.
- Ishbosheth (Saul's son) was 40 when his reign began.
- King David, Solomon's father, ruled for 40 years.

Solomon knew that he himself could only reign for 40 years, and so it transpired.

There was only one astral power greater than Venus and its 40-year cycle and that was the holy *Shekinah*. This brilliant 'star' would appear in the sky at periods of every 12 Venus cycles – every 480 years – and then it would shine down several times over a few years before disappearing once again.

In fact the Shekinah was (and still is) caused by the planets Venus and Mercury rising in conjunction – meaning that, viewed from Earth, they overlap and look like a single, extremely bright star.

The appearance of the Shekinah, it was believed, heralded the greatest moments of Israelite and Jewish history. However, particular significance was attached to every third appearance of the Shekinah – which took place every 1,440 years – when the brilliant object is in exactly the same place within the zodiac (the background stars). One such appearance of the Shekinah was due to fall at the winter solstice in 967BC, and Solomon ordered the land to be cleared on the hilltop to the north of the city in preparation for the laying of the foundation stone of his planned temple on that very day. According to priestly calculations, the divine Shekinah would appear in the dark morning sky like a brilliant beacon shortly before dawn.

This date was said to be precisely 1,440 years after Noah's ark, with its cargo of surviving animals, had come to rest on dry land after the great biblical Flood, when the storm clouds of the Flood finally parted and the divine light had shone through, bringing a new covenant between God and humankind. Moreover, Solomon and his astronomer-priests believed that the previous Shekinah appearance, 480 years earlier, had occurred as Moses led his people through the Red Sea.

The Shekinah was something greater than Yahweh, Ashtoreth or any other single god alone. Solomon understood that the light of the glorious Shekinah heralded the mating of the total godhead with the entire world of men. The forces of the god and goddess merged as one. This was the entire world of humans linking with the realm of the gods – Earth and heaven united as one.

It seems that the 'male' shaft of light from the star above was understood to pierce the 'female' and fertile soil; as the interchange reached its climax, the identities of the male and female merged as one. As in the sexual act, they became a single entity with all attributes blurred and united. Softness and hardness, physicality and intellectuality, aggression and love, pain and ecstasy. All polarity between the female earth and the male phallus of the beam of channelled light changed so fast they became one – male and female simultaneously, exploding in an orgasm of power and fertility.

Since the fifth millennium BC temples had been built to channel the light of Venus through openings to carry them deep into the earth at astronomically important moments. Perhaps the greatest of them all was the structure which still stands today at Newgrange in Ireland. A thousand years older than the Great Pyramid and more than two thousand years older than Solomon's Temple this extraordinary building allows the light of Venus to penetrate into its central womb once every eighth winter solstice.[3]

Solomon's motive was certainly more complex than a desire simply to fulfil the wish of his father David by building a temple in Jerusalem to worship Yahweh. He wanted more than that – a temple that would act like a machine to produce a response to the light of the Shekinah. This was quite different to a temple of simple worship – it was a carefully constructed mechanism that would act as a conduit to all gods. A kind of telecommunications centre between mankind and the realm of the divine beings that controlled the future and could deliver success or failure to earthly kings.

To become a 'real' king with unquestionable power Solomon needed a Shekinah communications device that would connect him, through his god Yahweh, to the cosmos above. Unfortunately, neither he nor any of his priests knew the secret of building such a structure.

Hiram the Mason

The Ark of the Covenant and its divine contents had to be in place to receive the light of the glorious Shekinah. However, whilst Solomon knew all about the importance of these Shekinah appearances, neither he nor any of his people had the astronomical knowledge to build a temple that would work as a perfect Shekinah observatory. For this reason, Solomon had to ask Hiram, the new king of the Phoenician city-state of Tyre, on the coast of present-day Lebanon, to help him with suitable timber, qualified workers and a priestly engineer who understood the workings of the gods. In return Solomon taxed his people mightily, extracting economically disastrous amounts of produce such as oil, corn and wine to be shipped to Tyre.

The sophisticated people of Tyre were wealthy and highly educated. Ashtoreth, or Astarte, was their chief deity and their understanding of the movements of Venus was unparalleled, even in comparison to the astronomer-priests of Egypt and Babylon.

The man sent by the Phoenician king to take charge of creating the new Temple in Jerusalem was Hiram Abif, a master craftsman and a high priest, perhaps descended from the Kenite clan. All of the stonemasons he selected to build the Temple were also priests – most probably with veneration for all gods as well as the mighty Ashtoreth and their own tribal god, Yahweh.

It seems possible that Hiram Abif had Kenite ancestry because he was above all a skilled metalworker, and it was he who created the two free-standing decorated bronze pillars known as Boaz and Jachin that were erected in front of the Temple, marking the solstice extremes of the Sun on the horizon.

With the aid of Hiram Abif, the foundation stone of the new Temple was duly laid in 967BC, four years after Solomon had taken the throne in Jerusalem and two years after Hiram had become king of Tyre. It seems probable that one of King Hiram's first official acts was to send his namesake to plan out the Jerusalem Temple. It would have taken at least one full year to make the astronomical observations and calculations required to design a temple that would work with the coming Shekinah.

The exact centre of the Temple had to be erected on the high ground to the north of the city, on what is now part of the Temple Mount, so that the light of the rising Sun would break the horizon at precise points on the hillside to the east throughout the year. The Sun rises due east twice a year, once in the spring and once in the autumn, on the two equinoxes, when there are exactly 12 hours of daylight and 12 hours of darkness.

An observer visiting the proposed site of the Temple at dawn every day for a year, beginning with the spring equinox, would see the Sun rise earlier and further to the north on the horizon each morning for precisely three months until the summer solstice – the point in the year with the most hours of daylight. From that point, the time of dawn would get later and the point of sunrise would return towards the east, reaching the centre point (due east) again three months later at the autumn equinox. The dawn would continue to be later and later as the Sun rose each day a little further to the south until, after another three months, it reached its extremity at the winter solstice – the shortest day.

If one were to take a photograph of the sunrise each morning and make a film of it, the effect would be like a pendulum swinging with the equinoxes at the centre and the solstices at the extremes of the Sun's swing across the horizon. Such knowledge was fundamental for astronomer-priests 3,000 years ago.

The location of Jerusalem was no accident, because it is an ideal place from which to observe sunrises and sunsets. The angle of shadows cast by the rising and setting Sun vary by longitude. At the equator, every day is more or less equally divided into light and dark and the Sun rises due east and sets due west. At the poles, the Sun never sets in summer and never rises in winter. In between these extremes, the angle between the two solstices increases the further one travels away from the equator. The latitude of Jerusalem is 31° 47′ north, which means that the angle of the shadows cast by the winter and summer solstices is precisely 60 degrees.

To observe this, all that was necessary was to draw a circle on the ground and place a vertical stick in the east and another on the other side in the west.

On the morning of the winter solstice the easterly stick would cast a shadow 30 degrees north of centre and that evening the westerly stick would cast a shadow 30 degrees south of west. The reverse would be the case at the summer solstice, creating a diamond shape inside the circle. A north-south line across both angles produces a signature that is unique to this latitude – and at Jerusalem it forms the perfect six-pointed star that is known as either the Seal of Solomon or the Star of David.

So, the symbol that has relatively recently become the emblem of Judaism and of the modern state of Israel is a solar diagram that celebrates the remarkable geographical position that the city of Jerusalem occupies.

Hiram Abif would have understood this perfectly well, because Jerusalem had been a famous place of worship for this very reason since the Stone Age. But his interest was in more than just the basic sunrise and sunset patterns. The name 'Jerusalem' in the Canaanite language means 'foundation for observing Venus rising', and Hiram wanted to calculate the movements of Venus and of the highly complex patterns of the Shekinah as it rises ahead of the Sun.

Any visitor to Jerusalem today will be told that Solomon's Temple was built on the Dome of the Rock where the Al-Aqsa mosque has stood for around fourteen and a half centuries. This is the very highest point of the hill – but it is not the place where the Jewish Temple once stood.

We believe that Solomon's Temple was built a little further to the north, at a site now known as the 'Dome of the Spirits'. The reason for this belief is the alignment to the hillside to the west, which had always made Jerusalem special. This tiny dome is only a few hundred years old but beneath it is the holiest spot on Earth. It marks the east-west line running from the peak of the Mount of Olives (Olivet), viewed through the Golden Gate, through to the two domes of the Holy Sepulchre in the west. It was upon the peak of Olivet, according to the Mishnah, that the high priest used to stand when he sacrificed the Red Heifer. During this ceremony it is said he would have had to look into the holy of holies of the Temple and sprinkle the blood of the sacrifice in its direction. More importantly, the light of the Shekinah would rise in the east above the peak, pass through the Golden Gate and penetrate the dormer window of Solomon's Temple, where it would shine on the Ark of the Covenant.

Quite independently of Chris Knight's researches in this area, Professor Asher Kaufman from the University of Notre Dame has argued exactly the same theory without any reference to the Shekinah.

The early Muslims under the Caliph Omar first occupied Jerusalem and the Temple Mount in 638CE with the intention of building a great mosque on the holy spot known to them as the *Shtiah* rock. The Caliph's men discovered the exact spot among the ruins of the Temple thanks to helpful Jews who pointed out the correct place amongst the piles of rubble. Later, Abd el-Malik built the Dome of the Rock in this place. This fact is recorded in many sources of both Jews and non-Jews, such as in the Cairo Geniza. Elsewhere in the Geniza, it is written that Jews came to Jerusalem with Omar and showed him the location of the Temple. A similar source to the Geniza states that Jewish guides helped to expose the *Shtiah* rock.

However, the Jewish people are passionate about their devastated Temple, which is the most sacred site in Judaism. Surely, common sense would suggest that they would *deliberately give the wrong information* to any non-Jews intent upon building on such a holy spot?

Perhaps we, and Professor Asher Kaufman, are causing some small problems by raising this issue, but none of the authorities of any religion in Jerusalem is going to admit to such a fact. Old conventions, however wrong, tend to have a life of their own and only the real cognoscenti will ever care anyway.

But let us return to the time of Solomon.

One can imagine the moment when the Shekinah arrived, as predicted, in 967BC, 1,440 years after Noah's Flood – at the moment that the foundation stone of the new Temple was laid. The blazing star rose quickly in the east, its brilliant glow lighting the entire landscape, all present dropping to their knees as the light of heaven shone down upon them. It lasted for ten minutes or more before the red orb of the rising Sun spilled across the horizon.

Secrets of the Temple

Then, as now, knowledge is power. The Israelites expected the Phoenician craftsman, Hiram Abif, not only to build the Temple but also to explain to them the secrets of astronomy and the rituals required to make it work as a conduit to the gods.

The Old Testament does not elaborate on the details of the construction work of the Temple but perhaps surprisingly, the oral traditions of Freemasonry do. They describe events surrounding the building of King Solomon's Temple in considerable detail and the Masonic ritual of the Third Degree is an important part of that information.

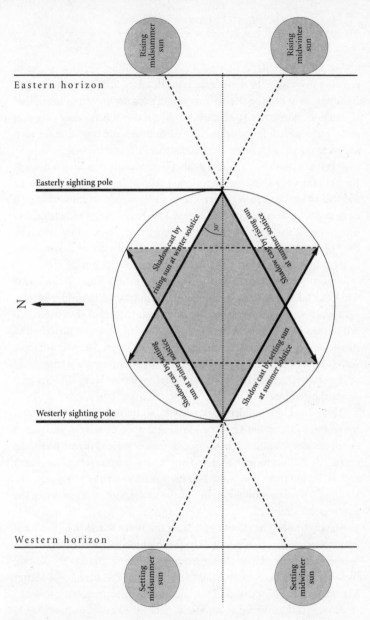

Figure 1 How the symbol of the Seal of Solomon, or Star of David, derives from the solstice sunrises and sunsets at the latitude of Jerusalem

We fully understand that most people would be highly sceptical of evidence from something as arcane as the rituals used by a secretive organization that has been accused of everything from devil worship to political subversion. But the rituals have been shown to contain knowledge that should not have been available to a relatively modern organization such as Freemasonry, which can be no older than 550 years at best.

It is said in the Third Degree ritual of Freemasonry that King Solomon, King Hiram and Hiram Abif were three Grand Masters. This suggests that they held a rank in a secret order, which was in some way connected with or analogous to Freemasonry. They are said to have met in a secret chamber directly below the 'holy of holies' of the Temple – the inner sanctuary where the Ark of the Covenant stood. This subterranean chamber was connected by a passageway to Solomon's palace in the city to the south.

According to Masonic lore, as expressed in this Third Degree rite, when the Temple was nearly complete, 15 senior Israelite builder-priests, who were acting as overseers, became concerned that they were still not in possession of the secrets and they decided to obtain them by any means – even if that meant recourse to violence. The precise nature of these secrets is not described in Masonic tradition but in our view they could only relate to the knowledge of how to capture the power of the Shekinah inside the Temple.

These rebellious builder-priests decided to ambush Hiram and extract the secrets by force. But 12 of the 15 thought it too dangerous and pulled out of the plot. The three remaining conspirators placed themselves at the entrances of the almost complete Temple, which were in the east, north and south and there they waited for their master to enter to venerate the Sun god. They knew he always he did this at the hour of noon, when the Sun was at its zenith.

Having finished his devotions, Hiram attempted to return by the south entrance, where he was confronted by the first of the priests who, according to legend, had armed himself with a heavy plumb rule. Raising the weapon in a threatening manner he demanded to be told the secrets of a Master Mason, warning him that death would be the consequence of a refusal.

Hiram Abif answered that those secrets were known to but three in the world, and that, without the consent and co-operation of the other two (King Hiram and King Solomon) he neither could, nor would, divulge the secrets and that he would rather suffer death than betray the sacred trust vouchsafed to him. The overseer then aimed a violent blow at the head of Hiram but he missed his forehead and only struck him a glancing graze on his right temple, which caused the master to reel and sink onto his left knee. Recovering from the shock, he made for the north entrance

Here he was accosted by the second of the plotters, who was armed with a builder's level. Hiram again rebuffed his demands to know the secrets and was immediately struck with a violent blow, this time on his left temple, which brought him to the ground on his right knee. Finding his retreat cut off at both these points, Hiram staggered, faint and bleeding, to the east entrance, where the third conspirator was waiting, armed with a maul (a heavy hammer). After Hiram had again refused to divulge his secrets, the third man struck him a fatal blow to the forehead. The master fell lifeless at his feet.

The three conspirators panicked when they realized that they had killed their master and still had no knowledge of the great secrets. They wrapped the body and headed out into the hills, where they buried Hiram Abif in a hastily prepared shallow grave, which they marked with a sprig of acacia.

The absence of Hiram was soon noticed and, concerned that something terrible had happened, some of the senior priests went to tell Solomon of their master's disappearance. The king immediately ordered a general muster of the workmen throughout the different departments, and it then became clear that three of the overseers had also gone missing. On the same day, the 12 craftsmen who had originally joined in the conspiracy came before the king, and made a voluntary confession of all they knew, down to the time of withdrawing themselves from the number of the conspirators.

King Solomon quickly selected 15 of his best men and ordered them to make a diligent search for Hiram to ascertain if he was still alive, or whether he had suffered death as a result of the attempt to extort from him the great secrets. Many days were spent in fruitless search until one of the men caught hold of a shrub, which to his surprise came easily out of the ground. On a closer examination he found that the earth had been recently disturbed and, with his companions, he dug down a short distance and found the roughly interred body of Hiram. They covered it again with

17

all respect and reverence, and to distinguish the spot, they stuck a sprig of acacia at the head of the grave. The group then returned directly to Jerusalem to give the sad news to King Solomon.

It is said that when the king's rage and grief had subsided, he ordered the men to return, and bring Hiram Abif's body back for proper burial. This done, their mission then was to find those responsible for the murder. They travelled in the direction of Joppa (present-day Jaffa) and were about to return to Jerusalem, when, passing the mouth of a cavern, they heard sounds of moaning inside.

On entering the cave the party found the three men answering the description of those missing. The moaning is said to have been due to their grief at the realization of the enormity of their wicked crime. On being charged with the murder, and finding all chance of escape cut off, they made a full confession of their guilt. They were then bound and led to Jerusalem, where King Solomon sentenced them to a dreadful death.

The Temple was eventually completed but it is said within Masonic ritual that the genuine secrets remained lost, even down to today.

Solomon's New World Order

Subsequently King Solomon held a council of all priests in his land and decided that all beliefs and gods were part of a whole single truth. However many names we give to the gods, he declared, there is, in truth, only one divine presence despite many manifestations. He is She, and She is Him. And the light of the Shekinah is the true light of all truths.

We deduce that what Solomon said (or is being credited, in this account, as saying) was that all of the gods are just fragments of a whole singularity that is the one and only divine. Just as all people are merely facets of the force that is humanity.

For us this is a powerful concept. Today Freemasonry accepts anyone who believes in a single God – and that includes Hindus, for example, who name many gods. But the Hindu deities are only splinters of a great force that runs through the universe and so they have, ultimately, only one God.[4]

For the Israelites, even the devil was part of God. In the Book of Jubilees, which was purportedly revealed by an angel to Moses on Mount Sinai, bad things happen because of the works of Mastema – which was simply the dark side of Yahweh.[5] The devil, as he is now called, was therefore originally God on a bad day.

Solomon's deepest respect was for the traditions of Enoch, which were once even more important to many Jews that those of Moses.

According to ancient tradition, Enoch (who is mentioned, briefly but somewhat enigmatically, in Genesis 5:18–24) was on Earth almost 2,000 years before Moses was born and Enochian priesthood appears to have existed right back in the depths of time long before there was any concept of 'Judaism'. There is a Masonic degree called 'The Royal Arch of Enoch' which dates back to 1740, and there is also a very ancient document known as the Book of Enoch. This document was known to have been popular among very early Christians (it is quoted in the Letter of Jude, in the New Testament), but it fell from favour by *c.* AD500 and most copies were destroyed. The work was lost to Western Christendom for over 1,000 years. However, it remained popular in isolated Ethiopia, where it forms part of the Ethiopian Bible to this day. It was to Ethiopia that an 18th-century Scots Freemason, James Bruce, went in search of the long-lost book. He discovered it in 1774 – nearly three decades after the Masonic ritual of the same name had come into existence.

This Masonic degree has not been 'worked' (used) for more than 200 years, yet it uses a 60-degree triangle which is described as the 'Delta of Enoch'. This is, of course, the angle of the solstices at Jerusalem (*see* page 12). The ritual claims that Enoch originally used this particular triangle on the exact spot where Solomon's Temple was built thousands of years later. It also states that some great secrets were buried in an underground vault at this location which were later discovered during the building of the Temple.

The copy of the Book of Enoch brought back by Brother Bruce was considered by the world of academia to be too weird to be the original article. It was full of scientific material relating to observational astronomy and the effects of latitude on sunrise, sunsets and the solstices. It also appears to indicate very clearly that Enoch visited the Megalithic structures in Stonehenge in England and Newgrange in Ireland.[6]

However, when the famous Dead Sea Scrolls were discovered and deciphered more than 50 years ago, it was found that most of them were copies of the Book of Enoch – and they proved that Bruce's copy was entirely accurate.

The Masonic ritual tells how King Solomon decided to inaugurate a new priestly order based upon the mysteries and rites of the Enochian priesthood. And it appears that their mission was nothing less than to bring about a new world order. This, we deduce, was to be a world where all gods were viewed as a part of the same. Quite simply it appears that Solomon invented the modern concept of monotheism – an all-embracing godhead, based on Yahweh as one supreme force, an amalgamation of every inter-pretation of the creative force. This new supreme deity is the God of modern Judaism, Christianity and Islam.

The members of Solomon's priestly order were to be in possession of secrets that would be passed on from father to son. The priesthood was to be unseen to the common man. Their mission was to build a world in which they would use their influence to ensure that all gods were honoured to the glory of the ultimate Godhead. Their task was to unify the entire world in a single, peaceful and tolerant society where God ruled through the king, his regent on Earth. They were to achieve their objective by any means, including the judicious use of money, political influence and, if all else failed, force.

Naturally, the centre of this new great order was to be Jerusalem.

These Enochian priests were to become a hereditary priesthood that would carry their ancient knowledge down the generations. And, as we will demonstrate, 2,500 years later this priesthood would continue its works under the guise of an order called Freemasonry.

According to tradition, Solomon then made a 'seal' that would be the mark of his holy task force. He created the device of a star made up of a pyramid and an inverted pyramid to form a symbol of the Shekinah. As we have seen, this device – the Seal of Solomon – was the astronomical mark of Jerusalem, derived from the angles created by the shadows cast by the sunrise and sunset at the two solstices. For Solomon, it represented the power of heaven reaching down to Earth, and the power of the king and his people reaching up to heaven.

The Seal of Solomon was to become the seal of the force that would invest 3,000 years attempting to build the 'New Jerusalem' – the ideal state and society – across the entire planet. The bloodlines that would carry this mission forward came to be known as the 'Star Families': hereditary priests who would take their secret mission to the four corners of the globe.

After Solomon died his country broke up under the economic pressures he left behind. His territories split into two Israelite kingdoms, one named Israel, in the north, and the other Judea, in the south, fighting a long civil war.

Over time the northern kingdom grew to be politically and economically of much greater importance than its southern neighbour, and under King Jeroboam II (782–746BC), Israel reached a level of high prosperity. Yahweh was now acknowledged as the most important god, but Canaanite deities were still popular and worshipped at major temples such as those of Bethel and Dan and at other 'high places', which were prehistoric stone circles corresponding to those found in Western Europe, such as Stonehenge. The recorded rites performed here by the Jewish people were as ancient as the stone circles they danced around, and included mass indulgence in sexual acts, similar to those that took place at similar sites in the British Isles.

The lands of Israel and Judah descended into a wild decadence – and Solomon's secret priesthood was not happy. The prophets Amos and Hosea recorded the dire iniquity of these events:

> There is no truths and there is no mercy, and there is no
> knowledge of God in the land. Cursing, and lying, and killing,
> and theft, and adultery have overflowed, and blood hath
> touched blood. (Hosea 4:1–2)

There was a widespread belief that Yahweh would uphold his people as long as they paid him some homage of sacrifice from time to time. But others were already foretelling the destruction of the kingdom as the penalty for the wickedness of its people.

The Fall of the Israelite Kingdoms

After the reign of King Jeroboam II the kingdom of Israel began to disintegrate with a series of short, unstable reigns of kings who usually murdered their way to the throne only to be killed themselves by the next aspiring king. However, it is worth noting here that all truth rests with the victor. Much of the negative view of Israel comes down to us from the scribes of the kingdom's opponent – Judea. At the same time, the region's growing major power, Assyria, was hungrily eyeing the quarrelling little states that lay between it and the Mediterranean.

Eventually, in 722BC, the Assyrian king Sargon II overran the kingdom of Israel. An inscription found in the ruins of Sargon's palace at Nineveh tells how he carried away 27,290 captives from Israel. The northern Israelite kingdom became the Assyrian province of Samaria and thousands of outsiders settled in the lands. From the intermarriage of the various new peoples with the remnants of Israel arose the Samaritans, whose religion remains distinct from Judaism to this day.

The southern kingdom of Judah retained its independence for another century and a half, but in 586BC it succumbed to the might of Assyria's successor as regional superpower, the Babylonian empire, under Nebuchadrezzar (Nebuchadnezzar in the Bible). Nebuchadrezzar's army destroyed Jerusalem, and the majority of Judeans (certainly all those in positions of influence, from the king downward) were taken in captivity to Babylon. Many of Solomon's secret chosen priesthood fled to Egypt, mostly to the island of Elephantine in the River Nile near Aswan, where they constructed a Temple said to be identical to King Solomon's Temple.

These evacuations left only the poorest peasants remaining in the land of Judah. Israelite independence had come to an end.

After the Exile

In 538BC the Persian king Cyrus, who had defeated the Babylonians, issued an edict in which he allowed all the Hebrews in his domain to return to their homeland. However, many of the Judeans living in Babylon did not return at the end of the exile period, but became a part of the Jewish Diaspora, living among nations outside their own ancestral homeland.

Cyrus also decreed that the Temple in Jerusalem should be rebuilt, and directed that the sacred Temple vessels seized by Nebuchadnezzar be sent back. However, as recorded in the biblical Book of Ezra, work on the Temple was thwarted by various factions and did not get under way until a few years later, under the rule of King Darius. The Persian ruler allowed Zerubbabel, the heir of the Davidic royal line, to fulfil Cyrus's decree and rebuild the Temple of Jerusalem unhindered. An ancient document known as the Book of Esdras records how the young Jewish leader had to solve a riddle to be allowed to rebuild the ruined Temple of Yahweh – the answer to which was: 'Wine is strong, a king is stronger, women are even stronger, but truth conquers all.'

Within less than a year, in 487BC, the cornerstone of a new Temple was laid, an event that coincided with the reappearance of the Shekinah precisely 480 years after the founding of Solomon's original Temple. The Judeans faced a new and seemingly optimistic future.

A province of the Persian Empire, but once more free to run its own religious affairs, Judea became utterly dedicated to Yahweh. During the Exile, the Judeans had set about purifying their religion and laying the foundations of what we refer to as Judaism (it is strictly speaking from this point that we may speak of 'the Jews' – followers of the revitalized Judean religion.) They attempted to 'straighten out' the many collisions and contradictions within their historical morass of myth and legend. It was at this time that they wrote down the bulk of the Hebrew Bible (what Christians call the Old Testament) – merging different traditions together to produce something close to a cohesive story. From this new beginning devotion to Yahweh became central to Judean society, and foreign religions and deities were no longer tolerated as they had been before. Non-Jews were persecuted and foreign religions expelled. Judah became a land where Yahweh, and Yahweh alone, was worshipped.

Before the Exile, for many centuries all Israelites had believed that the human soul after death went to a grey and formless subterranean house of dust called *Sheol*, to abide there for a short time before slowly fading away into nothingness. After the Babylonian Exile, a new view developed among the controlling group of Solomon's priests, that evil was a dark force, which they called Satan, opposed to Yahweh. They also adopted a belief in an afterlife, where cosmic justice is delivered after death rather than during one's life, which had the effect of creating greater responsibilities for the actions of each individual.

The Coming Messiah

By the middle of the 2nd century BC the members of this clandestine group were pulling further and further away from mainstream Judaism in anticipation of great events to come. Getting on for a thousand years had passed since Solomon's rule, and throughout that time the 'Star Families' had tried to bring about change. They had suffered a great setback when the Babylonians had forced them into exile in Egypt. In 64BC they suffered another when the armies of Rome marched into their land.

However, the Star Families believed that an appearance of the Shekinah would herald the emergence of a great national saviour, or Messiah ('anointed one'). The Shekinah had duly returned in 487BC, 480 years after the cornerstone of Solomon's original Temple had been laid, but no great leader had arisen at that time. Now, another 480 years later, in 7BC, they were anticipating the next appearance of the great blazing 'star' over Jerusalem. Would the Messiah arise this time? No wonder the arrival of the Shekinah was keenly anticipated by everyone in the land – even including the puppet ruler put on the throne of Judea by the Roman invaders: King Herod the Great.

CHAPTER 2

The Star Child

By 8BC the imminent return of the Shekinah was an open secret. Just about everyone in the land of Israel was aware that it was 960 years since King Solomon had laid the foundation stone for his Temple, so the second appearance of the Shekinah was now due. More importantly, it was also one perfect Shekinah cycle of 1,440 years since Moses had led his people through the Red Sea, which has always been considered to be the birth rite for the entire Hebrew nation – the breaking of the waters at God's command being analogous to the gushing of amniotic fluids of a mother about to produce a child.

Because exactly 1,440 years had now elapsed, the Shekinah would appear in exactly the same place in the zodiac (against the same background stars). It would therefore have passed through each of the 12 zodiac signs, which were equated with the 12 Israelite tribes. This return to its starting place in the heavens was considered to mean that life in Israel would also renew itself and a 'new Moses' would step forward to lead God's chosen people out of the hands of their current oppressors.

A New Temple

When the divine Shekinah had last shone out of Sagittarius it was the Egyptians who had been the enslavers of the Hebrew people, but now it was the Romans who occupied their land and held the Jews captive on the soil that their God had given them. The ruler of Israel was a puppet king called Herod ('the Great', ruled 30–4BC), who had little time for, or interest in his subjects, but was famous for his ambitious building programme. Nothing like this had been seen since the time of Solomon, and Jerusalem was even beginning to look more impressive than Rome itself.

Eleven years before the Shekinah's return, in 19BC, Herod the Great instructed that the decrepit 500-year-old Temple of Yahweh be rebuilt and greatly enlarged on a hugely expanded Temple Mount. Mistrustful of Herod, the Jews only took his plan seriously when he had all the building materials required to start the construction of the new Temple Mount assembled in front of the building site. As much as they detested their king, this was an unmissable opportunity to restore their holy Temple.

The work on the new Temple was conducted exclusively by stonemasons who were also priests – just as it had been at the time of Solomon and again when it had been rebuilt in the 5th century BC by Zerubbabel. It is said that no fewer than 10,000 priests were used in the construction of the Herodian Temple, which was to take nearly 90 years. The complex was barely complete when it was destroyed in AD70, long after Herod's death.

According to Jewish Law, God had predestined the location and measurements of the Temple, so it was impossible for Herod to relocate it or build it wider or longer. However, the Temple could be taller, and built of more splendid materials. The major construction effort was therefore focused on the erection of a vast new platform to form a magnificent setting for the Temple. Enlarging the area of the Temple Mount to the north, the west and the south, Herod created a gigantic artificial plateau covering more than 36 acres (14.5ha). However, the eastern wall that overlooked the Kidron Valley remained as it always had been, due to the requirement for the light of the Shekinah to enter the holy of holies.

When the Shekinah did arrive as predicted shortly before dawn on December 21, 8BC construction of the foundations was still at an early stage and the old Temple was still supported in its original place thanks to carefully managed demolition and the use of temporary supporting structures.

The Coming of the Messiah

King Herod was painfully aware at this time that the Jews were expecting the coming of their 'new Moses' to dethrone him and establish a new 'kingdom of God'. This expected leader was referred to as the 'Messiah' – a term that had a very different meaning to the Jews 2,000 years ago than it does to Christians today.

The term Messiah (Hebrew *mashiach*) literally meant 'anointed' or 'smeared with oil' – a ritual act which was an indication of priestly and kingly righteousness. It had no otherworldly meaning and the Jews certainly did not consider that this Messiah was God himself or the literal 'Son of God'. Such concepts would only arise much later among foreigners with alien religious ideas. The people of Israel were looking for a man who would be their king and lead them to victory in a great war against their enemies in general and the Romans in particular.

The Jews had good reason to dislike Herod. Following his ascent to the throne he ordered the assassination of his rivals among the preceding Hasmonean dynasty (prior to the Roman takeover in 63BC, the Hasmoneans had ruled the last independent Jewish state before the 20th century) and proceeded to confiscate the possessions of the aristocracy of Jerusalem in order to pay his debts to Rome and to his army. Herod claimed to be Jewish himself but in reality his father was Idumean and his mother a Nabatean Arab. A century earlier, the Hasmoneans had conquered the Idumeans – the biblical Edomites, who lived south of Judea and were traditional enemies of the Israelites. Under Hasmonean pressure, the Idumeans had nominally converted to Judaism, but the Jews remained suspicious of them. Herod's Idumean father, Antipater, had been made procurator of Judea under Julius Caesar 40 years earlier, and now Herod served as local ruler on behalf of the Romans. He had recently been making life difficult for the Pharisees, a traditionalist Jewish sect, for their insistence that the new Messiah would bring about the end to his rule.

King Herod must have been greatly irritated by the universal belief that he would soon be out of a job despite everything he had done to give the Jews a world-class capital city. Whether or not Herod truly believed that a Jewish Messiah was on his way did not matter: his Jewish subjects believed it, and that could only lead to trouble. The king, like everyone else, knew what the ancient 'Star Prophecy' foretold. It appears in the Old Testament Numbers 24:17 where it foretold:

I shall see him, but not now: I shall behold him, but not nigh: there shall come a star out of Jacob, and a sceptre shall rise out of Israel, and shall smite the corners of Moab, and destroy all the children of Sheth.

This prophecy linked the coming of the Messiah with the return of the Shekinah – and that divine star did indeed appear on the winter solstice 8BC. Mercury and Venus were in perfect conjunction and shone like a beacon in the sky over Jerusalem shortly before dawn on 21 December.

The Shekinah appeared with such stunning brilliance that everyone was deeply impressed and the Jews began the process of trying to identify who would be their Messiah. The Shekinah (incorrectly called the 'Star of Bethlehem' in later Christian tradition) is described in the Gospel of Matthew (2:1) as an obvious reference to the fulfilment of the Star Prophecy:

Now after Jesus was born in Bethlehem of Judea in the days of Herod the king, behold, wise men from the east came to Jerusalem, saying, 'Where is he who has been born king of the Jews? For we saw his star when it rose [or 'in the east'] and have come to worship him.'

These wise men were Magi, which meant that they were astrologer-priests, originally from ancient Persia, but by this date the term referred to anyone with astrological/astronomical knowledge. Throughout history, people with the ability to predict the movements of the heavens have been considered to possess powers beyond normal human understanding and the modern terms 'magic' and 'magician' stem from this word, which ultimately comes from Persian. It seems probable that these particular astronomers were actually employed by Herod to calculate the date of the Shekinah so that he could be prepared for any potential uprising or general disobedience amongst the natives.

Matthew 2 also tells us that King Herod ordered the killing of all children aged two and under in Bethlehem and surrounding areas. However annoyed Herod might have been by the Messiah legend, the massacre story is almost certainly a fiction invented by early Christians. Nonetheless, it faithfully reflects Herod's notorious ruthlessness in protecting his throne; towards the end of his life, when the story is set, he executed several members of his own family.

The modern calendar is based upon an assumed year of Jesus Christ's birth and history is traditionally divided into two halves either side of this event, 'BC' ('Before Christ') and 'AD' ('Anno Domini', meaning 'In the Year of the Lord' in Latin). These terms are now increasingly expressed as BCE (Before the Common Era) and CE (Common Era). There was no year zero so, on this reckoning, Christ was born in AD1, which means that many people celebrated the recent millennium a year too early, since the 2,000th anniversary of Christ's birth fell in 2001 not 2000.

But it is certain that this calculation is wrong, because records clearly tell us that Herod died in Jericho shortly before his 70th birthday, around late March or early April in 4BC – directly following an eclipse of the Moon. This date once created a major problem for Christian scholars because Herod could hardly have tried to kill someone born four years after his own death. In our estimation and following the tradition of the Shekinah, Jesus was born in the year 8BC, not in AD1 as many Christians still assume, so their lives did indeed overlap.

So, Jesus could have been born in the year that the Shekinah was in the skies on 21December. However, it seems more likely that the accounts of Jesus' birth are all a fiction to justify the later claim that he was the promised Messiah. But Jesus is not the only figure for whom messianic claims were made. There is evidence that, while many Jews did indeed believe that a Messiah had come, his name was not Jesus, but John.

John the Christ?

According to the New Testament, many people considered that John the Baptist was the anticipated Messiah, and he was certainly a figure of great importance. In the Gospel of Luke (1:15–17) we are told of John that:

> he shall be great in the sight of the Lord, and shall drink neither
> wine nor strong drink, and he shall be filled with the Holy Spirit

> even from his mother's womb. And many of the children of
> Israel shall he turn to the Lord their God. And he shall go before
> Him in the spirit and power of Elijah, to turn the hearts of the
> fathers to the children, and the disobedient to the wisdom of the
> just, to make ready a people prepared for the Lord.

And we are further told in Luke 3:15 that 'the people were in expectation, and all men mused in their hearts of John, whether he were the Christ, or not'.

It is certain that many, if not all, of the 'Jerusalem Church' held John to be the promised Messiah (in Greek *khristos* – the Christ). He was a holy man and baptized Jesus as one of his followers, an event which has been turned around to imply that he was merely clearing the way for Jesus.

According to the New Testament, John was a member of Jesus' priestly family. However, one important group, the Mandaeans, dispute this claim. The Mandaeans are an ancient, secretive, monotheistic cult principally found in southern Iraq and the Iranian province of Khuzestan. They date back to Jerusalem at the time of Christ, and one researcher has described them as 'a small but tenacious community' which 'follows an ancient form of Gnosticism' and 'practises initiation, ecstasy and some rituals which have been said to resemble those of the Freemasons'.[1]

Mandaeans believe that John the Baptist, whom they call *Yahia* in the *Sidra d-Yahia* (Book of John), was the last and most important of all the prophets and they reject the idea that Jesus Christ (*Yshu Mshiha*) was either a Messiah or a prophet. For them John the Baptist was the only true Messiah.

We find it very interesting that a remote sect, with a direct cultural memory of Jerusalem in first few decades of the 1st century AD, should have rituals that seem Freemasonic in nature. No less interesting is the fact that there was a group that venerated John in preference to Jesus from the time before Jesus' ministry right through to the present day.

There is little doubt that many other groups once agreed with the general thrust of Mandaean thinking. According to Hugh Schonfield, one of the leading scholars working on the Dead Sea Scrolls, there can be no doubt that John was the first messianic personality and the founder of 'The Way' – the movement that became the Jerusalem Church.[2]

All of the available evidence from root sources suggests that John was held to be the promised Messiah and was executed for that very reason by the Roman-appointed authorities.[3] Josephus, the 1st-century historian of the Jews who is considered by most secular historians a more reliable witness than the Gospels, recorded that Herod (that is, Herod Antipas, a son of Herod the Great) killed John to quell a possible uprising in the year AD36. This has caused problems for Christian theologians who believe that John died before Jesus, yet Jesus is thought to have been crucified at least three years before this date. However, as we will show, there is no problem because the hard evidence demonstrates that Jesus did die after John.

In fact, it appears that Jesus was the *successor* to John as the leader of the Jerusalem Church, also known as the Ebionites. As such *both* were considered to have been the Messiah – and we can be sure that the Jewish people believed that the Messiah had definitely arrived. A contemporary document has come to light in recent times that tells us a great deal. This reads: 'A star has marched forth from Jacob, A sceptre has arisen in Israel, And he will shatter Temples of Moab, And destroy the sons of Seth.'[4]

This is from one of the Dead Sea Scrolls, the ancient Jewish documents hidden in caves in the Judean desert at Qumran and rediscovered in 1947. The first line confirms that the promised Messiah has duly arrived, and the second line tells the reader that he is about to begin the war with the enemy of the Jewish people. The sceptre is the symbol of kingship in almost all cultures and therefore confirms his status as the expected kingly Messiah. However, the arrival of this new Messiah could not have occurred in the settlement of Bethlehem, as the Gospel of Matthew mistakenly claims, because that little town is in the southern state of Judea. To arise from the ancient land of Israel, as prophesied, someone would have had to come from a region well to the north. Somewhere that is, like Nazareth in Galilee. (In this context we refer to Israel in terms of its original geographic location and not as a word for the entire Jewish nation, as it was ultimately to mean.)

Jesus the Mason

Now, the story behind Christianity centres on the arrival of a Jewish Messiah, born to a virgin under the light of a blazing star in the east. He went on to perform miracles and was eventually executed before being resurrected and returning to heaven.

It cannot be known whether the man we now call Jesus Christ was born at the moment that the Shekinah arrived, but we can be sure that he, or his followers, claimed that he was the kingly Messiah who arrived under the light of the divine star. The author of Revelation 22:16, writing at least 40 years after the death of both John and Jesus, quotes Jesus as follows: 'I am the Root and the Offspring of David, and the Bright Morning Star.'

Little is known of Jesus' early life but he was almost certainly born in Galilee, possibly in a tiny hamlet called Nazareth, and lived in Capernaum, which is in Galilee.

The English name 'Jesus' comes from the Latin *Iesus* and the Greek *Iesous*, a rendering of the once common Hebrew name spelled *Yeshua*, which is a contraction of *Yehoshua* (Yahoshua, Joshua), meaning 'help of Yahweh' but carrying the import of the English word 'saviour'.

The word 'Christ' is from the Greek *khristos*. This is simply the direct translation of the Hebrew word Messiah (*mashiach*) – which, as we noted above, meant 'smeared with oil' ('chrism') as a mark of priestly and kingly righteousness. Many people treat the word 'Christ' as a surname, as if 'Jesus Christ' were the equivalent of the modern English name 'Joshua King'. But 'Christ' was a literal title, so 'Jesus Christ' would be rendered not 'Joshua King' but 'Joshua *the* King'. For this Jesus was intended to be the king of the Jewish nation.

It is traditionally taught that Jesus was a carpenter like his father. However, the original Greek word used in the New Testament Gospels was *tekton*, which means simply a craftsman – most usually a master builder working in stone. There can be no doubt that if the priestly and Davidic bloodlines claimed for Jesus in the Gospels (Matthew 1:1–17, Luke 3.23–28) are anywhere near accurate, he would have been a hereditary priest, and it is extremely likely that he was one of the 10,000 holy men who came into Jerusalem to work as stonemasons on the great new Temple. The fact is that there were few carpenters in Jerusalem, because buildings there at the time utilized little wood, yet the place was teeming with countless priestly stonemasons working on Herod's new Temple. What is more there is no doubt that Jesus was a priest – so he could not have been a lowly woodworker.

In 1 Peter 2:4–9 we are told (allegedly by the man later revered as the first pope in Rome) in terms relating to stonemasonry that Jesus was a priest of royal descent, and his power is likened to the holy light of the Shekinah:

> To whom coming, as unto *a living stone,* disallowed indeed of men, but chosen of God, and precious, Ye also, *as lively stones, are built up a spiritual house, a holy priesthood,* to offer up spiritual sacrifices, acceptable to God by Jesus Christ. Wherefore also it is contained in the scripture, 'Behold, *I lay in Sion a chief corner stone,* elect, precious: and he that believeth on him shall not be confounded.' Unto you therefore which believe, he is precious: but unto them which be disobedient, *the stone which the builders disallowed, the same is made the head of the corner, and a stone of stumbling, and a rock of offence,* even to them which stumble at the word, being disobedient: whereunto also they were appointed. But ye are a chosen generation, *a royal priesthood,* an holy nation, a peculiar people; that ye should shew forth the praises of *him who hath called you out of darkness into his marvellous light. [our emphases]*

Today, even most scholars accept that the Greek *tekton* has a broader meaning, and it is our contention that the longstanding translation of the word as 'carpenter' is an obvious error. There is little evidence or even reasonable logic to support it and yet there is a weight of evidence to translate the word as stonemason. The Gospels in English use the word 'rabbi' 13 times and 'teacher' 47 times in reference to Jesus – and both of these modern words have equivalence to a senior priest. We are told that strangers walked up to Jesus and asked him to cast out demons, heal the sick, settle disputes, and probate wills. Logically he must therefore have *looked* like a priest, in manner or dress or both, and been considered as such.

So, now we have established that it is more reasonable than not to consider that Jesus was, or claimed to be, the following:

- Of a royal bloodline, descended from David and Solomon.
- Born at the moment that the Shekinah arrived as predicted in the Star Prophecy – exactly 1,440 years after Moses led his people through the waters of the Red Sea.
- The new Messiah who was expected to become king of the Jews and lead an uprising against the Romans.
- A high-ranking priest who worked as a stonemason on the new Temple.

The Essenes

Until the middle of the 20th century it was considered that the vocabulary of the Jerusalem Church represented something markedly new and original. But the discovery of the so-called Dead Sea Scrolls changed that view once and for all.

The original group of people involved with John the Baptist, and later Jesus, referred to themselves as followers of 'the Way' and met in what we would call churches. But so, as the Scrolls themselves revealed, did the group that left the tattered documents in caves above Qumran in the Judean desert. It seems very likely, an many biblical scholars agree, that these two groups, and John and Jesus themselves, were part of the same movement: the Essenes. The Essenes were a highly religious Jewish brotherhood who differed greatly from mainstream Judaism. The most fundamental difference was that they structured their calendar and holy days around the movements of the Sun, rather than the Moon as was the usual Jewish practice. In the Dead Sea Scrolls, the Essenes referred to themselves in several ways, frequently as the 'Sons of Light', the 'Pure of Mind', the 'Poor' and followers of 'the Way', whilst their enemies were described as the 'Sons of Darkness'. Their own records show how they thought of themselves as 'the holy ones' who lived in 'the house of holiness' because 'the Holy Spirit' dwelt with them. Their teachings were concerned with love of God, love of virtue, and love of one's fellow humans.

The writers of the Dead Sea Scrolls use ways to describe themselves that were otherwise exclusive to the followers of Jesus. They refer to the faithful as 'the elect' and the 'children of light' – phrases used in the New

Testament to describe Christians (Titus 1:1, 1 Peter 1:2, Ephesians 5:8).

Yet this group is not mentioned in the Christian Bible or in later Jewish religious writings. At the time of Christ there were several significant groups active in the religious and political life of Jerusalem and around the country in general. The most important were the Pharisees, Sadducees, Herodians and the Essenes. The New Testament makes not even a passing reference to the Essenes, although it does frequently mention the other groups. This is an extremely odd omission, especially when several important non-Christian writers of the time – Philo, Pliny the Elder and Josephus – did write about the Essenes.

An account of the Essenes by the Jewish historian Philo of Alexandria (20BC–AD40) estimated that there were rather more than 4,000 of them distributed widely across the countryside wherever Jews were to be found. His writings tell how only mature men were admitted to the sect and that they preferred to live in villages rather than towns. He said they cared for the sick and elderly and they were farmers, shepherds, cowherds, beekeepers, artisans and craftsmen but that they did not make weapons or engage in commerce.

Essenes rejected slavery, believing brotherhood to be the natural relationship of men but that it had been spoiled by covetousness. Though they read a great deal they were not interested in philosophy in general but only morals. They returned from work rejoicing, as if they had been partying all day and contentment of mind they regarded as the greatest of riches. The members were instructed in piety and holiness. Their love of man was proved, Philo said, by their benevolence and equality, and by sharing all possessions in common.

Pliny the Elder (AD23–79), the Roman naturalist, recorded that the purpose of the Essene was to receive 'the repentance of others' and he used other words to describe the Essenes stating that they gather in an 'assembly' and considered themselves 'born again'.

In short, the Essenes lived by what today we would call 'Christian' values and used terms that are now understood to be absolutely 'Christian'.

Essenes had no wish to possess worldly objects and distributed goods according to need. They were also passionate about scrupulous cleanliness – which involved washing in cold water and wearing pure white garments. They prohibited swearing, the taking of oaths – other than their own oaths of membership – and they rejected participation in trade or commerce.

It is recorded that the Essenes drew their recruits from the ranks of those who had renounced material things – those who were prepared to be 'born again'. But their main method of growth was through adopting children and bringing them up in the kingdom of God. This makes sense of the otherwise curious quotation attributed to Jesus in Luke 18:16:

> **But Jesus called them unto him, and said, 'Suffer little children to come unto me, and forbid them not: for of such is the kingdom of God'.**

This influential group of spiritual thinkers, centred on Jerusalem, had many names for themselves. One of those that became more widely used by others to describe them was the 'Poor Ones', which in Hebrew was *Ebyonim* – later giving rise to the term Ebionites.

Philo tells us that these holy people devoted all their attention to the study of morals, using as instructors the laws of their country, which, they suggested, would have been impossible for human minds to devise without divine inspiration. He noted how these laws were taught at all times but most especially on the seventh day, adding: 'For the seventh day is accounted sacred, on which they abstain from all other employments, and frequent their synagogues, as they called these places.'

Philo's use of the word 'synagogue', at first sight appears to confirm the Jewishness of these people – but that is not necessarily the case. At the time all Jewish worship in Judea was directed towards the Temple in Jerusalem and there were no synagogues in the modern sense. This is simply a Greek word used by Philo to translate a term in Aramaic (the language of Palestine at the time) used by the Essenes, which meant nothing more than 'meeting houses' for those that they considered to be the 'poor' and the 'people of God'.

It is likely that a 'meeting house' of the 'people of God' would have been called a 'house of God', or *domos kuriakos* – the root of the English word 'church'. The one operating in the capital city after the death of Jesus was the 'Jerusalem Church', known to have been overseen by James, the brother of Jesus.

Philo explained how these Essene churches were run:

> Then one, indeed, takes up the holy volume and reads from it,
> and another of the men of the greatest experience comes forward
> and explains what is not very intelligible, for a great many
> precepts are delivered in enigmatical modes of expression, and
> allegorically, as the old fashion was, and thus the people are taught
> piety, and holiness, and justice and economy, and the science of
> regulating the state, and the knowledge of such things as are
> naturally good, or bad, or indifferent, and to choose what is right
> and to avoid what is wrong, using a threefold variety of defini-
> tions, and rules, and criteria, namely, love of God, love of virtue,
> and love of mankind.

Here Philo is describing the use of parables by senior Essene priests – just
as Jesus is described as having done in the Christian Gospels; for we
believe that Jesus belonged to this sect.

Essene Life and Ritual

The most prolific 1st-century writer on the Jews was Josephus
(*c.* AD37–*c.* 100). He suggests that he was personally initiated into the Essene
brotherhood. In his two famous books, *The Jewish War* and *The Antiquities
of the Jews,* he states that most Essenes did not marry. Some orders of Essenes
did, although they maintained strict rules about sexual intercourse. They
regarded all pleasure as evil and disciplined themselves in continence and
self-control; they wore white robes and referred to themselves as 'Lebanon',
which in Aramaic means 'white'.

According to Josephus, these people started each day facing east and
praying 'as if in supplication for the sun's rising'. They frequently bathed
in cold water cisterns and assembled for a sacred meal in a room into which
only the initiates were allowed. Following a prayer of humility spoken by
the priest they partook of bread and a single type of food. They concluded
the meal with another prayer in praise of God as the provider of the food.

Josephus also stated that Essene lives were fully regulated by 'overseers'
(Greek *episkopos* – hence 'bishop') who directed their daily duties, leaving

the brethren able to do only two things of their own free will – to assist those in need and to show mercy. James, the brother of Jesus was known as the *episkopos*, or bishop, of Jerusalem.

To be admitted, a proselyte had to first live in the manner of an Essene for a year to prove himself before being baptized. He then had to continue to live in their fashion for two more years to prove his worthiness. It was at this advanced stage that he took solemn oaths to become a full member and participated in the sacred meal. He had to swear piety toward God, give justice to all men and never to harm anyone of his own accord or at the command of another.

The Essenes took vows that required them to

- exercise piety towards God;
- observe justice to all men;
- show fidelity to all men, especially those in authority;
- be perpetually lovers of truth;
- keep their doctrines secret.

Essenes considered themselves to be the 'elect' of God and show every sign of being part of the all-important Star Family priesthood that had survived from the time of Solomon. Anyone breaking the Essene oath or being found guilty of sin was punished by expulsion from the Church.

Being cast out was a terrible punishment, since the offender could not accept any succour from an outsider without the permission of their bishop, and they would ultimately die of starvation. Excommunication was therefore a death sentence because no Essene would forgo his vows, even when rejected by his fellows. In reality the community generally accepted transgressors back into the fold when it was felt they had been punished sufficiently.

An example of this Essene system in operation is given in the New Testament in a story that does not seem to make sense unless one knows about this rule and punishment. The event takes place after James, the brother of Jesus, orders all new members to sell their possessions and give the proceeds to the Church. One couple, Ananias and Sapphira, were caught keeping some of the money from the sale of their land for themselves. As told in Acts 5:1–11, the apostle Peter apparently effects a double execution of the couple for dishonesty. In reality, what happened is almost certainly as follows:

A man called Ananias and his wife Sapphira became 'born again' when they joined the Essene group led by James, the brother of Jesus. They duly sold their belongings to give the proceeds to their church, but the word went about that they had kept some of the money for themselves.

Ananias brought the money from the sale and handed it to the elder called Simon (Peter). 'Why has Satan filled your heart to lie when you know you have kept back part of the money from the price paid for the land?' Simon demanded coldly. Ananias looked terrified and did not reply.

'Whilst it remained, was it not your own – and after it was sold was it no longer yours? Why have you conceived this idea in your heart? You have not lied to men – but to God!' Simon said.

From this moment Ananias was considered 'dead'. His 'born-again' status had just been revoked as he was excommunicated from the Church. He was then escorted from the premises and thrown out amongst 'the dead'.

Three hours later Ananias' wife Sapphira came in, unaware that her wrongdoing had been discovered and that her husband had been excommunicated. Simon was waiting for her:

'Tell me whether you have sold the land and, if so, for how much?' he asked.

Sapphira confirmed that the sale had happened but then lied about the amount.

'How is it that you have conspired to tempt the Spirit of the Lord?' Simon asked, pointing again towards the door. 'Look, the people who have put your husband amongst the dead are at the door and waiting to take you out also.'

The woman was immediately considered to be 'dead', like her husband.

The later, non-Essene, writers of Acts mistook Peter's action for a literal killing of Ananias and Sapphira rather than as an excommunication for dishonesty. This misunderstanding of the way words were used by this group of Jews has led Christians to falsely brand their Prince of the Apostles as an executioner of his own people. To ascribe the killing of these people, for a relatively minor misdemeanour, directly to God would appear to make a total mockery of the Christian concept of a loving, forgiving deity.

There is a similar misunderstanding in the idea that Jesus went around arbitrarily reviving corpses here and there as a favour to his friends. The story of Lazarus is a clear example. It seems clear to us that Lazarus did not literally die, but was excommunicated for four days until Jesus allowed him back amongst the living. Jesus, like all of the Essenes, believed in the resurrection of the dead – something that was going to happen to all of them at the end of time when the kingdom of God was established. His followers certainly did not expect their Messiah-king to revive dead bodies in the current world. Such an idea would have seemed crazy to them.

But being excommunicated from the Church was not good news in this life or the next. Unlike other Jewish groups, the Essenes believed that after physical death the 'the Sons of Light' would be resurrected into the kingdom of God on the third day. They alone would be resurrected into an ideal world because they were God's perfect people. Everything would seem as it had been in life, except that it would be perfect – the Kingdom of God would be on Earth but it would be free from sin. They would live forever in incorruptible bodies as their reward for being the righteous ones.

The Essenes were fundamentally different from all other Jews, most especially, as we have noted, because they regulated their holy days by the movements of the Sun rather than the Moon. Josephus recorded how they taught science to the children they took in, and they were famous for their knowledge of medicines. Their clean and caring lifestyle, plus their medical wisdom, meant that they lived long lives. Josephus recorded that many of them lived to an age of over 100 years.[5]

Jesus: the Would-Be Essene Messiah

These peace-loving people were dispersed over a wide area from Alexandria to Damascus. but their most famous location was on the shores of the Dead Sea on the lowest land on the planet, over 1,300 feet below normal sea level. Here, on the northwest shores of this poisonously saline lake – at the point nearest to Jerusalem – lies Qumran, a settlement that existed from the middle of the 2nd century BC until *c.* AD68. It had been briefly deserted the year that Herod had assumed the throne of Judea because a devastating earthquake had brought walls tumbling down in this desert outpost– an event that must have increased the hatred of Herod and the desire to see the promised Messiah arrive.

It was in the caves overlooking Qumran that the famous Dead Sea Scrolls were discovered between 1947 and 1956. The remains of somewhere between 825 to 870 separate scrolls have been identified. These priceless documents reveal that the Essenes were indeed a messianic, apocalyptic sect that used baptism and believed that they had a 'new covenant' with God. The scrolls describe how they followed a leader they called the 'Teacher of Righteousness', a man who was opposed, and possibly killed, by the establishment priesthood in Jerusalem.

A recently released Dead Sea Scroll fragment known as the 'Messianic Apocalypse' (4Q521) contains three important references that link the Essene community with the very early Christian Church. First, the text talks of a Messiah who will rule heaven and Earth. After this it clearly describes the expectation of the resurrection of the dead during the time of this Messiah. Finally, it gives instruction in how to identify the coming Messiah when he arrives. The Essene scroll reads:

> He will heal the sick, and resurrect the dead and bring glad tidings to the poor.

Jesus arrived in Judea from Galilee claiming to be the promised Messiah by saying to the disciples of John the Baptist:

> The dead are raised up, the poor have the glad tidings preached to them.[6]

There can be no serious doubt that once Jesus had succeeded John he knew that he had to fulfil the messianic expectations that are spelled out in the Essene tradition. The Essenes considered themselves to be the 'living' and all outsiders to be the 'dead'. And Jesus was converting ordinary Jews in droves to the new idea of churches, which were for the 'People of God'. Jesus was the warrior Messiah – the new king who would lead them into the expected apocalyptic war between the great Satan (the Romans) and the Sons of God.

The new world order was coming at last.

Jesus' words about the dead being raised up simply meant that he was indeed the promised Messiah who would lead all of his people in the way of light. He knew he had to fulfil all of the criteria:

- He would have to have been born at the moment the

Shekinah rose in the east;
- He would command heaven and Earth as his eternal kingdom;
- His spirit would be over the poor;
- He would resurrect those with faith;
- He would restore sight to the blind;
- He would show loving kindness;
- He would heal the sick;
- He would bring glad tidings to the poor;
- He would be the 'shepherd' to his 'flock' of holy followers;
- He would be called 'the son of God'.

According to the ancient rules of Israelite kinghood, everything happened in blocks of 40 years. Saul, David, Solomon and other great kings ruled for 40 years and Moses led his people out of Egypt at the beginning of his third 40-year block aged 80 before dying at 120.

Because Jesus was born in 8BC, we can see that if he began his campaign for kingship in his 40s, he was truly active around AD35 or 36, the year in which John the Baptist was probably killed.[7] Jesus himself was crucified within months of John's death.

This dating explains why in John 8:57 the following words are spoken to Jesus:

Thou art not yet fifty years old.

Whilst this is a reasonable comment to someone in their early or mid 40s, it is not logical to say this to someone still in their early 30s.

Like all Essenes, Jesus taught a gospel of peace and love but he and his followers knew that a terrible war was unavoidable. This he expected to lead and the war was expected to last for 40 years. The wisdom of the Messiah included calendrical lore whereby every act had to be performed at exactly the right time as well as in the right way. Since Jesus was born under the light of the Shekinah, when he turned 40 Venus had completed exactly one 40-year cycle. The Essene document from Qumran known as 'The Community Rule' dictates that members of the sect were not to 'depart from the command of God concerning their appointed times; they shall be neither early nor late for any of their appointed times'.[8]

They were required to keep in harmony with 'The laws of the Great Light of Heaven'.[9]

Those that followed the way of the Shekinah were 'the Sons of Light' – 'those born of truth' who followed the way of peace, humility, patience and goodness. Everyone else, including those Jews who followed the ways of the Moon (including the official Jerusalem priesthood of the time) were the 'children of darkness' who were 'born of falsehood'.

The Dead Sea Scrolls tell us how, under the command of the prince of the congregation, the Sons of Light would attack the army of Satan – first eliminating the ungodly Jews and then the Romans themselves. The war would be hard and bloody before God himself would intervene to bring victory to his children. Then would truly arrive the age of the Messiah, 'who shall teach righteousness at the end of days'. At this point the righteous dead would be resurrected to share the final, everlasting glory.

Jesus began his final phase by spending 40 days being 'tempted' by Satan. Each day represented a year, and the word 'temptation' meant 'trial of strength'. Jesus understood what was to be done. The Earth with its humans was mirrored exactly by the heavenly host. God was about to restore His intended order between heaven and Earth. Christians across the world today use elements of Essene messianic prayers without a jot of understanding:

> Thy kingdom come. Thy will be done on Earth as it is in
> Heaven.

This surely was the moment for which King Solomon had created the hereditary priesthood. His chosen Star Families were about to turn the ancient king's vision into reality. Jesus knew that his time was right – long ago prophesied by wise men, delineated by the movements of the heavens and with God's specific authority. His troops might be thin on the ground but the Romans had no chance against the power of the Shekinah – the light of God. As a result of his confidence Jesus did the unthinkable and actually went into the Temple and caused a riot when he and his associates smashed up the trader's stalls (remember, the Essenes rejected commerce).

Whilst Jesus, and all those who followed the Way, spoke of peace, they remained aware that the war was going to be frighteningly real. Jesus appointed five principal associates: two Simons, a Judas, James and John – who he described as 'sons of thunder'. One of the Simons was a *sicarius*, a specialist 'knifeman'. In Luke 22:35–38 Jesus instructs his associates that it is time for the peaceful to arm themselves:

> 'When I sent you without purse, bag or sandals, did you lack anything?' 'Nothing,' they answered.
>
> 'But now if you have a purse, take it, and also a bag; and if you do not have a sword, sell your cloak and buy one.'
>
> …
>
> 'See, Lord, here are two swords.'

In Matthew 10:34 Jesus adds: 'I came not to send peace, but a sword.'

But it was not to be. Jesus was not the promised Messiah insofar as he would not live to see the great war against Satan. The Romans arrested the would-be Messiah on what we would call charges of terrorism almost as soon as he went public about his mission. Jesus was executed with little delay and the Jerusalem Church had to regroup itself under the leadership of Jesus' younger brother, the holy man James. James the Just, the brother of Jesus, was now the group's Messiah.

Paul of Tarsus

Life went on and the Essene Jews wondered how they were going to bring about the kingdom of God. James was also to prove a failure as Messiah and would have probably been forgotten to history but for a stranger who arrived in Jerusalem a few years after the Crucifixion. He was from Tarsus, the provincial capital of Cilicia in Asia Minor where the principal religion was Mithraism – a form of Persian Sun worship that was popular throughout the Roman Empire at the time. This background was to have a profound effect on the man's particular version of Judaism. The stranger had been born to a Mithraic couple who had converted to Judaism. As Greek-speaking Jews they gave their son a Hebrew name, Saul, as well as a Greek name, Paulos. He is usually known as Paul. Paul was a physically powerful man as he was tentmaker by trade but he was prone to certain problems of the mind. Upon arrival in Jerusalem he found employment with the Sadducee high priest in Jerusalem, as a political 'enforcer' to keep various religious opponents in their place. He quickly became well known for his harsh dealings with a troublesome sect of Jews that had been followers of a recently executed rebel who claimed to be the promised Jewish king – the Messiah. But then, this Sadducee muscleman suddenly underwent a personal 'mystical experience'.

Paul must have had heard much about the Essene man who had claimed to be the Messiah, the resurrector of the dead, who had died a terrible death himself. The echoes of his Mithraic upbringing in Tarsus ran around in his head and the ideas of Essene Judaism suddenly came to life in his imagination as he welded the two concepts together.

Here was a wonderful fit – he alone could understand what it all meant. The family and followers of Jesus did not understand at all, but in a blinding flash of inspiration Paul believed that he had unlocked profound truths that God had spoken to him, and him alone.

From descriptions of Paul's 'divine' experience and his temporary blindness on the road to Damascus, medical experts have suggested that his hallucination was probably triggered by an epileptic fit. Whatever the cause, the idea that entered this tentmaker's head was an event that led him to create a new religion: Christianity.

It seems as though his medical problem led him to believe that God had given him an understanding of Jesus' mission that was totally at odds with that of James, the brother of Jesus, and the other close followers of Jesus who were still alive at the time. This foreigner proclaimed that the God of the Jews had revealed the truth to him alone and that his mission was to take the message to non-Jews: most likely because he knew that the people who knew the truth would not listen to him for one second:

> It was the good pleasure of God… to reveal his Son in me,
> that I might preach to the gentiles.[10]

He proudly announced how he was prepared to be all things to all people, that he was a Jew when it suited his purpose and that he was not interested in playing second fiddle to anyone – not even Jesus' brother James, who was now the leader of the Church. He would win by any means available.[11]

Whilst the idea of Jesus' death and physical resurrection are at the heart of the Christian faith, serious scholars know that it is built on sand rather than rock. One highly respected expert on the origins of Christianity said:

> [Paul's] phrase 'to reveal his Son in me' is admittedly a curious one... the words really constitute a tremendous, indeed preposterous, claim for any man to make, and especially a man of Paul's antecedents... The position which we reach then is that Paul is the exponent of an interpretation which may be best described as the traditional or historical one.[12]

Another leading thinker on the early Church has said:

> The Gospels demonstrate a belief or assert a claim that Jesus was a semi-divine being who was born contrary to the laws of nature and who conquered death. This is not the belief of the original followers of Jesus, nor did he himself make such claims.
>
> The letters of Paul are the earliest documents, Christian or otherwise, relating to the origins of Christianity that have survived; yet they are the least useful in establishing the facts about Jesus.[13]

From the very outset Paul had been directly at odds with James, who led the Jerusalem Church after his brother's crucifixion. James, like Jesus himself, was a priest of the Star Families and was fully conversant with the true teachings of his late brother. Paul, on the other hand, had not been an eyewitness of the events that had taken place involving Jesus or his followers. He was an outsider and had not the faintest idea about the entire concept of the true mission of the Jewish Messiah. He knew nothing of the Shekinah and had received what little information he had about Jesus from at least third-hand sources, at a time when the heady cocktail of religious sects and political infighting in and around Jerusalem were at their height. Paul was a man looking for a cause and if he could not find one that already suited his own individual tastes, he wasn't beyond 'rewriting' the story of Jesus to suit his needs.

However, Paul was not very original regarding his fictitious account of Jesus. Every aspect of the 'new' story already existed as a description of Mithra – the deity that had been popular in his hometown of Tarsus. According to Mithraic belief, Mithra had been born to a virgin mother in a stable on 25 December, 600 years earlier. He had died and was resurrected at Easter so that he could act as a mediator between mankind and God on Judgment Day.

This entirely non-Jewish, fictitious account of Jesus' mission and his death from Paul, a man who until recently had been the sworn enemy of Jesus' followers, outraged the Jerusalem Church. What followed was a period of ferocious encounters between James and Paul but the wily tentmaker was a man of great personal charm and was far wiser in the ways of the Roman world than James, a man who represented a pure but complex Jewish theology. Unable to find any real influence within Judea itself Paul had set out on a series of protracted journeys. Over a considerable period of time he had visited communities across a fair section of the Roman-ruled world and especially in Asia Minor, perverting the original message of Jesus and gradually creating what we call Christianity, a belief that he correctly estimated would better suit the sensibilities of non-Jews. He could only succeed by talking to people to whom James had never vouchsafed the true secrets of Jesus and the original message. Paul claimed that he was preaching the gospel to the uncircumcised – meaning non-Jews; leaving James to preach to the circumcised.

Paul spread the word of a Jewish man-god who had died and resurrected himself and who had then returned to heaven. His story was obvious nonsense to the people of Judea but the non-Jews of the Roman world identified with the theme that Paul related to them. And so they would, because it was a very familiar story he was telling.

Well after Paul had disappeared in Rome, the gospels that were later selected for inclusion in the New Testament were written in Cyprus, Egypt, Turkey and Rome by people who had never even set foot in Jerusalem, perhaps with the exception of St John's Gospel, whose author may have known the city on account of his accurate descriptions of it.

The Destruction of the Temple

Meanwhile the priests of Jerusalem were still working on the last phase of the new Temple of Jerusalem. The Temple itself was a relatively small affair but the platform constructed around it was truly gigantic. The retaining walls of the Temple Mount were made of large, well-cut stones – even the smallest ones weighing more than two tons. At intervals along the base of the retaining walls, such as at the southwest corner, particularly sturdy construction called for the use of single stones of up to 50 tons. They were laid in alternating rows aligned east–west, above it north–south, and so on. The walls go very deep, resting on bedrock, and neither mortar nor any other binding material was used between the stones, as stability was attained by the great weight of the stones and by the mildly graded recession of each course of stones by three to five centimetres.

The stone-dressing method used was so widely practised in Herod's day that it is referred to as 'Herodian' and it was also used as a decorative theme on ossuaries of the period found in the Jerusalem area.

Even as the priests toiled to complete their great new Temple, they knew that it would be destroyed in the coming war that was prophesied. Under the Temple were great vaults and chambers, the layout of which was only known to the priests who built them, and it was here that they constructed 'secret places' ready to take important artefacts that would be required when the Kingdom of God duly arrived.

The expected the 'great war' against Satan did come – some 30 years after the death of Christ – in AD66.

For the Jews, Roman oppression and tyranny reached its climax in AD64 under the proconsul Gessius Florus. The seeds of the 'great war' were planted and the Jews were confident that God would come to their rescue and vindicate their cause. In AD66 they launched a concerted attack on their oppressors. The conflict started in Caesarea and Jerusalem, and by November Roman forces had been driven out of the holy city, leaving more than 600 Roman troops dead and the high priest of the Temple slaughtered as a Roman sympathizer.

The Roman emperor, Nero, was highly displeased and responded by issuing two commands: destroy Jerusalem and level its Temple. Nero selected a seasoned 57-year-old general, Vespasian, for the task of dealing with the Jewish uprising, who would later be assisted by his son Titus. The general had built an awesome reputation when he had dealt with trouble in Britain, and now he headed for Judea with plans for a siege of Jerusalem.

Eventually the Jews were so close to winning the war that Rome was forced to use her full military weight against them in order to ensure victory. The Romans knew that if the Jews were to win their independence the whole empire would soon be in revolt.

A man called Joseph ben Matthias was given the task of commanding the Jewish forces. However, the extreme Jewish patriots were not satisfied with the relatively tame manner in which this peace-loving man reluctantly waged war. The bloody business of massacre and counter-massacre succeeded one another with unimaginable cruelty.

The Jews fought with a bravery and intelligence that matched the finest skills of the Roman legions. They caused the Romans huge losses but the might of Rome pushed on and city after city began to fall. The Romans had suffered and they took revenge by massacring the population of each city, making surrender an impossible option, even if the Jews had wanted it. By the end of the first year of fighting, Gabara, Jotapata, Japha, Tarichaea, Gischala, Gamala and Joppa were ghost towns and the Romans had regained control of Galilee, Samaria and the seaboard west of Judea. Over the next year Vespasian took virtually every city, leaving only the strongholds of Herodium, Machaerus, Masada and Jerusalem itself to be dealt with.

The Essenes believed ancient predictions that suggested the war would almost be all but lost before God would bring them final victory, so they began the process of hiding their documents and the important Temple treasures that they had seized.

As time went on, Joseph ben Matthias began to despair of the war, foreseeing a catastrophe for the Jews. He changed sides to work for the Romans in an attempt to limit the disaster that was being wreaked upon his nation. Under the Romans he became known as Josephus and was later to become the famous historian of the Jews.

The war looked almost lost for the Jews. But at this point the ancient prophecy seemed as though it might be coming true. The Roman war effort suddenly abated, and word spread that there were serious problems in Rome itself. The Gallic and Spanish legions, together with the Praetorian Guards, had rebelled against the emperor Nero, forcing him to flee Rome. The Senate declared the emperor a public enemy and he committed suicide on 9 June, AD68.

The lull in the fighting in the Jewish war resulted from the Roman general Vespasian returning to Rome to be proclaimed emperor, leaving his son Titus to continue battle plans in Judea. The respite was short-lived and Titus began the siege of Jerusalem in the spring of AD70 .

Jerusalem was crowded with people because of the Passover festivities and when Titus cut off the water and food supply the besieged masses suffered terribly. Those who tried to escape were crucified in front of the walls as an example to others and, according to Josephus, the famine was so severe that in one instance a mother ate the flesh of her own small son.

Titus did not want to see the Temple destroyed and he promised to spare the Jews if they would stop their resistance. Josephus was sent in to try to persuade his countrymen to surrender – but they refused, in the belief that their God was about to intercede in their great cause.

The Jewish commanders, John of Gischala and Simon ben Gorius, fought with great skill, creating tight 'killing areas' so that when the walls were breached the invaders would be forced into small pockets that could be picked off quickly. But the tide of Roman soldiers pushed relentlessly forward and fire soon consumed many buildings. On the Sabbath of 10 August, AD70, the Temple itself was ablaze.

From that day the Jewish people would never again offer up sacrifice to their God.

After bitter fighting the entire city fell in September of AD70. The Holy City was taken and burned, and the Tenth Legion encamped on the site of the ruined Temple, which had been levelled to the ground. Then the Romans proceeded to put every man, woman and child to the sword as they were found. Josephus records that of the 2½ million people assembled in the city at the Passover, 1 million perished in the siege and 347,000 died in other places. Of the remainder, 97,000 were carried into captivity and 11,000 starved.

However, Josephus tells us that even after the Temple was destroyed, the underground maze of tunnels in the giant platform provided hiding places for many of the Jewish fighters:

> This Simon [bar Giora], during the siege of Jerusalem, had
> occupied the upper town; but when the Roman army entered
> within the walls and were sacking the whole city, he, accom-
> panied by his most faithful friends, along with some stone
> cutters, bringing the tools required for their craft and
> provisions sufficient for many days, let himself down with all
> his party into one of the secret passages.

Josephus goes on to say that Simon and his team suddenly emerged in the
midst of the Roman camp on the site of the Temple itself:

> Simon... dressed himself in white tunics and buckling over
> them a purple mantle arose out of the ground at the very spot
> whereon the Temple formerly stood. The spectators were at
> first aghast and remained motionless; but afterwards they
> approached nearer and enquired who he was... His
> emergence from the ground led, moreover, to the discovery
> during those days of a large number of other rebels in subter-
> ranean passages.[14]

Simon had dressed himself in the white garb of an Essene, covered with
the purple mantle of a king. The white robes and the purple mantle had
obviously been prepared in advance because, even at this dire moment,
Simon and his followers still believed that God was going to intercede and
turn a horrible defeat into a glorious victory for the Sons of Light.

Simon was wrong. But neither he nor any of his men ever gave the
Romans a hint of the glories that lay concealed deep in the secret passages
below the Temple Mount.

Between AD66 and 70, a huge proportion of the population of the Jewish
homeland had been put to the sword, yet the New Testament fails to give
even a passing mention to the loss of the very people at the heart of the
Christian story, many of whom had been eyewitnesses to the baptism,
sermons and crucifixion of Jesus. We believe that this omission, except
perhaps in the case of Luke 21:20, where reference is made to these events
in the form of a prophecy by Jesus, demonstrates how the new gospels of
Christianity owed virtually nothing to the Jews and their search for their

Messiah. The deluded tentmaker from Tarsus had unwittingly created a revised wrapper for an old mystery religion that would eventually become one of the world's great faiths.

The gentile Christians of the Diaspora who had been taught Paul's strange interpretations of the life and death of Jesus were free to spin their invented history because there were very few people left to tell the true story. These people adopted 'the Jewish Messiah' as their own but never thought of themselves as a Jewish sect at all. Having taken a garbled version of the story of the Sons of Light, they turned their backs on the nation of the Jews, even falsely holding them responsible for the murder of their own Davidic Messiah.

The Son of the Star

But not all of the priests of the Star Families were dead. Many made their way to Europe and a few stayed on in Judea hoping for an opportunity of fighting the war again. A little over half a century later, in AD132, another member of the Star Families believed the time had come to march forward as the Messiah. His family name was Simon bar Kosiba, but he took the title *Bar Kokhba*: 'Son of the Star'.

To make sure that his army consisted solely of the toughest warriors, the Son of the Star said that only men who would bite a finger off their right hand would merit being in his army. No less than 200,000 people passed this gruesome test.

The test was later dropped but, after recruiting had finished, Bar Kochba had an enormous and ferocious army of about 580,000 people. This new Messiah started his attack by taking areas of the country one at a time, sacking fortress after fortress, city after city and eventually retaking all of Palestine for the Jews and their God.

The Roman emperor, Hadrian, responded by bringing his top general, Julius Severus, all the way from Britain to lead his army against the Jews. By that time, there were 12 army legions from Egypt, Britain, Syria and other areas ready to do battle. Due to the large number of Jewish rebels, instead of waging open war, Severus besieged each Jewish fortress and held back food until the Jews grew weak. Only after he had broken these key hubs did he escalate into outright war. The Romans demolished all 50 Jewish fortresses and 985 villages. The Romans also suffered heavy casualties and Hadrian did not send his usual message to the Senate saying that 'I and my army are well'.

Eventually the Roman army forced Bar Kochba into a small fortified area in Jerusalem called Betar, which was considered impenetrable – but it too fell.

Half a million Jews lay dead on the battlefield. The rest of the Jews were sold as slaves, hid in caves, or fled to other countries. The existence of the Jews as a nation in their own homeland came to an end

Hadrian reconstructed Jerusalem in the name of Jupiter and renamed it Aelia Capitolina. All Jews were forbidden to go near the city.

But the Jerusalem Church was not gone. A small but important number of the followers of John, Jesus and James had survived. The group, generally identified under the title of the Ebionites (from Hebrew *Ebyonim*, 'the poor ones') continued in the Roman province of Iudaea (a larger region than Judea centred on Jerusalem) during the early centuries AD.

The Ebionites were in theological conflict with Pauline Christians and Gnostic Christians even before the destruction of Jerusalem. Several modern scholars, including Hyam Maccoby, Robert Graves, Hugh Schonfield and Keith Akers, contend that the Ebionites rejected the teachings of Paul of Tarsus and stuck with the authentic teachings of John, Jesus and James the Just.

Away from the turmoil of the Holy Land the priests of the Star Families lived on. They were to wait for the right time to continue their holy mission to build a new world order of God. In the coming centuries the power of imperial Rome began to wane, but the might of the empire was being transferred to the cult of the tentmaker. The Star Families now had to contend with the powerful religion of Christianity.

CHAPTER 3

To Rescue an Empire

If Paul of Tarsus was the most important person in the history of Christianity then, arguably, the second most important was another Roman citizen by the name of Gaius Flavius Valerius Aurelius Constantinus, better known as the emperor Constantine I.

Constantine was born at Naissus (now Nis in Serbia) on 27 February, AD272. His father, Constantius Chlorus, was a general in the Roman army and his mother, Helena, was a 16-year-old innkeeper's daughter who had become a camp follower.

In AD305 Constantius was made co-emperor of Rome but he died the following year on 25 July at Eboracum (York) in Britain, where he had stopped on his way to an expedition against the Picts in Scotland. The 34-year-old Constantine was at his father's deathbed and the troops loyal to his father's memory proclaimed Constantine emperor on the same day. Relations between Constantine and his co-emperor, Licinius, eventually broke down, and a struggle for power followed which was resolved with the defeat and death of Licinius in AD324. Now emperor of both the eastern and western halves of the Roman Empire, Constantine began many important administrative reforms, including restructuring the army and separating civil and military authority, a move specifically designed to reduce the possibility of military commanders seizing power. The new centralized government was run directly by Constantine and his council, known as the *sacrum consistorium*.

Constantine and Religion

Having made major changes to the workings of military and civil life, Constantine turned his attention to religious affairs, with the aim of achieving as much unity and stability amongst his citizens as he could. Constantine was a follower of a solar religion centred on Deus Sol Invictus ('the Unconquered Sun God'), generally called simply Sol Invictus – a faith that was either very closely related to or perhaps synonymous with Mithraism. The emperor Aurelian had introduced this cult as the premier official religion of the empire around the time that Constantine had been born. Aurelian had dedicated the Sol Invictus Temple at Rome on 25 December AD274, in a festival called *Dies Natalis Solis Invicti* or 'Birthday of the invincible Sun'.

On 7 March AD321, Constantine decreed that Sunday (the Roman *Dies Solis*) should be a day of rest in honour of the Sun god. He stated:

> On the venerable day of the Sun let the magistrates and
> people residing in cities rest, and let all workshops be closed.
> In the country, however, persons engaged in agriculture may
> freely and lawfully continue their pursuits because it often
> happens that another day is not suitable for grain-sowing or
> vine planting; lest by neglecting the proper moment for such
> operations the bounty of heaven should be lost.

There is no doubt that Sol Invictus and the mystery religion of Mithras were extremely popular at the heart of Roman Empire when Constantine came to power, but they were not alone. Christianity was also prospering, though it was far from organized. It had exploded into many forms after the time of Paul and countless 'gospels' and other religious texts were in circulation.

We can be sure that the Star Families remained active during this period, not only in and around Jerusalem but also much further west. Historical and archaeological investigations into the remote past of Gaul (France) and Britian shows that Christianity was present in these locations from a very early date. There it began to follow a very different pattern to the Pauline model established closer to the centre of empire in Rome. As we shall presently see, the development of Culdean Christianity in the Celtic margins of Europe offered a safe harbour for Star Family priests within provinces that were so remote they could not be effectively controlled by developing bishoprics much further east.

Persecution of the Christians had officially ended in AD313 when Constantine and his once co-emperor, Licinius, had jointly issued the Edict of Milan, which essentially made Christianity legal in the Roman Empire. The fact that Helena, Constantine's mother, was a Christian may have been an influencing factor.

Rome had generally been rather tolerant of the various beliefs adopted by its many citizens. Earlier Roman rulers had not only accepted the right of the individual to believe what he or she wished in a religious sense, but Rome itself had frequently subsumed local deities from far off, and had come to include them in its own rich pantheon of gods and goddesses. As far as successive emperors were concerned, Christianity would have been no different, were it not for the fact that its followers stubbornly refused to accept that emperors themselves could be divine, or to believe that one's first allegiance was to Rome and its rulers. Jesus had famously put space between worldly emperors and his God when he said: 'Give unto God that which is God's, and give unto Caesar that which is Caesar's.'

Most Christians would have been content to live in peace as law-abiding citizens, but successive emperors had burned with indignation when Christians refused to accept either their divinity or their supreme position of authority. Tens if not hundreds of thousands of Christians had died in the jails of the empire or were sacrificed in the amphitheatres and along the roadsides – many of them followers not of the Jewish Jesus, about whom they knew virtually nothing, but rather of the almost entirely fictitious, resurrected Jesus created by Paul of Tarsus.

Constantine was a pragmatic man and he did not care what religion was popular amongst his people, but he did strive for conformity. He sensed that Christianity might represent the foundation of a stable and universal religion that could be controlled from Rome. But he also knew that this could never happen whilst Christianity itself represented a vast array of different cults, even within the group that believed that the man Jesus was a god.

Moulding a Faith: The Council of Nicaea

In AD325 Constantine personally presided over the first ecumenical council of the Christian Church at Nicaea (present-day Iznik, Turkey) which was the largest gathering of bishops and other Church leaders that had ever been convened up until that time. The council began on 14 June and across the next few weeks decisions were taken that would mould the shape of religion in Europe.

The bishops from Europe, North Africa and Asia who met at Nicaea were to have huge influence on the development of a religious cult that was still only three centuries old. In this comparatively short time, Christianity had learned to adapt itself to whatever circumstances prevailed and had maintained a very 'local' feel in many of the geographical settings where it had taken hold. In some areas, for example in Rome itself, the new belief system had taken on a distinctly 'Latin' feel, as Paul's Mithraic interpretation of the story of Jesus had fitted well with the beliefs of Sol Invictus.

Not only was Sunday (the day of the Sun) to be the Christian Sabbath, the images of Jesus and the various saints came to be depicted with the blazing Sun behind their heads to indicate holiness. These personal Sun images became known to Christians as 'halos'. Some of the earliest images of Christ represent him as the Greek Sun god Helios, who rode his golden chariot across the sky each day. Helios was the direct equivalent of the Roman god Sol, the centre of the religion Sol Invictus.

The key task for Constantine was to decide which documents should constitute the 'Holy Book' of this new Roman religion, which would be simply called the 'Bible' – the word being simply Greek for 'books' (*biblia*). With so many versions available, a proportion of the already existing gospels had to go completely and some of the material in the remaining gospels would need to be carefully edited. For example, the Gospel of Philip, which had been widely accepted among Gnostic groups until this point, was rejected, along with Gnosticism itself, as heretical. The Gospel of Philip contains a remarkable passage in which the disciples complain about Jesus appearing to favour Mary Magdalene over them, and which almost implies that she was Jesus' wife.

The Gospel of the Ebionites, popular among the Solomonic Star Families, was another rejected writing. The 4th-century Christian scholar Epiphanius wrote about this work, which he claimed was a 'forged and mutilated' version of the Gospel of Matthew, lacking the nativity story of Jesus and the resurrection episode.

However, Solomon's Star Families, the hereditary Jewish priests, who had been fully involved in the true Ebionite Jerusalem Church, knew that Jesus had been an important teacher – but not as important as the founder of The Way: John the Baptist. They believed that leadership of the Jerusalem Church had passed from John to Jesus and then to his brother James, and they repudiated all the Mithraic trappings that had become attached to the life of Jesus. So the truth may be that the Ebionite so-called 'forgery' is the earlier version of the gospel, championing John the Baptist and lacking fanciful passages that derived from the alien, Mithraic cult developed by Paul. It is likely that Matthew's gospel – which scholars accept as the most Jewish of the Christian gospels – became dramatically changed to include passages that Matthew himself never penned.

And, of course, another volume hugely popular among many Christians up to this point, and especially the Jerusalem Christians, was the *Book of Enoch*. This book was at the heart of the ancient traditions that underpinned the Star Families. It too failed to gain entry to the canon and every known copy destroyed.

More than 50 books were either dramatically altered or destroyed by Constantine and the bishops, leaving what is essentially the New Testament as we know it today. Every book that was included became 'gospel truth' and those that were removed were henceforth pronounced 'heretical'.

Nicaea represented a more-or-less open meeting between Constantine and the bishops, though it seems likely that many of the major decisions regarding the intended direction of Christianity were taken behind closed doors. The ultimate shaping of the Christian canon took place both at Nicaea and during the years that immediately followed it.

The Roman-sponsored, and therefore Pauline, Council of Nicaea had to play down the role of James, the brother of Jesus, and greatly exaggerated the importance of the disciple Simon Peter. Constantine's secretaries concluded that, with judicious editing, they could create an irrefutable line of succession based on a dubious saying of Jesus that is almost certainly a later addition to Matthew's gospel: 'This is the rock upon which my church is built.' (Matthew 16:18). They then claimed that Peter had ultimately travelled to Rome to become overseer (bishop) of the Roman Church, becoming what would later be called the first pope. By this means the bishops of Rome acquired a mandate from Jesus himself, which could henceforth be seen to be irrefutable and undeniable. What is more, this construct favoured Rome, which was Constantine's intention.

However, one thing could trump Rome's claim to power and control over the faithful: the claim of Jesus' own descendants. It is almost certainly the case that no dishonesty was intended by the actions of the delegates at Nicaea, because at the time there was no concept of 'truth' being an absolute – truth was that which best served political needs. Documentary evidence in front of these men strongly suggested that Jesus had been married and had children – but such a fact would make the line of Peter completely meaningless, as the bloodline of the Messiah would trump Rome's claim to power. As a result the Gospel of Philip was rejected, along with every other document or passage that contained references to anything that could suggest that Jesus may have had a wife and family

Rites of Mithra

Despite his interest in sorting out Christian affairs, it is uncertain whether Constantine ever became a Christian himself – tradition has it that he was baptized on his deathbed on 22 May AD337, but this may be a wishful legend that arose in a Church which owed its power to his intervention. A close look at the emperor's life before and after Nicaea demonstrates that he stuck rigidly to the 'Sol Invictus' variant of Mithraism that he had adopted as a very young man. Even after the Council of Nicaea, Constantine maintained the traditional title of *Pontifex Maximus* as the high priest of Apollo and his coins continued to be inscribed in favour of the old religion: *SOLI INVICTO COMITI*, 'To The Invincible Sun, the Companion [of the Emperor].'

The god Mithra sprang from Zoroastrianism, the old Persian religion whose supreme deity was Ahura Mazda. With the passing of time it was considered that Mithra was actually equal to the supreme deity. Centuries before the birth of Christ, Mithra had acquired a biography. It was said that Mithra had been born in a cave of a virgin mother on 25 December and received the adoration of shepherds at his birth. He was credited with the personal ability to save souls and it was preached that he had been put to death at the time of year we now know as Easter and that after three days he had risen from the dead.

By way of the Sol Invictus cult, Mithraism became merged into Christianity in almost every respect, for example, in the ideals of humility and brotherly love, baptism, the rite of communion, the use of holy water and the belief in the immortality of the soul, the last judgement and the resurrection. Mithraists also believed in eternal life in heaven, and in the torture of the wicked after death. Many of these beliefs and rituals were exclusive to Mithraism and were not officially affirmed as part of the Christian faith until the 4th century.

There can be little doubt that Constantine's great idea was to unify the minds and the souls of his subjects by amalgamating as many beliefs and practices as possible into one single religion, then to make the resulting faith the property of the empire. He brilliantly reasoned that a disciple of Jove in Rome, a Druid from the far west, or a worshipper of Isis, Demeter or Mithra would eventually come to accept the Jesus myth because aspects of it were already familiar. Mithra was not worshipped openly, on street corners, as was Jesus. On the contrary, in order to become a follower of Mithra it was necessary for an aspirant to be 'introduced' to the various forms of worship, all of which were secret. Mithraism had originally been confined to Roman soldiers and civil servants, so there was a strong martial aspect to his worship and access to the Mithraic Temples was restricted to men, with women playing no part in the ceremonies that took place there. Mithraism had much in common with the other mystery religions that proliferated across the empire, but like them it was of no use as a political tool.

Temples to Mithra were small affairs, often subterranean or made to look like caves. They have been found all over the old Roman world, as far west as Britain, but it is only fairly recently that the purpose of these little rectangular structures has been recognized. Mithraic Temples had rows of seats down each of two sides and empty areas both in the centre and on the east side, where little-understood ceremonies took place. It is unlikely that more than about 40 people could have fitted comfortably into any of the Mithraic Temples that have been excavated.

It is known that there were various 'degrees' of initiation into Mithraism. These were probably seven in number, one for each of the known heavenly bodies at the time: the Sun, Moon, Mercury, Venus, Mars, Jupiter and Saturn. Once initiated into the first degree of this religion, aspirants were allowed to take part in basic ceremonies, but those officiating were drawn from the ranks of those who had undertaken all seven degrees. The only part of any of the ceremonies that is even remotely understood is the ritualized recreation of Mithra killing a sacred white bull, but even this strange ceremony essentially remains a mystery.

Mithraism was a male-only religion but it did have a female counter-part and this was based on Cybele, the Phrygian goddess, known to her followers as 'the Mother of God'. The priests of Mithra were known as 'Fathers' and the priestesses of Cybele as 'Mothers'. And not surprisingly, the early shapers of the Romanized Jesus cult became known as the Church Fathers. To this day Roman Catholic priests are still addressed as 'Father'.

After baptism into the mysteries of Mithra, the initiate was marked on the forehead with the sign of the cross formed by the elliptic and the celestial equator. The Mithraists also celebrated a love feast, which consisted of loaves of bread decorated with crosses, and wine – the body and blood of Mithra.

As time went forward Constantine's re-labelling of Mithraism as Christianity would become almost forgotten, yet the obvious lack of any originality for crucial aspects of the story of Christ caused the early Church authorities to issue a papal bull (decree) to explain this away. The bull claimed that the story of Jesus had actually originated first but the devil had falsely placed Mithra further back in history than he really should be, specifically to cause mischief and to confuse true Christians! Clearly this is nonsense and it remains a fact that birth in a stable, virgin birth, crucifixion and resurrection after three days – and a host of other traditions and beliefs attached to the life of Christ – arose first in Mithraism and were added to the Jesus myth.

The Roman Church Triumphant

In a period of only a few months Constantine achieved all his chosen objectives. He doubtless hoped that Christianity would spread even further across the known world but it had now been ordained that the centre of Christian worship would not be in Palestine, where the religion developed, but rather in Rome itself. Henceforth anyone looking for religious guidance and regulation would have to respond to the Church in Rome, the city that was also the centre of civil and legal administration. In this way Constantine sought to re-establish the importance and relevance of Rome and to add significant props to the ailing empire.

It seems almost certain that some of the representatives at Nicaea were familiar with the Jerusalem Church, but these were men who had learned to keep their mouths closed. The true nature of Jesus' life and ministry were anathema to Rome and were so closely associated with the constant rebelliousness of Judea, and its eventual destruction by the Roman legions, that to speak about them – even three centuries on – would mean certain death. Priests of the Star Families learned early that they must be both patient and manipulative if the New Jerusalem was ever to become a reality. They were well aware that the Roman form of Christianity was every bit as much their enemy as the empire itself. The Families' influence was strong, but as would prove to be the case in the many centuries that followed, it was subterranean and deliberately subtle.

The Sacred Feminine

By the time of the Council of Nicaea, Christians already worshipped a mysterious Trinity, which is known to us today as the Father, the Son and the Holy Ghost or Holy Spirit. From its earliest days Christianity had been much influenced by Greece and the Greek language, which was the lingua franca in the east of the Roman Empire. The third component of the Trinity, prior to the Church finally adopting the term 'Holy Spirit', had often been referred to as *Sophia*, a Greek feminine noun meaning (Holy) Wisdom. This ancient concept is found in the Old Testament and was also central to Gnostic systems.

Followers of Mithra may have accepted what early Christians seem to have also taken for granted and something that was self-evident to the Star

Families – that one cannot have a Father and a Son without the presence of a Wife and a Mother. There is nothing unique about this state of affairs. It was an important component of other mystery religions that proliferated at the same time as that of Mithra and early Christianity. Probably the most popular of these, and one that flourished well into the Christian period, was the Mystery of Demeter, the celebration of which took place annually in Greece.

Demeter, which means simply 'Earth Mother', was a form of an age-old deity that had been worshipped across most of Europe and large parts of Asia as far back as the Old Stone Age. Although she must have had hundreds of names in different locations she is generally referred to these days as the 'Great Goddess'. There is no doubt that her form reigned supreme in the spiritual lives of individuals for tens of thousands of years. Her worship had come from Europe to Minoan Crete and on to the shores of the land of Canaan, where the Phoenicians in particular had embraced it with enthusiasm. It was fully understood by the ancestors of the Jews and was enshrined in the 'Holy Union' of masculine and feminine that was believed to take place at the time of the Shekinah (*see* page 10).

By the time Demeter rose to prominence, during that period we now refer to as Classical Greece (beginning *c.* 500BC), the Great Goddess as a concept was already thousands of years old and Demeter reflected much of what had been central to the goddess's worship. A popular story suggested that Demeter was the goddess of vegetation and that she had shown specific concern for humanity. It was said that she had a daughter, Persephone, who had been abducted by Hades, the god of the underworld. Incensed, Demeter had turned to Hades' brother Zeus, king of the gods, and demanded that her daughter should be released. Zeus agreed to intervene, but warned that Persephone could leave the underworld only if she had eaten nothing during the period of her captivity. It turned out that she had been tricked into eating a single pomegranate seed and Zeus decreed that henceforth Persephone must spend one third of the year in Hades and the other two-thirds with her mother in world above.

So grief-stricken was, and is, Demeter at the annual loss of her daughter that, it was said, while Persephone was locked in her prison far below the ground, Demeter weeps and all vegetation in the world ceases. This was the Greek explanation for winter and is probably a variant of a story that was told in Minoan Crete and doubtless across much of the world in very ancient times.

In addition, Demeter was associated with another character, who in different stories is sometimes her husband but just as often her son. His name was Dionysus and he became one of the most popular of the Greek deities. His special concern was for growing things and especially for wine. Stories about Dionysus relate that he was set upon by brigands who killed him and then roasted and ate his flesh. Through the intervention of Demeter his body was reconstructed so that the episode became a cyclic event, celebrated annually.

The worship of Demeter herself took place twice each year in and close to Athens in Greece. The ceremonies celebrated there became known as the 'Mysteries of Demeter' because no accurate account of the rites has ever found its way into common knowledge. This is a mark of the respect given to the ceremonies and the awe that they inspired. In addition, the secrets had to be kept by initiates on pain of death.

Further east, in Egypt, another version of the all-pervading Goddess had arisen. Her name was Isis and she was extremely popular not only in Egypt itself but also eventually across the whole Roman world and beyond.

Isis had originally been a lunar deity and her presence in Egyptian religion was so old that she had probably existed right back at the start of civilized life along the River Nile. Popular stories made her the wife of Osiris, the most beloved of all Egyptian gods, whose special responsibility was for the dead and the afterlife. Osiris ruled on Earth until he was deceived by another god, Set, who arranged for Osiris to be locked into a sealed sarcophagus, which was set adrift on the Nile. Isis was heartbroken and searched diligently for her husband. The coffin had drifted ashore in far-off Biblos and become entangled in a tamarisk bush, which had eventually grown into a tree, with the sarcophagus inside its trunk. The king of Biblos had so admired the tree that he had it made into a pillar to support his palace. Isis eventually tracked it down and released her husband from his imprisonment.

Set, though, was not finished. Whilst Isis was away he arranged for the body of Osiris to be cut into 14 parts, which he distributed throughout the world. Isis travelled for a long period, gathering together the various pieces, which she eventually reconstructed. Then she magically restored

Osiris to life for long enough to conceive her son, Horus. However, some of the stories relate that Isis found every part of her husband except his penis, and that in order to conceive Horus she manufactured a phallus from beeswax. Osiris entered the *Duat*, the underworld, where he supervised the afterlife of all who believed in him and his faithful wife.

There are several common threads in the stories told about Isis and those of Demeter. In each case there is some ambiguity about the relationship between the goddess and the god. Sometimes the god is the consort of the goddess, and at other times he is her son. In each case, though, the body of the god is ripped asunder and then reconstructed by the goddess, and there is no doubt as to why such stories exist. What we find in the character of Osiris and that of Dionysus are representatives of a common god from ancient times who is collectively known as 'Corn God'. While the Great Goddess is perpetual and represents the forces of nature, the Corn God is annually reborn as the corn, which grows, is cut down and dismembered because humanity must eat. In this respect both Osiris and Dionysus are representative, not of nature itself, but of the bounty that springs forth each spring.

The Corn God also lies at the very heart of Christianity, at least as far as the Gospels are concerned. This becomes clear close to the end of Jesus' life at the time of an event known as the Last Supper. This ritual meal is described in detail in the Christian Bible. It is supposed to have taken place the day before Jesus was arrested, tried and crucified by the Roman authorities. At this special meal Jesus took wine in a cup and passed it around his disciples. According to Luke 22:17: 'He took the cup, and gave thanks and said, "Take this, and divide it among yourselves".'

Jesus went on to explain that the wine represented his blood. He then turned his attention to the bread. According to Luke 22:19: 'He took bread, and gave thanks and broke it and gave it unto them, saying, "This is My body which is given for you. This do in remembrance of Me".'

It is unlikely that this event ever took place. Such an idea would be totally disgusting to all Jews at the time as blood and dead flesh were anathema to them. As a would-be 'King of the Jews', Jesus would have lost all support if he had even made such an outrageous statement. This scene was a much later embellishment designed to appeal to Romans who had, for centuries, been drinking the blood of their gods.

Most likely, the Last Supper was the usual communal meal enjoyed by most Jews on the eve of the Passover. The concept of the bread and wine was far older than Christ, as the Bible itself records. In Genesis 14:18 we read that hundreds of years before the first Jews existed, Melchizedek (meaning 'king of righteousness') the high priest and king of Jerusalem, brought forth bread and wine.

There can be no ambiguity here. Both Melchizedek and Jesus, or whoever first wrote down these stories, were clearly making reference to the Corn God from extreme antiquity. What makes the New Testament incident even more important is the fact that part of the analogy specifically relates to bread, which is of course made from corn.

If Jesus either equated himself, or was equated by his followers, with the Corn God, then we would also expect to find a representative of the Great Goddess somewhere in this story, and indeed we do. She is none other than the Virgin Mary.

Mary the God-Bearer

The Virgin Mary's importance to specific denominations of the Christian Church remains an essential and even perhaps a paramount part of the whole Christian religion.

Mary was already venerated by the time of the First Council of Nicaea. In specific locations, and especially among the Greeks of Asia Minor (Turkey) she was already referred to as *Theotokos*, the 'God-Bearer'. By AD553 this was a title that was officially bestowed on her across the whole Christian world. Nevertheless her actual position within Christianity has always been somewhat ambiguous for a couple of very important reasons.

The emperor Constantine used the Council of Nicaea to push through the version of Christianity that best suited his purposes. It was decided at Nicaea that Jesus was indistinguishable from God – in other words, he was 'of the same substance' as God, as the Nicene Creed puts it. This being the case – and it is something absolutely repudiated by the Jerusalem Church – there could be little doubt about the divinity of the Virgin Mary because who could give birth to a genuine god except a genuine goddess? What made matters even more complicated was the fact that if God was Jesus' father and Mary his mother, Mary must also have been the wife of

God. And if Jesus himself was also God then Mary was his wife also. In this respect she closely resembles both the Greek Demeter and the Egyptian Isis.

The implications were not lost on either Constantine or those who came in his wake, and the Christian Church has spent many centuries puzzling over Mary's actual position within the faith. Constantine himself does not seem to have been unduly troubled by these implications and it is possible that they exist as a legacy of Mithraism. The Virgin Mary is still referred to within the Catholic Church and the Orthodox Eastern Churches as both 'Mother of God' and 'Queen of Heaven'. She has also constantly been referred to as either the 'Bride of Christ' or the 'Bride of God', which, if Jesus is indivisible from God, are merely different versions of the same thing. All of this was accepted and understood by the Star Families, though not in the way Roman Christians believed. To the Star Families the association of the Goddess and the annually sacrificed and re-born Corn God was part of a belief that went way back before the advent of Judaism, to a time when God and Goddess were indistinguishable in importance. They saw such stories as that of the Goddess and the Corn God as important allegories – ways in which people could eventually come to accept a much deeper message regarding the nature of gender and Godhead.

Christianity Triumphant

Despite Constantine's best efforts, even an official faith could do little but delay the inevitable. Within 200 years the greater Roman Empire crumbled, imperial power surviving only in the east and centred upon Constantinople. But Pauline Christianity, with its strong structures and hierarchies centred on Rome, survived the incursions of the 'barbarians' that destroyed the Roman secular infrastructure in the west. The barbarians were themselves soon converted, and the faith continued to gain ground, eventually reaching the very extremities of Europe, for example Ireland, where people had held out against this potpourri cult for many centuries. Ultimately it became the undisputed belief system for all of Europe.

As it spread, Christianity gradually lost its tolerance for other beliefs that had at least been evident at the time of Nicaea. In particular, Christianity found ways to demonize Venus, a planet that had been held sacred for so long that nobody could know when the practice began. Venus formed part of the Holy Shekinah and it had been the sacred 'hour hand' of time. It represented the supreme power of the Goddess, and in fact the planet still bears her name because Venus was merely the Roman counterpart of the Egyptian Isis and the Greek Aphrodite, who was herself just another version of the Great Goddess. Venus was also the symbol of the Holy Virgin, something that would not be forgotten by Freemasons many centuries into the future, suffused as their practices would be with the beliefs of the Star Families.

Christianity eventually shunned Venus-worship altogether. True, it persisted on the fringes of the Christian world, in particular in Scandinavia, where Lucifer, Lord of Light, became St Lucy, whose winter solstice celebrations, candles and fires became embedded in local Christian practices. But in the main, Venus, as either a male or a female representation, was viciously attacked. Lucifer, who had originally been a deity or sub-deity associated with Venus was now treated as just another name for Satan. The magical mathematical association between the movements of Venus and those of the Sun as seen from Earth became the stuff of forgotten and forbidden legend as the Christian Church persecuted those who merely looked at the heavens with an intellectual curiosity. The tall pointed hats worn by the 'seers' – those learned hierophants that had once been astronomer-priests were now considered to be the headgear of witches and their astronomical shadow staffs were labelled 'broomsticks'.

Anything deviating at all from the official line of the Church was 'sinful' and 'heretical'. Everyone's ticket to a happy afterlife was dependent on unquestioning obedience to the newly merged Mithra-Jesus cult.

The light of Lucifer had been extinguished. Ignorance had triumphed over wisdom and superstition had replaced logic. The Church spread a veil of darkness across Europe as truth became turned on its head. Religious intolerance became the norm and subscribing to blind faith was praised as a great virtue. Those who maintained a religion based on an understanding of nature and astronomy were called pagans, a term which the Church still falsely uses as a label for those it sees as being uneducated and wicked.

The Dark Ages were about to begin.

CHAPTER 4

The Rising of the Star Families

The families of the Jewish priestly line that had survived the great slaughter at the hands of the Romans in First Jewish War (AD66–70) and Second Jewish War (AD132–5) (*see* Chapter 2) had headed far away from their beloved homeland. From foreign shores they watched and waited. Some gave up all hope of the coming of the kingdom of heaven, some slowly retrenched and others assumed that it must be God's will that their day would come on some future auspicious date of his own choosing. Direct confrontation against the perceived oppressors seemed hopeless and the last group that tried to remove the Romans from their land by force had followed their leader, Bar Kochba, the 'Son of the Star' … into oblivion.

The Revelation of John

A famous, but paradoxically unknown, Star Family member by the name of John put his thoughts into words. He wrote a powerful and deeply passionate document about the plight of his people that somehow managed to find its way into the New Testament, providing the closing words of the Christian scriptures. In the Book of Revelation, probably written within 10 or 20 years of the First Jewish War, this mysterious John laments the loss of the holy city but he pens his words in hope and speaks of resurrection and of the coming of further struggles between the powers of good and evil. The writing is certainly Enochian in character and utterly different to the rest of the New Testament; it also resembles works in the apocalyptic parts of the Old Testament, such as Ezekiel and Daniel. Somehow it managed – just – to avoid being put through the Pauline filter.

It is rather strange that Revelation survived the cull carried out under Constantine but the debate about its Christian credentials has never gone away. It was centuries before the Roman Catholic Church finally drew a line under questions of its authenticity. Five hundred years ago, Martin Luther, the theologian and instigator of the Protestant Reformation, recognized that Revelation was unconnected to the rest of the New Testament. He said:

> There is no prophet in the Old Testament, to say nothing of
> the New, who deals so exclusively with visions and images.
> For myself, I think it approximates the *Fourth Book of Esdras*;
> I can in no way detect that the Holy Spirit produced it.
>
> Many of the [Church] Fathers also rejected this book a long
> time ago … Christ is neither taught nor known in it.

The fact that Revelation is Enochian in style makes it highly probable that it came from someone who was close to the Jerusalem Church and certainly connects it with the Essenes. As we have noted, the *Book of Enoch* was a popular work amongst early Christians, but it disappeared almost entirely for around 1,500 years.

Enoch was lost to the world by the time of Martin Luther but it is highly significant that he identified a strong commonality between Revelation and what he referred to as the *Fourth Book of Esdras* (*4 Esdras*). This work is now known as *2 Esdras*, and proved to be of central importance in the formation of Freemasonry in Scotland – well before Luther's time.

In Revelation 5:10 John says:

> And hast made us unto our God kings and priests: and we
> shall reign on the earth.

This appears to be a description of the Star Families; the people who were God's bloodline of kings and priests – the ones whose divine duty was to create a new world order to guide humankind to its ultimate destiny.

In chapters 20 and 21 John makes a prophecy that 1,000 years after the fall of Jerusalem, evildoers, referred to as Gog and Magog, will attack the city of Yahweh. But at this time the holy ones will rise up and retake their homeland. John says:

> And I saw an angel come down from heaven, having the key of the bottomless pit and a great chain in his hand.
>
> And he laid hold on the dragon, that old serpent, which is the Devil, and Satan, and bound him a thousand years, and cast him into the bottomless pit, and shut him up, and set a seal upon him, that he should deceive the nations no more, till the thousand years should be fulfilled: and after that he must be loosed a little…
>
> …But the rest of the dead lived not again until the thousand years were finished. This is the first resurrection… and when the thousand years are expired, Satan shall be loosed out of his prison, and shall go out to deceive the nations which are in the four quarters of the earth, Gog, and Magog, to gather them together to battle: the number of whom is as the sand of the sea.
>
> And they went up on the breadth of the earth, and compassed the camp of the saints about, and the beloved city: and fire came down from God out of heaven, and devoured them.
>
> And I saw a new heaven and a new earth: for the first heaven and the first earth were passed away; and there was no more sea. And I John saw the holy city, new Jerusalem, coming down from God out of heaven, prepared as a bride adorned for her husband.

The Temple of the Jews had fallen in AD70. The precise origin of the term 'Gog and Magog' is unknown today but biblical scholars know that it was used as a term for unspecified invaders from the north. So, John saw that another invasion would arrive after 1,000 years and that 'the dead' would be resurrected after the intervening millennium. This can only be a reference to an expected resurgence of the Star Families, implying not that they were dead in the literal sense of the word but rather in terms of their influence and success. The attack would be followed by a victory of the resurrected ones that would bring about a New Jerusalem – a *global* "New Jerusalem" with the God of the Jews ruling the world. This would be a world, as John says, with 'no seas' – in other words a united world with no international barriers.

For rational people the idea of predicting the future seems impossible and it is not surprising that long-range prophecies that describe detailed events, invariably end up being plumb wrong. Of course, those who believe in the supernatural (as most people did before the age of science) feel that there are ways to transcend the laws of nature. The prophet Elijah had foreseen the rising of a new Messiah when the Shekinah returned. As an astronomical event, the Shekninah was certain to happen on a known date and because people then *looked* for a Messiah, Elijah's prophecy seemed sound – until it crumbled to dust with the death of Jesus.

But, as we shall see, no matter how or why he came to write the words, John's vision of the future given in Revelation was to prove to be startlingly accurate.

The Star Families in France

At the time that John wrote his Revelation a substantial group of his compatriots had wandered the fringes of the empire before slowly regrouping in southern Gaul (France) – a location that was reasonably prosperous but remote enough to be safe for the exiles. The seaports of the region were significant but secondary trading centres, being close enough to Rome, the seat of power, to be considered fully subjugated but far enough away not to matter very much.

In these cosmopolitan areas around the southern seaports of Gaul, the Star Families were just another group of foreigners who soon integrated into European life, taking on the mantle of any cult that allowed them to remain fairly invisible. The eventual rise of Christianity must have been a blessing as they could readily present themselves as Jews who had converted to the new faith of the empire. Some of them also doubtless retained their Jewish trappings because Jews were generally accepted, especially in areas given to trade.

Even to those who had, outwardly, accepted the new faith there was a difference in their intentions. When they praised Jesus Christ they offered genuine veneration for a man who had almost been their Messiah, rather than the Pauline human manifestation of Yahweh. With their Jewish heritage they must have despaired of the incredible idea that a man could be God, but the northern peoples amongst whom they were now residing saw gods reflected everywhere – especially in the persons of their frequently deranged emperors. To the Star Families Jesus fell short of being a God, but he was without doubt one of Yahweh's true prophets and his influence had been, and would prove to be, pivotal to the world.

However, Jesus was not the only prophet they venerated and even though John the Baptist had been sidelined by Pauline Christianity, he remained paramount as the first and most important of the Star Family prophets. It seems entirely possible that these Solomonic priests shared the same view as the Mandaeans and held John the Baptist to be the true Messiah – the real Christ. Indeed the future activities of various bodies connected to the families greatly strengthens this possibility.

A quarter of a millennium after the fall of the Temple these descendents of the Jerusalem Church must have been disgruntled yet entirely unsurprised when Constantine and the Christian bishops formally approved their dead leader's designation, not only as a god but *the* God. Constantine and his bishops, mainly outsiders with no Jewish background, had not only taken Yahweh as their own – they had officially merged Him with the failed Jewish Messiah.

For Constantine, as we have seen, the whole purpose had been entirely political rather than theological, because he was determined to try and hold the creaking Roman Empire together. If he could no longer control the population by physical force he would do it by psychological means.

It was to no avail. Despite the strenuous efforts of Constantine and the emperors that followed him, nothing could save the huge, unwieldy Roman Empire. Hordes of warriors from the east began to pour into the western Empire, and even local tribes that had been kept at bay by the power of the legions found open revolt possible. By the second quarter of the

5th century the legions protecting both Gaul and Britain were withdrawn so that all possible strength could be focused on the protection of Rome itself.

As Jewish priests presenting themselves as Christians, the Star Family members living in Gaul exploited the changes that surrounded them. Taking advantage of the Frankish invasions that followed the collapse of Roman power, slowly but surely they began to assume positions of power and influence in region after region under new, Germanic rulers. They remained in southern areas for many generations but they progressively moved north into Burgundy and Normandy. Through trade and judicial marriages they gradually infiltrated the seats of feudal counts and other post-Roman aristocrats.

In particular they gained real power in the region of Champagne, a small but crucially important area sandwiched between the Frankish kingdom (Francia, hence 'France') to the north and Burgundy to the south. And although we do not know the names of the people in question, a series of clearly related events that took place between the 11th and the 13th centuries bear witness to the Star Family's manipulation of Western European and even Near Eastern politics from their base in Champagne.

There is strong evidence that the counts of Champagne and the leading aristocratic families of the region were Ebionite Christians – representatives in Western Europe of the original Jerusalem Church. They betrayed their origins by their concerted actions. Star Family priests stood in their midst and were the ultimate controllers of events that would eventually change the face of the world.

The Star Families and the Normans

Other Star Family priests gained influence further west, in the region that would become known as Normandy. Here they eventually came across another group of incomers. These were the Norsemen, or Vikings, from Scandinavia. Led by their desire for conquest, the Vikings had invaded the region in the 9th century, and as in other regions, hit-and-run raiding had been followed by settlement. The French throne ceded a large area in the west of the royal domains to the Vikings in 911 and the duchy of Normandy – the land of the Northmen – was born.

Somewhere around the beginning of the 10th century the undercover Jewish priesthood came face to face with the Vikings and discovered that their secrets were not quite as exclusive as they had always imagined. It must have amazed the Star Families' members to discover that these outwardly uncouth Norse people had much in common with themselves. Like their Jewish counterparts the Normans were not Christians – at least not in any normal sense of the word.

Duke Rollo (or Hrolf) was the first of the Norman Vikings to be christened but there is strong evidence that he and his most important followers retained a significant interest in their ancestral beliefs. Their tutelary goddess was named Freyja, and how startled the Star Family priests must have been to discover that she represented the planet Venus and was known as 'Queen of Heaven' – the same appellation that had been given to Venus by the Jews, right back to Canaanite times.

The Normans had largely abandoned their native language in favour of the local form of French, but had lost little or nothing of their ancient theology. It transpired that they fully understood the cycles of Venus and that they also recognized an astronomical phenomenon known as 'the horns' – an idea that that the Star Families must have assumed belonged exclusively to their own tradition.

In ancient times the Jews (like all the peoples of Canaan) saw horns on a human head as a badge of holiness and priestly power because the rising of Venus as a morning star and its alternative role as the evening star caused it to trace a pair of horns through the heavens on either side of the sky – in the east at dawn and the west at dusk. It was as though Venus created horns for the entire planet.

Whilst horns were of great symbolic importance to the Normans, the idea that Vikings routinely wore horned helmets is now recognized as being quite wrong. This was a misunderstanding of the Viking *religious* interest in horns that grew up in popular mythology in the early 19th century. It then became popular in many romanticized paintings of the period and so the 'horned helmets' of the Vikings became fixed in the minds of later generations.

The Star Families were no doubt less communicative about their core beliefs than their new soul mates, and one can imagine how they must have argued and debated amongst themselves exactly how much they should tell outsiders – even outsiders with a directly comparable theology. Eventually they must have elected to explain how the movements of Venus were at the heart of the appearance of the divine Shekinah and how the great prophets such as Enoch and Moses were often depicted as sporting a pair of horns to mark their godliness.

The religious imperatives of the early Normans and the Star Family Jews were inexplicably close and their shared mistrust of the Roman Church must have quickly created a powerful bond. Both groups realized that after the Roman Church had taken control of Christianity, unwanted ideas had been banned, books and entire libraries destroyed and non-conformists dispatched. The knowledge of astronomy that had underpinned Jesus' mission was labelled as evil and the holy symbol of horns had been, quite ridiculously, associated with Satan. By the 10th century the proud bringer of light and knowledge, the archangel 'Lucifer' had been given the horns as a mark of his evil. The badges of all that had been good and godly were now firmly attached to an idea that became known as 'the Devil'. The very heart of the belief system brought forward by Jesus Christ had been replaced by magical stories from an ancient Persian cult that no longer even survived.

But the Star Families and the Norsemen knew better.

Both groups had ancient traditions that centred on megalithic structures – the prehistoric stone circles and dolmens found across the western fringes of Europe and the land of Israel. When Moses and Joshua took Jews into the land of Canaan they found it to be covered with stone shrines used for astronomical observation. The very first place where the Jews of the Exodus chose to enter the 'promised land' from across the River Jordan was at a place called Gilgal – a word which means 'circle of stones'. The Enochian Jewish priesthood appears to have developed out of ancient Canaanite theology centred on observational astronomy at aligned stone sites.[1] Saul, the first king of the Jews, was acclaimed at this stone circle shrine.

The areas known to the Vikings were similarly covered with tens of thousands of these extremely ancient stone structures; particularly the British Isles.

Over time, their shared secrets led the families to intermarry and a strange allegiance grew based on a common mistrust of the Church and a desire to allow more rational, wiser ideas to rise to the surface. The Normans were famously open to new ideas and particularly keen to join in the plan to build a New Jerusalem.

In Revelation 5:5, the author states:

> And one of the elders saith unto me, Weep not: behold, the Lion of the tribe of Judah, the Root of David, hath prevailed to open the book, and to loose the seven seals thereof

The Lion of Judah is a traditional symbol of King David and the city he founded as his capital, Jerusalem. The term 'root of David' is a messianic term associated with the hereditary priesthood and thereafter the building of a New Jerusalem. The lion appears on the emblem of Jerusalem.

Perhaps unsurprisingly, the Norse/Star Family alliance, centred on Normandy, adopted the same lion, doubled up, as its symbol. (An otherwise strange choice of animal for a northern European people).

In 1066 William, Duke of Normandy, successfully invaded England and the Lion of Judah soon became the crest of their conquered land – the

Figure 2 The lion emblem of the city of Jerusalem

Figure 3 The heraldic badge of Normandy (two golden lions on a red field)

Figure 4 The lion of England (also gold on a red field, like the emblem of Normandy)

Figure 5 The royal arms of the United Kingdom

badge of the 'New Jerusalem' spoken of by John in the Book of Revelation.

Today the British royal arms includes nine animals – eight of which are lions. The chained unicorn of Scotland is the only other creature.

Yet despite the unicorn imagery, the single lion rampant first used by the Normans is still the principal heraldic symbol of Scotland.

The Family of Earl Rognvald

One Family, more than any other, stands out as critical in this Norse/Star Family union. The Norse family concerned was from the line of Earl Rognvald who ruled More (pronounced *mo-ray*), the part of Norway around the present city of Trondheim. The family was given the northern Scottish islands of Orkney and Shetland and Rognvald's brother, Sigurd the Powerful, ruled the islands as Rognvald's regent.

It was Rognvald's son Hrolf (Rollo) who invaded France and took control of Normandy before marrying the daughter of a Star Family member, Popa, the daughter of Count Berenger of Bayeux. Their offspring were therefore descended from the Viking rulers and the Jewish priesthood. In 912, at a village on the River Epte, Hrolf signed a peace treaty with King Charles the Simple of France that was later known as the Treaty of St-Clair-sur-Epte and established Hrolf as duke of Normandy. To seal the treaty Hrolf married his second wife Gizelle, the daughter of King Charles.

It was at this time that Hrolf More and his cousins decided formally to adopt the name 'St Clair'. The name had been created a short time earlier by a family member who called himself Guillermus de Saint Clair – which translated into English means 'William of the Holy Shining Light'.

There can be little doubt that the 'holy shining light' in question was the holy Shekinah.

In 1057 a member of this St Clair branch of the More family left Normandy to join the English court of Princess Margaret, granddaughter of King Edmund Ironside and a first cousin to King Edward the Confessor. William 'the Seemly' St Clair was a cousin of Duke William of Normandy, and when the duke conquered England in 1066, William St Clair escorted Princess Margaret to exile in Hungary. There, King Stephen gave her a fragment of the 'True Cross' as part of her dowry for her marriage to King Malcolm III Canmore of Scotland. When the bridal party finally arrived in Scotland, King Malcolm gave William St Clair lands across his kingdom. William is regarded as the ancestor of the Scottish Sinclairs.

Here, in ancient Albion, through their merger with the Norse bloodlines, the Star Families believed they had laid the foundation of the New Jerusalem.

Crusade: The Star Families take the Initiative

As the year 1070 arrived, the Star Families, now spread out across France, England and Scotland became increasingly aware that 1,000 years had passed since Jerusalem and its Holy Temple had been destroyed by the troops of Titus in AD70. They picked up their Bibles and read again how John, the writer of the Book of Revelation, had said that their holy city would again be attacked by the forces of Satan after one millennium. The words of Revelation 20 were impassioned but the meaning seemed clear:

> And he seized the dragon, that old serpent, which is the Devil, and Satan, and bound him a thousand years, and cast him into the bottomless pit, and shut him up, and set a seal upon him, that he should deceive the nations no more, till the thousand years should be fulfilled: and after that he must be loosed a little.

And so it was.

In 1076 the news must have spread like wildfire through the ranks of the Star Families now dispersed across France, England and Scotland. Seljuk Turks had taken Jerusalem, destroying much of it. The first part of the prophecy had come true and now it was their duty to deliver up the second part: they, the scions of the priests who had defended Jerusalem a millennium ago had to retake their Temple and recover the secret documents and treasures that lay beneath it. Once the real Jerusalem was in their possession they could reinstate the authority of Yahweh and build a world fit for him to rule.

But how could they possibly achieve victory across such a great distance and against the huge forces available to the Muslim Turks?

Taking England with the help of their Norse friends had been one thing, but even if every Norman family agreed to fight alongside them, they would be still be too few in number to reach across the breadth of the world and dislodge the Muslim hordes from their homeland.

The plan that was hatched must rate as the greatest stroke of military genius the world has ever known. It involved years of debate, negotiation, plotting, blackmail and power play of every kind. The idea was audacious in the extreme. If they were to succeed they would have to begin by taking control of the Holy See – and by using the authority of the pope to mobilize all of Christendom in a great war to win back Jerusalem.

Now the accent swings back to the Star Family priests living in Champagne. Events that were to unfold across the next two centuries show conclusively that the infiltration of Ebionite beliefs and Star Family membership within the ruling elite of Champagne was almost total. One of their number, a man by the name of Odo of Lagery, himself a kinsman of the counts of Champagne, was in exactly the right position to supply exactly what was required – a Star Family pope. With the help of the Normans this became a reality.

Born *c.* 1042 at Châtillon-sur-Marne in Champagne, Odo sprang from a high-ranking and influential aristocratic family. At an early age he was dispatched to a life in the Church and had soon become a canon and an archdeacon at the great cathedral in Rheims, which was also in Champagne. After a spell in the Benedictine monastery of Cluny (which across many centuries showed itself to be the springboard for Star Family manoeuvring), Odo was sent to Rome to serve under Pope Gregory VII. Odo shone like a star in the midst of an ailing Roman Church. Odo also gained in stature by supporting Pope Gregory in his tenacious fight to wrest control of the Church from temporal hands, such as those of the Holy Roman Emperor.

Gregory VII was succeeded in 1087 by Victor III who, for unknown and quite suspicious reasons, died after only four months at Monte Cassino. At his death he was surrounded by cardinals who had arrived in Italy to attend a Church council at nearby Benevento. The greater proportion of cardinals present when Victor died were either from Champagne or Burgundy or were Normans, and they emerged from his deathbed to announce to the world that the dying pope had proposed Odo of Lagery as his successor. The absolute truth of these events will never be known, but Odo was ultimately made Pope Urban II on 12 March 1088.

His entry into Rome, which was contested in some quarters, was made possible by a contingent of Norman troops. This took place in November 1088 but despite the assistance of the Normans, Urban spent nearly three years in exile in southern Italy, an area that at the time was under Norman rule. He had innumerable problems with the Holy Roman Emperor and was often in fear of his life but as soon as circumstances allowed, in November 1095, Urban called a council at Clermont in France. There, amidst the nobility of Europe and the assembled ranks of cardinals and bishops he called for a solemn, holy war to be waged against the Turks, who were threatening to overrun the Eastern Church. He made it plain that the ultimate objective was to win Jerusalem for Christianity.

The pope outlined a plan for a Crusade and called on his listeners to join its ranks. He then commissioned the attending bishops to return to their homes and enlist others in the Crusade. Urban also outlined a basic strategy in which individual groups of Crusaders from countries across Europe would begin the journey east in August 1096. Each group would be self-financing and responsible to its own leader and would make its separate way first to the Byzantine capital Constantinople, where they would join together into a massed army. From there, together with the Byzantine emperor and his army, they would launch a counter-attack against the Seljuk conquerors of Anatolia. Once that region was under Christian control, the Crusaders would campaign against the Muslims in Syria and Palestine, with Jerusalem as their ultimate goal.

Plans went ahead more or less as Urban had proposed. The armies marched through Anatolia and Syria and by May 1099, the Crusaders had reached the Holy City of Jerusalem. Siege was laid and siege engines – built from Genoese ships owing to the lack of wood – were wheeled forward to attack the city's impressive defences of Jerusalem. The city finally fell on 15 July 1099. Once inside the walls, the Crusaders began to destroy everything and everybody. One eyewitness, Fulk of Chartres, wrote afterwards of what he saw:

> At the noon hour on Friday, with trumpets sounding, amid great commotion and shouting 'God help us,' the Franks entered the city. When the pagans saw our standard planted on the wall, they were completely demoralized, and all their former boldness vanished, and they turned to flee through the narrow streets of the city.
>
> Those who were already in rapid flight began to flee more rapidly. Count Raymond and his men, who were attacking the wall on the other side, did not yet know of all this, until they saw the Saracens leap from the wall in front of them. Forthwith, they joyfully rushed into the city to pursue and

> kill the nefarious enemies, as their comrades were already
> doing. … Many fled to the roof of the Temple of Solomon
> [Al-Aqsa], and were shot with arrows, so that they fell to the
> ground dead. In this Temple almost ten thousand were killed.
> Indeed, if you had been there you would have seen our feet
> coloured to our ankles with the blood of the slain. But what
> more shall I relate? None of them were left alive; neither
> women nor children were spared.[2]

Many Jews, who were seen as having sided with the Turks, misunderstood the seriousness of their situation and were brutally slaughtered.

Once again God's city was the scene of unbridled human savagery.

A week after the Holy City had been taken, the central areas had been cleansed of the mounds of bodies, and the Valley of Hinnom, to the south of Jerusalem and in front of the Gate of the Essenes, was being used as a charnel house. Acrid smoke rose from the large fires that burned night and day to consume the decaying flesh of the piles of recently dead. This valley had long ago been the place where children were sacrificed to Moloch before the first Temple was built and since the time of Christ it had been the refuse burning area for the entire city. It was fitting that this little valley had been the inspiration for the idea of the fires of hell.

In the Al-Asqa building (no longer a mosque at this time) Godfrey of Bouillon, the leader of the part of the crusading army that had breached the city walls, was offered the crown of Jerusalem. He was the grandson of Godfrey III, duke of Lower Lotharingia (Lorraine) who had been centrally involved in creating the radical group of priests at the monastery of Cluny. Godfrey had previously fought against the papacy yet he was present when Urban II proposed the Crusade and he famously sold all that he had to join and lead the expedition to take Jerusalem.

As a Star Family member, Godfrey knew that he could not presume to take the title 'king of Jerusalem' for he was certainly not the Messiah. Instead he asked that he be called *Advocatus Sancti Sepulchri*, meaning 'advocate' or 'defender' of the Holy Sepulchre.

Problems immediately arose when a Norman priest named Arnulf of Chocques, the temporary patriarch of Jerusalem, was replaced by a non-Family member called Dagobert of Pisa. Dagobert wanted to make the new kingdom of Jerusalem a theocracy, with the pope at its head, and the patriarch as the pope's representative. Godfrey stalled the issue by promising to turn over the crown to the papacy once the Crusaders had conquered Egypt – which he knew would not happen.

Struggles for Power

Word of the glorious victory in Jerusalem reached the ears of Urban II on the afternoon of Saturday 29 July 1099, just two weeks after the storming of its walls. The pope was doubtless ecstatic, as were the Star Family members who had drawn up the plans presented by Urban. But it appears that Urban then underwent a change in attitude that threatened to spoil everything. He announced that he was considering moving the seat of Christianity from Rome to the Holy City of Jerusalem. This may have been because the security of successive popes in Rome had been in doubt and Italy as a whole was a hotbed of conflicting families and political interests. On the other hand it is possible that Urban's pride simply got the better of him and that he wanted to be the first Christian pope based in Jerusalem, the city of Christ. In the end it didn't matter. Later the same evening Urban felt unwell, retired to his bed, and quickly fell asleep. He never woke.

In 1100, just three days after the first anniversary of the taking of Jerusalem, Godfrey of Bouillon also died suddenly. The patriarch, Dagobert, may well have been responsible for Godfrey's death. Whether or not this was the case, Godfrey's passing caused brief confusion among the Star Families, particularly when Dagobert attempted to claim Jerusalem for himself. The Families quickly stepped in before he could succeed and proclaimed Godfrey's brother, Baldwin of Boulogne, to be the new king of Jerusalem. Baldwin was doubtless as reluctant to accept such a title as his brother had been, but the political realities of the situation meant that only the authority of a king could secure the city for the future. Perhaps he consoled himself with the observation that there were many kings in the world, none of whom also proclaimed themselves to be Messiahs. He could be a secular king without considering himself guilty of blasphemy.

Dagobert was absent at the time and on his return he reluctantly crowned Baldwin in Bethlehem, since he absolutely refused to undertake the ceremony in Jerusalem itself without papal authority. Baldwin and

Dagobert continued quarrelling for a further two years until Dagobert went to Rome. Whilst he was absent, King Baldwin tried to replace him with a Star Family member, a minor priest named Ehremar. However, Ehremar was disposed of soon after Dagobert's return.

The Normans retained a strong interest in events that were taking place in the Holy Land and many of them had fought alongside the Crusaders. However, their new base in England was proving to be a tougher nut to crack than William the Conqueror, duke of Normandy, had envisaged. He had defeated the Saxon king of England, Harold II, at Hastings in 1066, but winning the hearts of the English people was not nearly so easy. Throughout most of his reign as king of England, from 1066 until his death in 1087, he ranged across the country, putting down revolts and enforcing his authority on the realm.

Slowly but surely, William prepared England for the creation of the New Jerusalem. Church building went ahead at an unprecedented rate and William was wisely careful to reassure the popes of his day that he was a true son of the established Church. Unfortunately the same could not be said for his choleric and impatient son and successor, William II, popularly known as William Rufus because of his ruddy complexion. William II had his father's ferocity but none of his diplomatic skills. He thought nothing of desecrating English churches and stealing Church property when it suited his aims, and he made no bones about his hatred for the established Church. No matter how much sympathy Star Family priests in Champagne might have had for the beliefs of William Rufus – for they were no more enamoured of the Church than he was – they knew that matters would very soon run out of control.

William was pushing for the Church of Rome to be replaced by a new English version, with himself as its head, based on ideas drawn from the Star Family's private theology. This was dangerous. The Families certainly did not want a schism developing in the Western Church because no matter how much they may have disliked the Roman form of Christianity, its continuation was, for the moment, central to their plan.

On Thursday, 2 August 1100, William II had organized a hunting trip in the New Forest, a hunting ground that his father had established near Winchester, the seat of the royal treasury. It is recorded that William had slept badly the previous night and dreamed that he had gone to heaven.

He awoke suddenly, commanded that a light to be brought, and bid his attendants to stay with him. An account from the period describes the preparations for that day's hunt:

> An armourer came in and presented [the king] six arrows.
> The king immediately took them with great satisfaction,
> praising the work, and unconscious of what was to happen,
> kept four of them himself and held out the other two to a
> friend by the name of Walter Tyrell... saying 'It is only right
> that the sharpest be given to the man who knows how to
> shoot the deadliest shots'.[3]

The party chased their prey but somehow William and Walter Tyrell, lord of Poix, became separated from the main group. It was the last time that William was seen alive. It was claimed that Walter had let loose a wild shot at a stag but, instead of hitting the animal, had 'accidentally' struck William in the chest.

Political circumstances were much more settled in Champagne and the next part of the plan to undermine the Pauline, Roman Church and to replace it with something much more in keeping with Star Family intentions had already been underway for a year before the forces of the West conquered Jerusalem, and a full two years prior to the assassination of William Rufus. It involved another aristocrat from Champagne, and his name was Robert of Molesme.

CHAPTER 5

The Sleepers Awake

Organizing the First Crusade had been an undertaking of mammoth proportions but it was not the only major project that would have to be carefully orchestrated by the Star Families. Their greatest desire was to excavate below the ruined Jerusalem Temple in order to retrieve their treasures and sacred documents, which they knew to be buried there. They were well aware that this would be an extremely difficult and time-consuming task, for the treasures were deeply buried and any obvious excavation would draw unwanted attention to their mission.

The New Essenes

As plans for a Crusade were being mooted, in the period following the Seljuk capture of Jerusalem in 1076, the leaders of the Families had therefore decided to establish a new order of Essenes. From the start this was intended to be a network of holy, pious men who would remain objective and who would have no hint of personal interest in wealth for its own sake. The new order would be established in northeast France, the powerbase of the crusading Star Families, and would provide a network of spiritual – and political – support for whoever was eventually selected to undertake the excavation of Essene treasure.

The creation of such a trustworthy group in the run-up to the Crusade was essential because the Families knew that, if the crusade succeeded, Jerusalem would soon be awash with men from the West who could best be described as 'privateers'. It was accepted practice among all medieval armies that when a city fell, the victorious soldiers had free range to thieve and plunder all they could.

The last thing the Star Families needed was for word to get out amongst the booty-hungry, thieving hordes of soldiers from across Christendom that there was hidden treasure below the Temple Mount in Jerusalem. The very Church itself was riddled with corruption. Absolutely no one outside their own closed circle could be trusted.

By the 11th century the wider world knew little or nothing of the long-forgotten Essenes. But the Star Families had not forgotten them and they put their knowledge to good use.

The Star Families needed a springboard to launch their new order, which would obviously have to be, or appear to be, entirely Christian. Such an organization had to be planned very carefully because orthodoxy would see to it that the infant organization was destroyed before it began if it displayed the slightest hint of heresy. What was required was a high-profile monk who was totally honest and dedicated to true godliness. Such an individual would not need to know anything regarding the true agenda and ideally he would be an old man who could engender passion for the cause and respectability to the outside world – though without living long enough to get in the way of future developments.

There was one obvious candidate, well known to the Star Families. His name was Robert of Molesme, the son of Champagne nobility. In 1068 he had became abbot of the Benedictine abbey of St Michel de Tonnere, where he found the monks to be lax and lazy. He had sought to impose greater solitude, better discipline and harder work on his monks but his efforts failed completely. He had then created a reformed Benedictine abbey at Molesme. This had proved to be highly successful – in fact too much so, because it became so wealthy that the monks of Molesme grew as lax and lazy as their contemporaries elsewhere. By 1098 Robert was a bitter and lonely man approaching his 70th year and he must have been somewhat surprised to receive a visit from a small group of Champagne nobles suggesting that they could arrange funds if he might like create a totally new order of monks – an order that would remain true to its calling and which would repudiate worldliness in all its forms.

Robert can only have been delighted to hear that money and land were to be made available to him to build a new, respectable order for God's own sake. Accordingly he left Molesmes with 21 handpicked monks and headed to land granted to him by Duke Odo II of Burgundy. Here, with financial support from both Burgundy and Champagne, he founded a totally new order of monks which, his patrons had suggested, should wear pure white habits and be named 'Cistercians', after the site of their new abbey, Cîteaux.

The wearing of a white habit was the first obvious connection to the Essenes who had dressed in an identical fashion. The name 'Cistercians' itself was another possible direct connection to the Jewish holy men of more than 1,000 years earlier. According to some authorities the word Cîteaux derives from an old French word, *cisteaux*, meaning reeds, which were abundant in the marshy location of the new abbey. However, other commentators have suggested that the word Cîteaux was derived from the Latin word *cista*, meaning a water tank. Water was also abundant at the site of the new abbey, and it is certainly a fact that Cistercian monks regularly washed. This was far from being the norm at the time, even for monks, and this could easily have been in recognition of the Essene habit of ritual and actual cleanliness.

Despite its financial assistance the modern order of Essenes more or less spluttered into life, gaining speed extremely slowly – but that did not matter for the time being. A great game of chess was being played out on a board that spanned most of the known world and many great men of the age found themselves to be mere pawns, sometimes to be sacrificed as the plan unfolded. The pace of the game was breathtaking.

Within months of the founding of the Cistercian Order, Jerusalem was taken by the forces of Christendom and four days later Godfrey of Bouillon was its new ruler. As we have seen (*see* page 84), within two weeks Pope Urban II was dead and within the year Godfrey of Bouillon himself had succumbed – some said to disease, others suggested he had been shot by an arrow, and a few asserted that he had been poisoned. Just two weeks after Godfrey had died he was followed to the grave by King William II of England, 'accidentally' shot down with an arrow in his chest.

The Search for the Temple Treasures

Three years later, the circle of Star Families selected the man who would be charged with the task of leading the team to find the Essene treasures and scrolls beneath the Temple ruins. He was Hugues de Payen, a cousin of Hugues, count of Champagne, who held lands within the French city of Troyes. Hugues de Payen had fought in the First Crusade, most probably in the vanguard of Godfrey of Bouillon's force.

In 1104 the count of Champagne held a meeting in Troyes at which Hugues de Payen is known to have been present along with some fellow veterans of the battle for Jerusalem, including a knight called André de Montbard. (André's 14-year-old nephew, Bernard, was destined to become one of the most influential people of all time.) It is likely that members of the new Cistercian order were also present, owing to their close interest in the project to recover the treasures.

Exactly what was discussed at this meeting is not recorded but within weeks Count Hugues was on his way to Jerusalem together with Hugues de Payen and André de Montbard. Hugues de Payen remained there for four years before he returned to Troyes. What he was doing for all that time is not known for certain, but the events that follow strongly suggest that he may have been carefully surveying the gigantic platform on which the Jerusalem Temple had once stood.

That nothing happened for the next ten years must have been due to a political and religious gridlock. There were two people with the power to block the planned excavation: King Baldwin I of Jerusalem, the brother and successor of Godfrey of Bouillon, and Pope Paschal II, who had succeeded Urban II shortly after the capture of Jerusalem in 1099.

The pope himself almost certainly had little to do with the delay because most of his time and effort were spent trying to fend off the German dynasty of the Holy Roman Empire under Henry V. Having forced the abdication of the existing emperor, in 1111 Henry compelled Paschal II to crown him emperor in Rome. This was only achieved after he had thrown the aging pontiff into prison and then fought off an attempted rescue by the Normans. The pope's difficulties with the emperor did not ease and he died on 21 January 1118.

If Baldwin of Jerusalem was blocking the excavation he must have also been watching his back very carefully. He is certain to have required reliable and trustworthy food tasters to avoid being dispatched by Star Family members who wished to see more rapid progress. In the event, Baldwin survived the pope by barely two months. On 2 April 1118, Baldwin died on a visit to Egypt after eating a meal of fish freshly caught in the River Nile. Whether it was a bad fish or whether someone had added something lethal to the meal we will never know. But it is clear that his demise opened up the way for Hugues de Payen and his team.

The news of Baldwin's demise had barely reached Europe when Hugues de Payen and an entourage of eight other knights left Troyes once more and set out on the dusty roads to the east. Their avowed intention – at least according to one later chronicler, William of Tyre – was to form a brotherhood that would guard the roads from the coast of the Levant to Jerusalem, in order to safeguard the passage of pilgrims to and from the Holy Sites. However, such a small force of middle-aged knights would have been totally unable to fulfil such a remit – and in any case they did nothing of the sort.

The men involved are recorded as being: Hugues de Payen, André de Montbard, Geoffroi de St Omer, Payen de Montdidier, Achambaud de St Amand, Geoffroi Bisol, Gondemare, Rosal and Godfroi. Where the points of origin of the original knights is known they can be shown to be of Champagne extraction, with the exception of the Payen de Montdidier and Achambaud de St Amand, who were from Flanders.

Baldwin I, the late king of Jerusalem, had had no sons and had been replaced on the throne of Jerusalem by his cousin, Baldwin II. King Baldwin II was from the Ardennes, an area whose rulers had blood ties to Champagne, and he was apparently fully supportive of the plan to excavate below the Temple.

The nine knights camped on the part of the ruined Temple known as 'Solomon's Stables' where they remained for nine years thanks to the direct financial and logistical support of Baldwin II. Hugues de Payen and his team quickly began digging massive workings, often tunnelling through solid rock.

Seven and a half centuries later, another group of people decided to investigate beneath the Temple Mount. In 1867 a British Army expedition led by Lieutenant Warren of the Royal Engineers began to cut their way downwards under the giant platform of the Mount.[1] All they discovered was a maze of tunnels left by the small band of Star Family excavators. A number of artefacts identified as belonging to Hugues de Payen's group were recovered by the British engineers and are now kept in Edinburgh.

How much Hugues's team knew about the layout below ground we cannot know, but they must have known that their first task was to locate the Copper Scroll. This document inscribed on metal must surely count as the most fabulous treasure map ever created. Two Copper Scrolls were created by the Star Families at the time of the holy war against the Romans in AD66–70. The 'junior' version was found at Qumran in 1952 amongst the Dead Sea Scrolls and was opened three years later to be read for the first time in nearly two millennia. This scroll states that at least 24 important scrolls were secreted beneath the Temple Mount along with vast treasures and a second, more detailed, copy of the Copper Scroll. It states:

> In the pit adjoining on the north in a hole opening
> northwards, and buried at its mouth: a copy of this
> document, with an explanation and their measurements, and
> an inventory of each thing, and other things.[2]

A total of 61 locations are described and the precious items listed. The late John Allegro, a passionate and objective Dead Sea Scroll scholar, recorded his amazement when he realized what the document contained:

> As word after word became plain, and the import of the
> whole document inescapable, I could hardly believe my
> eyes ... the Qumran caves had produced the biggest surprise
> of all – an inventory of sacred treasure, of gold, silver, and
> jars of consecrated offerings, as well as sacred vessels of all
> types...[3]

John Allegro also explained the purpose of the Copper Scroll:

> The Copper Scroll and its copy (or copies) were intended to
> tell the Jewish survivors of the war then raging where this
> sacred material lay buried, so that if any should be found, it
> would never be desecrated by profane use. It would also act as
> a guide to the recovery of the treasure.

It seems doubtful that any of the people involved in burying these
documents and treasures could have ever imagined that it would take their
descendants more than 1,000 years to return for them. But return they
did.

The Copper Scroll led Hugues and his party to their treasures. For
example one entry reads:

> In the inner chamber of the twin pillars supporting the arch
> of the double gate, facing east, in the entrance, buried at three
> cubits, hidden there is a pitcher, in it, one scroll, under it
> forty-two talents.
>
> In the cistern, which is nineteen cubits in front of the
> eastern gateway, in it are vessels, and in the hollow that is in
> it: ten talents.
>
> In the Court of [illegible], nine cubits under the southern
> corner: gold and silver vessels for tithe, sprinkling basins,
> cups, sacrificial bowls. Libation vessels, in all six hundred and
> nine.

The nine knights must have found their scrolls, vast amounts of money
and cartloads of gold and silver artefacts. Their success was such that in
1125 Hugues, count of Champagne suddenly renounced his titles in
Champagne, sailed to Jerusalem and put himself under the guiding hand
of Hugues de Payen. The count had formerly been Hugues de Payen's liege
lord and such a total reversal of their roles was an unprecedented action
in feudal Europe.

There is another source of evidence that gives a description of the excavations carried out to recover the ancient documents and treasures beneath
the ruined Temple. And strangely, that account comes from the rituals of
Freemasonry, which we will deal with presently.

The Knights Templar: Soldiers of Yahweh

Having completed their allotted task, this small band of treasure-hunters in Jerusalem turned themselves into a military order of monks. With the help of their Cistercian brothers back in Europe, they also adopted a white mantle (later to bear a red cross on the front). Again with the help of the Cistercians they devised their formal title *Pauperes Commilitones Christi Templique Salomonis* normally translated into English as 'The Poor Fellow-Soldiers of Christ and the Temple of Solomon'. But they are usually known by a shorter title – the Knights Templar.

The longer title seems entirely Christian at first view – but it is nothing of the kind. Every Christian quite naturally assumes that the term 'Christ' refers to Jesus – but of course it does not. As we have seen (*see* page 32) the word is from the Greek *khristos* ('anointed'), and is a translation of Hebrew word 'messiah' (*mashiach*) – literally one who is 'smeared with oils' as a mark of Jewish kingship. 'Christ' is a title, not the name of any one individual, so the order's title does not refer specifically to Jesus but to John the Baptist and James or anyone else who was to lead the Jewish priests and their people to a new world order. At that time it perhaps even applied to Baldwin II, the king of Jerusalem. In fact history would show that the Knights Templar, as representatives of the Star Families and therefore Ebionites, ultimately showed far more reverence for John the Baptist, as the founder of their sect, rather than his successor, Jesus. This heightens our suspicion that the entire order, or at least its leaders, thought of John as the original Christ or Messiah – and not Jesus.

We can be sure that the Knights Templar intended the words to have this meaning because they describe themselves as 'Poor *Fellow*-Soldiers of the Messiah'. The use of the term 'fellow-soldiers' (*commilitones*) implies that they saw themselves as equals with this person, rather than his 'followers'. One would have expected any normal Christian monks to simply describe themselves as 'Poor *Soldiers* of *Jesus* Christ and the Temple of Solomon'. The word 'fellow' subtly changes the import. Fortunately it appeared that nobody questioned precisely what the Temple of Solomon had to do with Jesus Christ. Solomon's Temple has no direct connection to Jesus Christ, according to the Christian canon. In any case the Templars had been based very close to King Baldwin's palace in Jerusalem, so it also appeared that their name could, in part at least, have merely originated in the location of their headquarters in the Holy City.

The world was fooled. No one noticed that the title the new order took was intended to celebrate the Star Families' mission, ordained by King Solomon, to create the New Jerusalem that had been promised for centuries. The 'Children of Israel' – the real army of Yahweh – were on the march again.

Bernard of Clairvaux

Back in France the Cistercian Order had developed well, owing initially to an Englishman called Stephen Harding and latterly to Bernard, the young nephew of André de Montbard.

Bernard was the son of Tescelin, lord of Fontaines in northern Burgundy, and of Aleth, a noblewoman from Montbard in Champagne. They had many children but Bernard was quickly recognized as being particularly intelligent and shrewd. Though small of stature, he would prove to be a match for the mightiest kings, princes and popes.

In 1113, at the age of 23, Bernard had ridden the few miles south from Fontaines to Cîteaux, to join the first Cistercian monastery. Within the year he was followed by no fewer than 30 of his relatives – in fact they did not so much 'join' the order as take it over. Three years later the 26-year-old Bernard had an abbey of his own, this one very close to Troyes in Champagne. It was called 'Clairvaux', which means 'Valley of the Light' and although Cîteaux remained the nominal motherhouse of the order, it was in Clairvaux that key decisions would be taken for the next 30 years.

Bernard (soon known as Bernard of Clairvaux) immediately began to play his part in Church politics, at first in Champagne but soon across all Christendom. When Hugues de Payen and his team started digging in Jerusalem, Bernard initiated a campaign to build up the reputation of the tunnelling knights from Jerusalem as though they were the world's finest warriors, rather than a band of burrowing recluses. His words owed much to poetic licence:

> **They go not headlong into battle, but with care and foresight, peacefully, as true children of Israel. But as soon as the fight**

> has begun, they rush without delay upon the foe ... and know
> no fear ... one has often put to flight a thousand; two, ten
> thousand ... gentler than lambs and grimmer than lions;
> theirs is the mildness of monks and the valour of the knight.

'Children of Israel' they certainly were.

It was Bernard, the Cistercian wunderkind, who had first brought the nine knights to the attention of Pope Gelasius II, asking that they be made into a monastic order by providing them with a 'rule' – a code of conduct and practice – which was effectively a version of the Cistercians' own rule, and as such would give them legitimacy and defined status within the Church.

The request appears to have fallen upon deaf ears but the pieces on the chessboard were soon to change again. Pope Gelasius II died suddenly after a year and five days in office, whilst visiting the monastery of Cluny. Cluny was always important to the Star Families in Champagne. It was a hothouse of reformed Benedictine ideas and the springboard for not one but several reformed monastic orders that the Star Families either created or else used to their own ends. It also seems certain that by this time most, if not all, Star Family incentives in Europe and beyond were being planned in Champagne, which can effectively be considered its headquarters between the late 11th and early 14th centuries. The monastery of Cluny was close by. Conveniently, the next pontiff was Guido, the son of the Duke William II of Burgundy, which made him a kinsman of Bernard and therefore, almost certainly, a Star Family member.

Guido became Pope Callistus II and was immediately sympathetic to Bernard's argument that the Christian world should have an elite fighting force to spearhead the fight against the Muslim threat. Bernard explained how the embryo of such a force for the Western Church already existed, in the form of Hugues de Payens and his colleagues. Bernard proposed that if this little group was well regulated and adopted a similar monastic rule to that of the Cistercians, it could grow rapidly and become exactly what was required – a committed and large group of well-trained and well-armed knights whose specific remit would be to protect the Holy Land – especially Jerusalem, which at this time was once again in danger of falling to Muslim armies.

However, the greatest incentive for the pope, was that these soldiers would also be monks. As such, Bernard suggested, and because of the intended international nature of the new order, it would be outside the regular Church hierarchy, owing direct allegiance to no bishop, archbishop or any other agency, spiritual or temporal. It would be answerable only to the pope himself.

It was a brilliant strategy. The official creation of the new order cost the pope absolutely nothing and yet the glory of the enterprise would reflect favourably upon him. What was more, at a time when popes were constantly besieged not only by weighty ecclesiastical problems but also often literally by foreign troops, the knowledge that he would possess what amounted to a powerful personal bodyguard, committed specifically to his service, must have seemed very attractive to Callistus. He was well aware just how quickly the Cistercians were growing and he could not have failed to know that much of the impetus of the order came directly from Bernard, who had already personally founded dozens of abbeys. If the little man from Champagne could achieve so much for the Cistercians, he could surely make the pope's new personal army into a reality.

However, Callistus died before he could officially instigate the proposed order and it fell to Pope Honorius II officially to turn the Knights Templar into a monastic order by providing them with a 'rule', or constitution. This was granted on 31 January 1128 when Hugues de Payen appeared before the specially convened Council of Troyes. This impressive body was presided over by the cardinal of Albano, the papal legate, and comprised the archbishops of Rheims and Sens together with no fewer than ten bishops and several prominent abbots, including Bernard of Clairvaux. The proposition to grant the Knights Templar the formal status of a monastic order was carried and the Templars were given their rule and the right to wear their own mantle, which was pure Essene white.

Through Bernard's influence, the band of aging knights who had spent almost nine years living in near poverty as they tunnelled their way under the Temple Mount were suddenly spectacularly rich, as the new order was inundated with gifts of money and land from pious donors. Quite soon they would change the world through their building programme and their invention of global banking which, along with the Cistercians' development of the wool trade and the huge international trading fairs in Champagne, were effectively to herald the 'modern' age.

Bernard the Mystic

Bernard proved to be of unparalleled importance to Christian thinking. He would eventually be beatified as St Bernard of Clairvaux, although he has gone down in Church history as being something of a 'mystic' and his approach to Christianity was, to say the last, highly unusual.

Bernard had two obsessions that shone through his life and which were reflected in practically all his actions. Firstly he was absolutely fascinated by the concept of the female nature of God personified in the form of St Mary the Virgin, for whom his apparent veneration knew no bounds. His respect for women had a massive impact on the courts of Europe, where the status of females became elevated thanks to his efforts. Bernard seemed to share the same view as Jesus Christ in believing that all people were equally valuable in God's eyes and everyone, both male or female, had to enter into a contract with God if the new world order was to be established.

Secondly, Bernard showed a highly unusual obsession with The Song of Songs, or Song of Solomon. Throughout his life he produced dozens of sermons relating to the Song of Songs, which remains one of the most puzzling books of the Bible.

The Song of Songs appears at first sight to be a long and complicated love poem between a bride and a bridegroom. It mentions King Solomon but it is very unlikely that the work owes anything directly to him, and most experts place its authorship in rural north Israel. They suggest that the Song of Songs started life as a series of traditional poems that were gathered together c. 300BC[4] – the precise time that the Essenes were first forming. The Song of Songs is, at face value, a beautiful erotic story with little or no religious content – it does not mention God once – but to the Jews it was considered to be an allegory of God's relationship with Jerusalem.

Christians of Bernard of Clairvaux's period adopted the Song of Songs, viewing it in a similar way to their Jewish counterparts, though in the case of Christianity as an allegory of the relationship of Jesus and his Church. On the surface this is the way Bernard dealt with the work, but it is likely that he actually viewed this extraordinary book more in the way it was treated by Jewish mystics. Like the Jewish scholars of his time Bernard almost certainly saw the Song of Songs as a thinly veiled story dealing with the recreation of Jerusalem and the relationship of the New Jerusalem with God.

It was public knowledge that Bernard had a fascination for Judaism. When Jerusalem had been taken by force, only a generation earlier, the Jews within the city had been slaughtered with as little compunction as the unfortunate Muslims. Within 12th-century Western Europe, Jews lived a sort of marginal existence.[5] They could take part in trade and were useful when it came to finance, simply because they were allowed to lend money at interest, which in principle Christians could not. The charging of interest on loans was known as 'usury' which to Christians was against ecclesiastical law. The Jews had no such law, and money lending was therefore one of the few means by which a European Jew could become prosperous. Unfortunately, Jews were quite frequently harassed as 'enemies of Christ' and 'pogroms' were common, in which the Church often played a significant role. Bernard of Clairvaux was different. On several occasions during his life, and despite his busy schedule, he walked for days to prevent pogroms against the Jews and it is suggested that he retained Jewish Cabalists and experts in Hebrew within his own monastery near Troyes.

Bernard's mystical leanings caused him to be more venerated than might otherwise be the case. He was undoubtedly one of the greatest intellectuals of his age – once describing God as being 'height and breadth and depth and width' – and he also suggested that God would be more likely to be found amongst the rocks and trees than in any church constructed by human hands.

It was in no small measure thanks to Bernard that by 1130 the Star Families were in the best position possible to begin building their new world order. After 60 years of manoeuvre and murder they had control of the West and the crusader lands of the East. Bernard was remodelling attitudes in both Church and the courts of Europe whilst the Knights Templar and the Cistercians were preparing to launch changes unparalleled in human history.

CHAPTER 6

The First New World Order

The Knights Templar quickly spread to every country in Christendom. In each case a Master of the order was appointed who would report to the head of the Templars, the Grand Master, a position that was held for life. Three junior ranks were established below the Knights themselves, which were the 'sergeants', 'rural brothers' and 'chaplains'. There was also a separate division of *Fratres conjugati*, who were married brothers. They wore a black or brown mantle with a red cross to identify them from the celibate, Essene-style members. The *Fratres conjugati* were not considered to be of the same status as the celibate brothers. (According to historical documents the Essenes also had a non-celibate component of married brothers.)

Initiation into the order involved a secret ceremony and rumours soon began circulating that the Templars were indulging in rituals that were not Christian. Such talk could have been very dangerous for a less prominent order but the extremely wealthy and well-connected Templars were well placed enough simply to ignore any such questions. They were not short of initiates, who had to be of noble birth, of legitimate heritage, because nobody of humble birth could be a Knight, and willing to sign over all of their wealth as well as give vows of poverty, chastity, piety, and obedience.

Whilst the publicly promoted purpose of the Templars was military, many brothers devoted their time to commerce and others to the order's massive building programme. The Templars soon used their wealth to construct numerous fortifications throughout the Holy Land and were undoubtedly the best trained and most disciplined fighting units of their day. The cardinal rule of the Knights was never to surrender. The fearless and uncompromising nature of the Templars, along with excellent training and heavy armament, made them a formidable and elite fighting force in medieval times. They are still remembered for their white garb adorned with a red cross on the chest, which today is incorrectly associated with all crusading knights.

Protecting the Temple Treasures

The first problem that the Knights Templar had to confront was the question of what to do with the Essene scrolls recovered from beneath the ruined Temple of Jerusalem. The physical treasures that they had excavated (*see* Chapter 5) needed protection from theft, but the items themselves would not have caused any suspicion. However, the documents were a different matter. They were precious in the extreme and, because of their content, in danger of being destroyed if they ever came to the attention of the Church.

Carrying them back to Champagne or any other part of France does not seem to have been seriously considered as an option. This could be because the area was considered vulnerable to an all-powerful Church elite, even within the areas where Star Family presence was strong. The considered opinion of those responsible for the documents appears to have been to search out a friendly location as far from Rome as reasonably possible. Their plans for these documents must have been top secret at the time but there is a record of what happened in the oral tradition of Freemasonry.

According to the narrative of the 20th degree of the so-called Ancient Scottish Rite, in 1140 one of the Templar lodges from Jerusalem travelled to Kilwinning, a small western seaport in Scotland. It is further stated that this group brought with them ancient documents to be stored in a purpose-built abbey at Kilwinning.

This is perplexing information, for how could those penning the relatively recent rituals of Freemasonry have known about the existence of Essene scrolls, let alone secret Templar activities? Until the Dead Sea Scrolls were discovered and the Copper Scroll deciphered in the 1950s no one is supposed to have known that anything lay beneath the ruined Temple of Jerusalem.

In 1921, a generation before the Dead Sea Scrolls were found at the Essene camp at Qumran, one famous Masonic expert, J S M Ward, wrote that 'the abbey [of Kilwinning] was not built till about 1140, and the legend does not state where [the documents] were during the period between 70AD and 1140AD'.

Using Freemasonic information, Ward was aware that these documents had existed before the destruction of the Jerusalem Temple and that they had arrived in Kilwinning 1,070 years later. The inescapable conclusion is that information from the Knights Templar eventually made its way into Masonic traditions.

This leaves the question of where the scrolls were for the period between the completion of the Templar excavations *c.* 1128 and the building of the abbey at Kilwinning in 1140 – plus the tantalizing question of what happened to them after that date.

Kilwinning abbey is usually referred to as having been 'Benedictine' but this is not exactly true. The abbey was built on land owned by the St Clairs (or Sinclairs), the Star Family which arrived in Scotland before William the Conqueror invaded England, and was granted to Hugh de Morville, a friend and confederate of King David I of Scotland. Hugh de Morville then brought a group of monks from Kelso to build and inhabit a new abbey on the site, but they were not mainstream Benedictines – rather they were from an order known as 'Tironensians'.

Mason-Monks: the Tironensians

The Tironensians remain one of the most mysterious of all reformed Benedictine orders. There has been only one in-depth study of the Tironensians, by Canadian author Francine Bernier, whose work appeared as recently as 2005.[1]

The greatest mystery surrounding the Tironensians lies in how such a successful monastic order, which once controlled over 117 monastic houses, could have disappeared so completely from the historical record. However, Bernier has spent years scouring books and documents in order to offer a detailed account of the Tironensians who, though now almost unknown, clearly had an important part to play in the development of both monasticism and architecture from the 12th to the 14th centuries.

The Tironensians were founded in 1107 and took their name from Tiron or Thiron, meaning 'high hill', their first abbey, 35 miles west of Chartres in France. They were founded by a Benedictine monk named Bernard of Tiron who, like his counterpart Bernard of Clairvaux and the founders of the Cistercians (*see* Chapter 5), believed that the mainstream order had become lax.

In 1113 the Tironensian brothers were invited by King David I to come to Scotland – a place where they would have found the prevailing form of Christianity very much to their liking, since Scottish Christianity still retained elements of its Culdean foundations, to which the Tironensians stuck assiduously. (Alan Butler has demonstrated[2] that Bernard of Clairvaux also had close associations with Culdean Christianity and that he often espoused its beliefs. It is almost certain that Culdeans, as the dominant Christians in post-Roman Britain and Ireland, were replete with Star Family priests and practices. The Culdeans regularly fell out with the Roman Church and it had been necessary to hold a Church synod at Whitby in AD664 in order to try and bring them fully into the Roman Catholic fold – an attempt that in the case of Scotland clearly failed.)

The Tironensians were also famous for their prowess as master builders – much more so than any other of the Benedictine-inspired orders. In their day they were at the leading edge of architecture. At Chartres they maintained and ran a college that was specifically funded and set up in 1117 by Count Theobald VI of Blois, Troyes, Champagne and Chartres. Although now largely forgotten, this college went on to supply the expertise necessary to create some of the greatest buildings of the period, including, according to some sources, the cathedral of Chartres, which was rebuilt between 1194 and 1250 (*see below*, page 108). Other experts claim that the money necessary to build the new cathedral in such a relatively short space of time was supplied by the Knights Templar[3] and it is further asserted that they supplied the necessary skill to complete this remarkable building.

This is entirely possible, but it is also likely that the Templars collaborated closely with the Tironensians in order to establish cutting-edge building techniques at their great college in Chartres.

From the outset Bernard of Tiron had sought recruits for his order who were already proficient in the sort of skills the new institution would most need – especially stonemasons. Both within the Tironensian abbeys themselves, and in the college in Chartres, these early masonic monks had passed on their own knowledge to new initiates, putting the novices through an ecclesiastical form of apprenticeship and training them carefully until they too became masters of their craft.

Of course the masons were not alone. The order needed carpenters, tanners, farmers, blacksmiths and every other conceivable craft that made 12th-century life possible. But it was within the ranks of its masons that the order achieved its highest accolades.

So, we now need to accept the fact that the creation and specialization of the Tironensian order of monks is almost certainly yet another example of Star Family manipulation, like the creation of the more famous Cistercians, another reformed Benedictine order (see Chapter 5) with whom the Tironensians had much in common, including an unusual approach to Christianity.

As we will see later in the chapter, it would appear that the task of the Cistercians and Templars was to lay the economic foundation of the New Jerusalem, particularly through the wool trade, with Cistercians controlling production and the Templars acting as the international financiers and soldiers of the enterprise. The now almost forgotten Tironensians, we believe, were given the specific remit of stonemasonry – it was they who would oversee the physical buildings of the New Jerusalem. It has even been suggested that the great innovations in architecture that began c. 1130 (see below, p.107) owed much to the Tironensians as it did to the Templars and Cistercians.

The Tironensians built many Scottish parish churches, as well as their own abbeys. The first Tironensian abbey in Scotland was Selkirk, founded in 1113, followed by Kelso in 1128, and then Kilwinning in 1140. It is interesting to note that the building of Kelso took place in the same year as the Council of Troyes and the return of the original Templars from Jerusalem. It was built at the specific request of King David I, who was also a great friend to the Cistercians. Kelso is said to have been the most beautiful of all the Scottish abbeys.

Since the documents found by the original Templars ultimately found their way to Kilwinning, which was a Tironensian foundation by the brothers from Kelso, and since Kelso was founded in 1128, it seems distinctly probable that the scrolls were in fact first brought to Kelso – an abbey that might even have been specifically built to house them. But history would prove that Kelso, being so close to the English border, was not safe from harassment and so a new abbey was constructed by the same strange order of monks, this time in the safer district of Kilwinning. It follows that if this was the case the documents were brought there in or after 1140.

Secrets of the Hidden Scrolls

The most important and fascinating question that remains to be answered is: what information did these scrolls contain?

We now know a great deal about the scrolls found at Qumran and it is likely that the documents under the Temple contained some of the same information as the scrolls known as the 'Manual of Discipline' and the 'Community Rule' which described how a group similar to the Essenes was expected to conduct itself. This stands to reason because of the similarities between the Essenes and the Cistercians and Templars.

Amongst the many rules is the call for everyone who wishes to join the community to pledge himself to respect God and man; to live according to the communal rule; to seek God; to do what is good and upright in his sight and to love all the 'children of light'. Initiates must bring 'all of their mind, all of their strength, and all of their wealth' into the community of God. They must maintain a sense of humility, charity and mutual fairness to fellow brothers as well as showing patience and compassion. They are to belong to the community in both a doctrinal and in an economic sense; they are to establish in Israel a solid basis of truth and unite forever in an indissoluble bond. As a means to these ends everyone is to obey his superior in rank in all matters of work and money.

Templar communities were run along very similar lines to those of the Essenes and their brothers, the Cistercians. Like the white brothers of ancient times and those of their own era, the Templars were democratic in structure. Exactly as the Essene 'Community Rule' spelled out, the officers, local and regional leaders and even the Grand Master of the whole order were elected at Chapter and any of them could be removed if they failed to achieve the objectives expected of them.

Other scrolls also told how the authors looked forward to the dawn of a new age when, as the elect of God, they would be his agents in the destruction of the ungodly and the restoration of acceptable worship in a purified Temple, served by a worthy priesthood.

One document known as the 'War Scroll' details the war that will be fought by the Sons of Light against the Forces of Darkness. It is not simply an overview of a hypothetical conflict but contains very specific details about the army that will fight the battles – how it will be composed, equipped and managed during the battle. According to the War Scroll, there would be both infantry and cavalry, all armed in a very precise way and subject to the will of a supreme commander. Each item of adornment, every shield, lance and sword is described in great detail and attention is given to the moral rectitude of those taking part. What the War Scroll describes is an entire army, marching and fighting according to Jewish beliefs and intentions. It seems entirely likely that the order of the Knights Templar was assembled along the lines described in the War Scroll.

But there are reasons to suppose that there were even more important documents placed under the Temple – being as close to the holy of holies (the spot where the Ark of the Covenant once stood) as it was possible to get. Given the breathtaking developments in architecture undertaken by the Knights Templar it has often been suggested that they must have somehow gained access to information on constructional geometry and a knowledge of secrets of some ancient lost art and science – probably from previously lost Judaic/Egyptian traditions. Whether or not this is founded in fact cannot be proven, but as soon as the Templars and the Cistercians began operating, the world of Western architecture changed, almost overnight.

Architectural Wonders

Both Templars and Cistercians were prodigious builders and they were at the heart of the great cathedral- and church-building period that was prompted across Europe by the new-found architectural 'secrets'.

The beauty and engineering excellence of the buildings erected from 1130 onwards, in what became known as the 'Gothic' style, are truly staggering. The cathedral builders created huge vaulted ceilings and flying buttresses, allowing for thin walls and huge window spaces.

John Ochsendorf, a structural engineer and historian of architecture and construction at the Massachusetts Institute of Technology, is amazed by what the medieval guilds of stonemasons achieved. He talked of the first time he stood on top of the vault of the chapel at Kings College, Cambridge: 'You're standing 80 feet off the ground on a thin piece of stone… You can even feel small vibrations. And you can't help thinking, the nerve of these people!'[4]

The chapel roof spans almost 50 feet (15m) and yet the vaulting supporting the roof is only 4 inches (10cm) thick – a similar relationship of length to thickness as that of an eggshell. Ochsendorf is adapting a computer program in an attempt to rediscover the secret knowledge behind the arches and domes of Gothic cathedrals in the hope that it could 'revolutionize' modern architectural designs and help develop environmentally friendly buildings. As Ochsendorf adds: 'These people developed a very real science of construction to attain a high degree of stability. I'm simply in awe of the fact that we haven't surpassed it yet.'

The word 'modern' itself is not a new invention. It was first coined in France, less than ten years after the Templars finished their excavations, to refer to the new-style Gothic cathedrals being built under Templar and Cistercian direction. Not only was the structural engineering a remarkable breakthrough, other aspects such as the creation of coloured glass for the stained-glass windows were a sudden and inexplicable leap forward in technology. The new cathedrals were being built to a far greater height than ever dreamed of before with more windows, larger naves and wide internal spaces uncluttered by pillars.

Scientific knowledge was truly entering the 'modern' age.

Many scholars now agree that the Templars were fully involved in the financing and planning of the construction of these Gothic cathedrals.

The Templar influence in geometry and design led to the creation of beautiful structures such as the cathedral of Chartres. The version of Chartres we see today was erected extraordinarily quickly, probably between 1194 and 1250. Chartres cathedral is described by the Church as the product of co-operative effort by the townspeople, financed by the pilgrim trade. This standard explanation totally fails to explain the massive and immediate input of financial resources that was made available to pay for the quarrying and transport of the stone and the enormous expenditure on the vast numbers of stonemasons, sculptors and other craftsmen who would have been employed to complete such a vast and complex edifice so quickly. It is highly doubtful that the proceeds of the pilgrimage to Chartres over the period of its construction could have paid for the creation and installation of the stained-glass windows, much less for the construction and decoration of the entire building. The only source of finance in Europe at that time which could have produced the resources necessary was the Order of the Knights Templar.

In France guilds of skilled artisans were known as *compagnonnages*, and the *compagnonnage* of stonemasons who built the great cathedrals were known as the 'Children of Solomon'. The Children of Solomon were instructed in the art of sacred geometry by the Tironensians,[5] the Knights Templar and Cistercian monks, and they acted entirely with the sanction of Bernard of Clairvaux. He gave a 'rule' to the Children of Solomon in March 1145, which laid down the conditions required for living and working.

These 'Children of Solomon' must have relied heavily on the 'Knights of the Temple of Solomon' for finance and instruction and there are strong grounds to believe that the Templars created rituals of initiation for the stonemasons. It stands to reason that if the original band of Templars did indeed find buried information detailing the secrets of the priestly builders who constructed the Jerusalem Temple, they would require strict vows of secrecy to be sworn by any initiate who was to be entrusted with these skills. In this way the guilds of stonemasons would have formed their own hierarchy – tied very closely to that of the Knights Templar.

Templar Wealth and Enterprise

Quite soon – in fact in a very short period of time considering the logistical difficulties – the Templars represented a truly multinational organization and this meant constant travel. Travel required better roads and, where possible, efficient river and sea navigation. The Templars faced each challenge as it came along. They built garrisons in remote areas where outlaws were known to operate, levelled tracks and built bridges. They constructed sturdy cargo ships and war galleys that were highly manoeuvrable. The Templar infrastructure grew, with presbyteries, farms, castles, seaports and even small towns creating an ever-stronger and more integrated Templar infrastructure, to the extent that the Knights Templar effectively became a society within a society. They were not subject to local taxes of any sort and, being answerable only to their Grand Master – who in turn was technically answerable only to the pope – lived outside the jurisdiction of the lords and kings upon whose land they thrived.

The Knights Templar came to own estates of varying size scattered throughout Europe from Denmark, Scotland and the Orkney Islands in the north, to France, Italy and Spain in the south. In England and Wales alone they had over 5,000 properties. They also extended their interests into Africa, establishing a major presence in Ethiopia, where the Essene *Book of Enoch* was eventually rediscovered many centuries later. There is also good reason to believe that the Knights Templar sailed west to the continent of America. In Europe they developed two principal naval bases; one on the island of Majorca to give them control of the Mediterranean and another at the port of La Rochelle on the Atlantic coast of France. From there, many people argue, they conducted trade with Greenland, the North American mainland and even Mexico.

Some years ago Chris Knight had a lengthy conversation with the Norwegian shipping magnate Fred Olson, who said that sailing to North America was far from unusual before Christopher Columbus was born and that he would be surprised if a trading force such as the Templars had not travelled there. He pointed out that there is a very safe route from northern Scotland across which one can sail to the Americas without ever losing sight of land.

Within 50 years of their foundation, the Knights Templar had become a commercial force equal in power to many states; within 100 years they had developed into the medieval precursors of multinational conglomerates with interests in every form of commercial activity, making the Templar institution far richer than any kingdom in Europe.

Meanwhile, under the guiding hand of Bernard of Clairvaux, the once struggling order of Cistercian monks was expanding in unison with the Templars. Within Bernard's lifetime the Cistercians established over 300 abbeys throughout Europe. Whilst the long-term mission of the two orders was the same, the approach of each was different. The Cistercians became known as the 'apostles of the frontier' due to their habit of refusing donations of land near major centres of population and opting instead to site their new establishments in marginal lands in the mountains and barren reaches of Christian Europe. The Templars, on the other hand, located themselves in centres of population with an emphasis on estates strategically situated near major trade and pilgrimage routes.

The Templars proved to be wise businessmen as much as they were feared warriors. They made substantial strategic investments in land and agriculture and invested in the industries that provided the essential ingredients for their massive building programme. As we have noted, Jews had always been the providers of credit to Christians because usury (lending at interest) was not acceptable for Christians themselves. But somehow these later Jewish priests with a Christian face managed to ease themselves into the role of the world's first international bankers. They developed the concept of financial transfer by 'note of hand' which was, essentially, what we would call a banker's cheque or credit note, and therefore also the precursor of the credit card.

Amazingly, these creative businessmen-cum-warriors-cum-builders-cum-monks also created the medieval equivalent of the 'package tour' industry. Having secured the routes to holy shrines, they were able to offer a complete service to pilgrims whether it be to Rome, Compostela in Spain or Jerusalem itself. The Templars set up arrangements with innkeepers, ship owners, ferrymen and people involved at every other necessary stage of providing a smooth 'vacation'. And they made a good margin of profit on each step of the way.

Part of the Templar package was their new invention – the traveller's cheque. The greatest worry for any pilgrim at the time was fear of robbery, and no pilgrim would have wished to be caught on the open road with substantial sums of money. Prior to the Templars, however, there had been little option because travel required money. The Templar infrastructure provided the perfect solution. The pilgrim simply went to see his local Templar treasurer and deposited funds to cover the expected cost of the entire intended journey, including travel, accommodation and the necessary giving of monies to shrines en route as well as at the destination. The treasurer would give the traveller a receipt, which was encrypted with a secret Templar code to prevent fraud – rather as an internet transaction would be today.

At each key point in his journey the pilgrim would hand his receipt to the local Templar representative who would then settle any dues outstanding, deduct the relevant amount, re-code the note and give it back to the traveller. Once home the returned pilgrim would present his much used 'traveller's cheque' back to the original Templar treasurer who then returned any outstanding balance or provided a bill for any overspend.

Templar bankers also arranged the safe transfer of funds for international and local trade for the Church and state as well as other businesses. They lent to bishops to finance church-building programmes as well as to kings and emperors to cover building projects, wars and, of course, the Crusades.

The key members of the Knights Templar were of Jewish descent and therefore in principal had no objection to usury. However, as it was imperative to the organization to maintain a 'Christian' face, it looked for a way to be able to lend money at a profit without being accused of usury. The way they achieved this was to argue that since it was quite permissible to charge rent for the leasing of a house, the profit they received on loans should be considered as 'rent' rather than interest. This 'rent' was payable at the time the loan was made and was added to the capital sum borrowed.

With this complex commercial infrastructure in place across Europe, a 'new world order' began to emerge and the Western Christian world became transformed into a more vibrant and stable place. The new-found benefits of financial security and safe travel, together with reliable and effective trade over great distances, led to the accumulation of capital and this gave rise to the emergence of a newly prosperous merchant class, the urban bourgeoisie. The arrival of city merchants shifted the balance of power towards towns and cities, which previously had emerged from the need for mutual safety rather than trade. The Order of the Knights Templar were like a modern multinational conglomerate, but they could also, in many ways, be seen as having established the first European Union – a Europe-wide institution with free cross-border trade and a movement of currency on an international scale.

Champagne Fairs

Nowhere do the changes brought about by the Templars and their Cistercian colleagues become more evident than in the creation of what became known as the Champagne Fairs. Since the 10th century, trade fairs had been held in Champagne, to which merchants would travel from a wide area to buy and sell goods. Champagne was conveniently placed in terms of ease of access, but though the early Champagne Fairs prospered, they were small-scale affairs. None of the cities of Champagne was especially large and visiting merchants had to set up tents wherever possible. As a result they and their merchandise were vulnerable to theft, and transactions involving large amounts of cash were highly risky. This situation changed with the accession of Theobald II as count of Champagne in 1125.

Theobald came from a prominent Star Family – and what an influential family it was. As discussed earlier, in 1125 Count Hugues of Champagne had decided to join his companions in Jerusalem, thereby becoming the first recruit to the fledgling Order of the Knights Templar. At that time Hugues had surrendered his noble rank and position – but not, we suspect, his influence.

Hugues had no sons but he did have three nephews – the sons of his brother Stephen, count of Blois and of Chartres, who had been one of the leaders of the Crusade before his death in battle in 1102. As the Templars emerged as an international power-base from 1128 onwards, the control that these Star Families exercised was utterly astounding.

When Hugues went east, his title of count of Champagne passed to his nephew Theobald (or Thibaud), who became Theobald II. Another nephew, Henry, count of Blois, who had been educated at the Star Family headquarters at Cluny, travelled to England, where he became the bishop of Winchester the year after the Templars received their rule. The third nephew, Stephen, also sailed across the English Channel; in 1135, following the death of his uncle Henry I, the son of William the Conqueror, Stephen took the throne of England. He quickly made his brother's post of bishop of Winchester superior to that of the archbishop of Canterbury, thereby giving Henry absolute control of the Church in England to match his own control of the state.

On Henry's death the succession had been hotly disputed and there is little doubt that Stephen was placed on the English throne for the sake of the kingdom's stability as a Star Family puppet, since he had neither the intelligence nor the political skill to have achieved such rank on his own accord. One contemporary writer, Walter Map, expressed a low opinion of King Stephen: 'He was adept at the martial arts but in other respects little more than a simpleton.'

Indeed, Stephen proved to be a loose cannon, since far from bringing stability, he only made matters worse. However, it was during Stephen's rule that the Templar insignia of a red cross on a white ground was adopted as England's national flag. It seems likely that his influential Templar uncle, Hugues, may have more than influenced this decision to make their mantle the badge of the New Jerusalem.

Theobald II, Hugues' nephew and successor as count of Champagne, was an exact contemporary of Bernard of Clairvaux, having been born in the same year, 1090. The two men appear indeed to have been great friends and Theobald conveniently acquired his title in Champagne just before Bernard began his rise to influence in the Church. In addition to being count of Champagne, Theobald was also count of Chartres, and he also held several important fiefs from the count of Burgundy, such as Auxerre, Maligny, Evry and Troyes (the city that was Theobald's capital).

From the moment he came to power, Count Theobald began to transform the Champagne Fairs into something much more remarkable than the small-scale affairs they had been hitherto. It is no exaggeration to say that Theobald's decisions at this time had a tremendous bearing on the eventual development of Western Europe.[6]

Very soon there were a total of nine annual Fairs held in Champagne. The main ones were held at Lagny in January and February, Bar-sur-Aube in March and April, Troyes in July and August, Provins in September and October and Troyes again in November and December. Eventually these were supplemented by four other smaller fairs and in the end there was barely a day of the year when one fair or another was not operating in Champagne.

Incidentally, it was these new 'super-fairs' in Champagne that gave rise to the introduction across Europe of the pound, that unit of weight that today is considered so Anglo-Saxon and a losing competitor to the metric system.[7] The unit was called the 'avoirdupois pound' and it was divided (as today) into 16 ounces. This was actually a very ancient unit that can only reasonably have come from the Star Families – and probably from the scrolls they had so recently rescued from beneath the ruins of the Jerusalem Temple.

It was the great American statesman Thomas Jefferson who first noticed something extraordinary about the 'avoirdupois pound'. On 4 July 1790 Jefferson drafted a report on weights and measures to submit to the House of Representatives in Philadelphia (then the capital of the new United States of America). He noted a number of oddities and then wrote:

> 'Another remarkable correspondence is that between weights
> and measures. For 1,000 ounces avoirdupois of pure water fill
> a cubic foot, with mathematical exactness.'[8]

Such a perfect fit suggests a connection between the modern foot and the pound – which simply should not be the case unless there was a forgotten mutual origin in ancient times. Certainly the British 'imperial' pint is connected to the avoirdupois ounce because 20 such ounces of water are precisely equal to 1 pint.[9]

Count Theobald took definite steps to make certain that merchants from as far away as possible would take advantage of the benefits the new Champagne Fairs could offer. Firstly he ensured that there was sufficient, safe lodging space for the visitors, as well as secure warehousing for their merchandise. His own forces offered safety of passage to and from the Fairs and he protected the Jewish community of Troyes, members of which acted as moneychangers and arranged loans and credit where necessary, prior to the Templars establishing their own network.

The First Crusade, which, it should be remembered was also engineered by the Star Families of Champagne, had opened up the Near East and had allowed a route for luxury goods from even further east. The great markets of the Levant offered goods from as far away as China. Exotic merchandise of all kinds now finds its way to Champagne, either via Italy and the Alps, via the ports of southern France or via Spain. Spices, silks, perfumes and a host of other commodities arrived at the Fairs from the south, whilst furs came from Russia and Germany and fine wines from all the regions surrounding Champagne.

Most important of all, and absolutely pivotal to the ultimate success of the Champagne Fairs, was woollen cloth that was brought down from Flanders to be traded in the Champagne Fairs for the goods arriving from the south and east. It was first and foremost upon the trade in wool that the Champagne Fairs depended and it is no exaggeration to suggest that wool was the engine of the international trade that drove the Fairs.

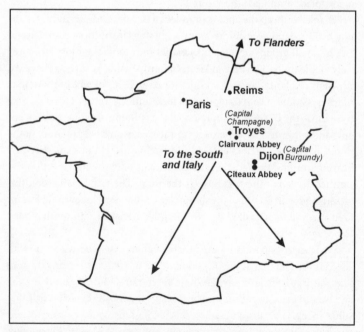

Figure 6 Map of France, showing Paris and the major cities of Champagne and north Burgundy

The Cistercian Sheep Economy

There was nothing remotely coincidental about the sudden availability of raw wool on a previously unprecedented scale. The Cistercians were building up huge flocks of sheep in Flanders and even more so in England. They had drained hundreds of thousands of acres of previously sea-washed land in Flanders to allow for the animals and in Britain they were opening up opportunities for sheep grazing in massive areas that had previously been wasteland.

The Cistercians herded sheep wherever they settled. It was a stroke of genius because sheep are by far and away the least demanding and most productive of all domestic animals.[10] They thrive on marginal land and cope well with great temperature ranges. It may be said that the herding of sheep fitted well with the Cistercian way of life but it might equally be suggested that the type of monasticism the Cistercians adopted was tailor-made to accommodate the sheep.

Thanks to sheep the abbeys founded in Britain, and specifically in the north of England, rose quickly from being small institutions founded and run by small groups of religious fanatics into some the most economically viable units anywhere in Western Europe. Abbeys such as Rievaulx, Kirkstall and Fountains in Yorkshire soon ran herds of tens of thousands of sheep. Grants of land to support all these animals were not hard to come by because the Cistercians represented the epitome of monastic zeal. For any landowner to give generously to the Cistercians was as good, in the minds of the benefactors at least, as a free pass to Paradise, particularly bearing in mind the fact that the Cistercians only sought land that was unfitted for any other purpose at the time. The Cistercians took this 'desert' and with the aid of the sheep, turned it into the green and pleasant land that well represented the New Jerusalem that Britain was intended to become.

What seems particularly bizarre in light of the Cistercian obsession with sheep is the fact that at the inception of the order and for many decades afterwards, Cistercians were absolute vegetarians. Only the aged and the sick were allowed to consume meat and this was mostly beef. It is true that some sheep were slaughtered so that their skins could be turned into parchment for the abbeys' scriptoriums – but this was a very tiny number in comparison with the size of the herds in question.

The Cistercians raised sheep for more than one reason. For example, once land had been enclosed to create large sheep runs, the animals would graze back the scrub, whilst at the same time dropping their manure onto the land, enriching the soil and making it suitable for crops. As an ultimate intention this was understandable in itself, but on the way great profits came from the crop of wool. Apart from the small costs of tending the sheep and clipping them when necessary, this wool cost the Cistercians almost nothing. Neither was its existence coincidental to events taking place elsewhere.

There was clearly a 'grand plan' being mapped out because the mechanisms necessary to support the Cistercian wool trade were put in place just before the Cistercians had established their sheep-led economic empire. The work of their fellow white-clad brothers, the Templars, had provided security of travel and guaranteed international payment methods.

And just as surely as Britain was a major plank of this well thought-out plan, Flanders was another.

Flemish Influence

During the 12th century Flanders occupied most of present-day Belgium, together with parts of the Netherlands and northern France. Like Champagne it was a county (that is, ruled by a count) that owed a nominal fealty to the king of France but in effect operated with a fierce independence. In 1125, when Count Theobald II came to power in Champagne, Flanders was ruled by Count Charles I. Although kind by nature and well liked, he does not appear to have been the right man for the job as far as the Star Families were concerned. He died under suspicious circumstances in 1127 and after a very brief struggle for power the county fell to Thierry, the youngest son of Thierry II of Lorraine and a man with whom the Star Families could do business.

Count Thierry was a Crusader and a close ally of the Knights Templar in his later life. His 40-year reign (1128–68) saw the region grow significantly in economic power. Thierry's first wife, Marguerite de Clermont, died in 1133 and whilst on Crusade in 1139 he married Sibylla of Anjou, daughter of the then king of Jerusalem, Fulk of Anjou, who was another Star Family member. Thierry was also a staunch supporter of the Cistercians and many abbeys were created on his land during his reign.

Whilst Theobald was busy organizing and arranging the Champagne Fairs, Thierry was occupied with consolidating his hold on Flanders and was promoting a period of peace that allowed the woollen industry, already evident in cities such as Ghent and Bruges, to grow and prosper. This was all happening whilst the Cistercians, especially in Britain, were making sheep-breeding into a major sector of the national economy. As the looms of Flanders became more numerous and efficient, so the supply of local raw wool was soon insufficient for the Flemish spinners and weavers. English Cistercian wool was welcome and the monks were soon exporting hundreds and then thousands of tons of raw wool each year to Flanders. Landowners in Britain were quick to follow the lead of the Cistercians and within a couple of decades Britain became the natural home for the production of good, long-staple virgin wool.

Bales of raw wool were shipped from all over Britain to Flanders, where the wool was carded, spun and woven into cloth all across the county. The finished cloth was taken in pack trains down to Champagne, where it was traded with goods that had come up from the south or across from the east. At first the cloth was also dyed and finished in Flanders, but as the desire for richer fabrics and more vibrant colours developed, so northern Italy and especially Florence provided the service of dying and finishing.

What eventually began to happen was the sort of situation in which a merchant from England might travel to the Champagne Fair in Troyes, where he would negotiate the sale of his raw wool to a merchant who had travelled to Troyes from Flanders. The English merchant might also arrange the purchase of luxury woollen cloth from Florence, which may well have been made from the very raw wool he had sold into the market a year or more ago.

Together the Cistercians and the Templars were driving commerce. Their distant ancestors, the Essenes, may have turned their noses up at the thought of 'trade' but the Star Families certainly did not. Their ancestors had been Jews who had prospered in the hostile surroundings of Western Europe only by acquiring the financial and business skills that made them an important element in the Christian economy.

Very few aspects of daily life could fail to have been affected by the dramatic changes that the Star Families were bringing about, and many of these changes have left a legacy that has come down to us today. A good example is the use of the symbol known as the *Agnus Dei*. This means the 'Lamb of God' and is usually depicted in the following manner.

In ancient Jewish times the Lamb of God was the paschal lamb slaughtered on the eve of the Passover. This festival celebrated the Exodus from Egypt and the birth of the Jewish nation and in Christian tradition was adopted as Easter – the 'birth' of the Christian religion brought about by the supposed resurrection of Jesus Christ. In the Christian liturgy Jesus is 'The Lamb of God who takes away the sins of the world'.

It was the Knights Templar who, from the 12th century onwards, placed the red cross of their order onto the Agnus Dei. It is regularly seen in churches, either carved in stone or wood, or else included in stained-glass windows.

St John the Baptist, whose emblem the lamb had been, became the patron saint of woollen weavers and took pride of place in their guilds. An interesting result of this relates to the town of Halifax in Yorkshire, England. Halifax lay in the heartland of Cistercian sheep-rearing and although originally only a small village, grew to be one of the greatest areas of woollen cloth production anywhere in Britain. Its town crest is a revelation (*see* Figure 8).

The church in Halifax was dedicated to St John the Baptist in the early 1100's and the woollen weaving guild was strong in the settlement from an early period. When the town crest was created the good burghers of Halifax created an image that might well be the best symbol of Star Family beliefs and operations ever made.

The town crest of Halifax contains the head of John the Baptist and the Agnus Dei, complete with St John's staff and the Templar flag. It also has the roses of Yorkshire (roses are one of the symbols of both the Goddess and of Venus) and a chequerboard background to the central shield that has distinctly Freemasonic overtones.

Perhaps most significant of all is the Latin motto: *Nisi Dominus custodierit civitatem* ('Except the Lord keep the city'). This motto comes from the opening verse of Psalm 127 (Hebrew numbering), which runs in full as follows: 'Except the Lord build the house, they labour in vain that build it. Except the Lord keep the city, the watchman waketh but in

Figure 7 Image of the Agnus Dei (Lamb of God)

Figure 8 The town crest of Halifax, Yorkshire, England, as depicted on the gates of the Piece Hall

vain.' The psalm is one of a distinct group of Psalms (120–34) that each bear the subtitle 'A Song of Ascent' ('Song of Degrees' in the King James Bible), and some scholars have proposed that these were originally chanted or sung during ritual processions to the sanctuary of the Jerusalem Temple. But the Songs of Ascent were also of special significance to the Essenes – who included them in the Psalms Scroll, a selection of around 40 Psalms found among the Dead Sea Scrolls. And it comes as no surprise to learn that the Songs of Ascent were, and remain, central to the liturgy of the Cistercian order. In this connection the 'house' and 'city' of Psalm 127 are not simply general terms but refer respectively to the Temple and Jerusalem – or, in the case of the Essenes and Cistercians, the New Jerusalem they were trying to bring about.

According to a very old local tradition, the head of John the Baptist was brought to Halifax and buried in, or close to, the church that carries the saint's name. Whilst this story almost certainly has no basis in fact, the combination of Star Family symbolism and ancient liturgy incorporated into the town's crest and mythology demonstrates how important the Cistercian and Templar influence was on these new wool-based communities from the 12th century onwards.

The 'modern age' began far earlier than many historians have ever suspected. The word 'modern' itself comes from Templar-inspired buildings and the banking and commercial developments created by the twin orders of the white-mantled new Essenes provided the foundations for the Industrial Revolution that would begin in Britain almost 700 years later.

In the 18th century the wool-producing regions of England moved from 'cottage industry' into the factory age with the development of coal-fired steam engines. In Yorkshire and Lancashire new factories grew up to spin and weave wool in bulk, as well as a newer material, cotton, which came from America. New canals and railways brought a movement of raw materials that encouraged the establishment of foundries and heavy engineering, all of which soon spread to Europe and America.

The Templars, in effect, changed the world forever. But by the end of the 13th century they had become too rich and powerful for their own good. Their end was in sight.

CHAPTER 7

A Wicked Act

On 29 November 1268, a child was born in Fontainebleau, France, who would grow up to become one of the Star Families' greatest enemies. Prince Philip was the eldest son of King Philip III of France and his wife Isabella of Aragon. The prince's childhood was far from secure and there were moments when factions fighting to control the crown made his very survival difficult. Perhaps as a result of this Philip grew to be suspicious, dark, brooding – and completely ruthless.

By the late 13th century the county of Champagne was proving a thorn in the side of the French kingdom, retaining near-independent status and prospering greatly from the Champagne Fairs. Its rulers eclipsed their nominal liege lords, the kings of France, in terms of their economic power and influence. Events during the reign of Louis VII, who had briefly invaded Champagne, had proved that a direct open assault on the region was not a practicable idea. Champagne still stood high in the estimation of successive popes and so if the irritant were to be brought to heel it would have to be done by stealth and diplomacy.

The perfect opportunity came along in 1284 in the form of a 13-year-old girl.

Joan of Navarre

Since 1135 the counts of Champagne had also been kings of Navarre, a small Pyrenean realm between France and Spain. The first joint ruler, King Theobald I (Theobald II of Champagne) was an active Crusader who supported the Templars and kept a court very similar to the one that flourished in Champagne. Theobald's son, King Theobald II, (Theobald III of Champagne) followed his father's example and proved to be a just and fair ruler. He began the process of dismantling the feudal state of Navarre and in order to do this he relied more on taxes gained from his ordinary subjects, rather than on the feudal dependencies of his barons. Though heavily taxed, the populace willingly accepted the situation because King Theobald II offered his ordinary citizens extraordinary rights, prestige and a greater political voice than had ever been granted elsewhere in feudal Europe.

All of these strategies were made possible because Navarre, unlike Champagne, was a kingdom and therefore owed no fealty to any other state. The political and economic impetus during the reign of both Theobalds in Navarre had its roots in Champagne and the Star Families. Navarre at this period represents the earliest example of what the Star Families were seeking – safe, secure states in which the population took a part in the running of their own affairs. When compared with examples of national structure in much of the modern world, 13th-century Navarre may not have been a haven of democracy but it was far in advance of anything that existed around it during the period.

King Theobald II was killed at Tunis during the Eighth Crusade and, since he had no children, control of Champagne and Navarre passed to his younger brother, who became King Henry I of Navarre and Count Henry III of Champagne. The new king was known as *Henri le Gros* by the French and *Enrique el Gordo* by the Spanish – because he was very, very large. This oversize monarch enjoyed a reign of just three years before dying of suffocation in July 1274. Henry's only surviving child was a daughter: Joan I, queen of Navarre and countess of Champagne.

At the time Joan (or Jeanne) was only three years of age and so responsibility for the government of Navarre and her other possessions passed to her mother, Blanche of Artois. Within weeks of Henry's death, the vultures began to circle around the kingdom and its infant ruler.

Blanche frantically looked around for support. Her ideal solution would have been for Joan to be betrothed to an English prince but none was available. In desperation, and probably to buy more time and at least some protection, in 1275 Blanche herself married Prince Edmund of Lancaster, a younger son of King Henry III of England. He had been born in 1245 and had previously been married to Aveline de Fortibus but she had died within a year of the marriage in 1272.

At the time he married Blanche, Edmund, known as 'crouchback' ('cross back') because he so frequently wore the Crusader's cross on his mantle, took the unusual step of proclaiming himself 'count palatine' of Champagne. A 'count palatine' was a feudal lord who exercised quasi-royal authority in his domains. But strictly speaking Edmund was walking on thin ice with regard to Champagne. It might be said that he exercised power on behalf of his wife, but of course Champagne did not belong to Blanche. She was simply governing it on behalf of her young daughter.

Despite Blanche's marriage to Edmund of Lancaster the dark clouds continued to gather and it began to appear that if she was to save her daughter's kingdom her only recourse would be to seek help from the one place she did not wish to turn to – the French crown. In the end there was no choice and so she sought refuge at the court of King Philip III, who could not have been more pleased to take her in.

Joan of Navarre was duly betrothed to the king's son, Prince Philip, and they were married on 16 August 1284 – he was 16 and she was 13 years old. Edmund of Lancaster was quickly persuaded to renounce his claim on Champagne by Philip III, who had to part with a number of castles to confirm the deal. The French king died the following year and the teenage Philip IV took the throne. His good looks earned him the nickname of Philip the Fair, but history has few other good things to say of him. As soon as he came to the throne, he set about proving himself one of the most ruthless kings that ever ruled France. His control over Champagne would not become total as long as his wife remained alive and he also needed an heir, both for France and for his wife's vast territories.

Philip Plots against the Templars

By the later part of the 13th century few kings of Western Europe could truly call their thrones their own. By this time the Templars had become so powerful that they could practically dictate their own terms. Like his immediate predecessors and his contemporaries elsewhere, Philip inherited a kingdom that was deeply in debt, in part to Jewish moneylenders but most of all to the Knights Templar. Not only did Philip owe money to the Templars, he also felt humiliated by them. He was unpopular with his subjects and on at least one occasion the Templars had saved him from an angry mob and taken him for safety to their headquarters at the Paris temple. There, he doubtless looked at the exquisite surroundings and ruminated on the potential wealth of the Templars. It is also said that his request to become an honorary Templar, a title that had been bestowed on other monarchs such as Richard I of England, was refused. Philip was an unforgiving scheming dictator and would doubtless have harboured a grudge on these grounds alone.

It would not have been hard for Philip to reason that if there was a way of expelling the Jews from France and of destroying the power of the Templars, he would suddenly owe money to nobody. Wealthy Jewish bankers and merchants were a relatively 'soft' target. But the mighty Templars were a very different matter – how could Philip possibly move against such a powerful multinational military-political-financial organization that was answerable to none except the pope?

But it so happened that circumstances played perfectly into Philip's hands.

Things were still not going well in the Holy Land, despite frequent attempts to bolster the remaining crusader states there. By 1290 the only remaining Christian stronghold in the Levant was the town of Acre. This was attacked by the forces of Sultan Al-Ashraf Khalil and in May 1291 it fell with tremendous loss of life amongst the Templars garrisoned there, including the Templar Master, De Beaujeu. Within weeks the outlying Templar forts had been abandoned and Western Europe's incursion into the Holy Land, which had lasted for almost exactly 200 years, was over.

Rumours spread in the West that the Templars had shown themselves to be cowards at Acre, having advised the commander there to sue for peace. But the Templars, who were skilled strategists and knew their Muslim opponents well, could probably see at once that negotiation was better than battle, since they knew the odds against the Acre garrison to be overwhelming. They were certainly not cowards; when their attempts to pursue a diplomatic solution failed, the Templars fought manfully to the bitter end.

Yet even if the Templars had been able to justify their actions at Acre, they could do nothing to counter the general reputation they had gained by this time. Many considered them to be high-handed bullies and their duties as tax collectors for both the pope and secular leaders had certainly not endeared them to the populace as a whole.

The increased unpopularity of the Templars after the fall of Acre was Philip's first stroke of luck. Still, it would be impossible for Philip IV to move against the Templars unless he could first persuade the pope to abandon them. The Templars were useful to popes, not only as tax collectors but in terms of the potential threat they represented to anyone who opposed the pontiff. As a result Philip was forced to take a leaf out of the Star Families' own book. If he couldn't influence an existing pope, he would create one of his own.

Philip was aided by yet another stroke of luck. In 1294, a pious and saint-like monk was prevailed upon to accept the position of pope as Celestine V. In his short reign Celestine created 12 new cardinals, 8 of whom were French. This action set the seal on what followed 13 years later.

Pope Celestine V resigned his office very quickly and was replaced by Benedetto Gaetano, who took the name Boniface VIII. It was not long before the new pope and Philip IV were at loggerheads over various issues. What it really amounted to was that Philip thought popes had too much power over himself and his subjects. Philip regularly confiscated the Church's property, appointed his own bishops and rejected Rome's ecclesiastical appointees. The series of disputes between Boniface and Philip escalated until the pope eventually formally censured the king and threatened to excommunicate him, thereby removing from his people their Christian obligation of loyalty to their anointed sovereign. Philip responded by sending a 'hit squad' headed by an aristocratic thug by the name of William Nogaret to confront the pope in Italy. Nogaret and his mercenaries did not kill Boniface, but so abused and humiliated him that it could nevertheless be suggested that they were responsible for his death in October 1303.

The next pope to be elected was Nicholas Boccasini, who took the name Benedict XI. On the pretext of bringing about reconciliation between the French crown and the papacy, Philip IV sent an embassy to Rome. Benedict, obviously assuming that it would be advantageous to all concerned, removed the censure from Philip and his court but he would not forgive William Nogaret and his colleagues. They were excommunicated and ordered to appear before the pope for punishment. This confrontation never happened because after only eight months in office Benedict XI died suddenly at Perugia. It was suspected at the time, and is still considered likely, that the pope was poisoned at Nogaret's instigation.

The conclave that met to decide Benedict XI's successor found itself facing a difficult task. King Philip had shown that he would not countenance the existence of a pope of whom he did not personally approve. Philip himself had seen to it that there were now many French cardinals present in Rome and they pushed for the election of Cardinal Bertrand de Got – who just happened to be a lifelong friend of Philip IV. Probably in desperation, the Italian cardinals eventually agreed.

It has been suggested that a private meeting was arranged between the new pope, now Clement V, and Philip soon after the pope's investiture in June 1305. This took place in the forest of Saint-Jean-d'Angély, France. From this moment on Clement was King Philip's man and, though they did not know it, the Templars' fate was sealed.

Meanwhile, Philip's wife, Joan of Navarre, had very conveniently died two months earlier in childbirth. Philip and Joan had several other children, including the heir to the throne, Louis, who had been born in 1289. With the death of his mother, Louis became king of Navarre and, more importantly from the perspective of his father, count of Champagne. But the boy was only 16 years of age when his mother died and during his minority his titles passed to his father.

To sum up the situation, Philip IV now had control of Champagne, the crucible in which the Templars had been created and where they still enjoyed their greatest support. At this time Champagne was almost certainly the place where most Star Family plans were laid and where its leaders were located. Philip also now had the papacy in his pocket – and to prove the fact he insisted that Clement V reside not in Rome but rather in Avignon, a papal territory in the south of France.

The Fall of the Templars

With no one now to prevent him doing as he liked, within months Philip had every Jew in France arrested and deported – minus their wealth. In a single strike he had written off much of his own debt and added hugely to his personal coffers. But he had no intention of using his spoils to pay off his debts to the Knights Templar.

At this time the Templars remained far from popular and many people were questioning the point of a huge monastic fighting force that had been dedicated to protecting the Holy Land, which had now been lost to the Christian West. Philip and his brother kings may also have wondered what the Templars themselves planned to do: what if they decided to create a state for themselves back in Europe? Where would it be and on whose land? The most likely place was surely France, where the order's founders, and probably most of its members, had originated, and where the Templars had vast lands and wealth. Moreover, Philip himself was hugely in debt to them. Destroying the Templars would allow him to wipe out his debts and seize the order's wealth for the French crown. Nothing now stood in Philip's way, and his mind was made up.

The Templars had to go.

But first Philip had to lure the Templar commanders to France. As it turned out the Grand Master, Jacques de Molay, was called to France in 1307, not by Philip IV, as is traditionally asserted, but by the pope. They were to have discussions about a possible merger between the Knights Templar and the other famous crusading order, the Knights of St John (generally known as the Hospitallers). A meeting took place at Poitiers, the results of which are not known. But in any case, the pope's idea of a merger very rapidly became irrelevant.

King Philip was keeping a keen eye on these events, planning his next move. Around this time, scurrilous accusations had begun to surface in France regarding the Templars and their supposed unorthodox or even heretical religious beliefs and practices. De Molay was keen to scotch these rumours and the pope agreed to convene a commission of enquiry on 24 August 1307. Whilst this was taking place, de Molay was in Paris and King Philip seized his chance. Shortly before dawn on Friday 13 October 1307, de Molay and all other senior members of the order were arrested on the king's secret orders. Philip's soldiers across his realms were also instructed to seize all Templar property and detain members of the order throughout the realm.

It seems very unlikely, however, that Jacques de Molay was taken entirely by surprise. The Templars had members everywhere, most likely even within the royal court. As far as they were concerned, the writing had been on the wall for some time and it would have been remarkable if they had not taken some sort of action to protect themselves and their assets well in advance of October 1307. Alan Butler and Templar historian Stephen Dafoe have argued that, unknown to King Philip, a sizeable proportion of the Templars in France had quietly slipped away to bases that the Templars already maintained in the Alps, well away from the influence of the French king.[1]

Tradition also has it, probably on good grounds, that the entire Templar fleet, moored at their French base of La Rochelle, weighed anchor and set sail for an unknown destination in darkness on the evening prior to the arrests.

Jacques de Molay and other senior officers of the order, together with many hundreds of ordinary Templar personnel, were most certainly tortured in order to extract 'confessions' regarding the Templars' heretical practices. Leading the assault in Paris was none other than William Nogaret, King Philip's ruthless 'enforcer'. Under torture the Grand Master himself admitted to a whole swathe of crimes (but de Molay later publicly, and dramatically, retracted his admission of guilt – *see below*, page 133).

Templar 'Crimes'

The list of charges eventually brought against the Templars in France is as follows:

1 The denial of Christ and defiling the cross
2 The worship of an idol
3 The performance of a perverted sacrament
4 Ritual murder
5 The wearing of a cord of heretical significance
6 The use of a ritual kiss
7 Alteration of the ceremony of the mass and the use of an unorthodox form of absolution

8 Homosexual acts

9 Treachery toward other groups amongst the Christian forces

King Philip urged his fellow monarchs throughout Europe to follow his lead against the Templars in their midst. But few were quick to act and it took great prodding from the pope to get them to comply. To be fair to the pope, he did initially condemn Philip's attack on the Templars in 1307, but was supposedly convinced of the Templar's guilt by the evidence presented to him. Whilst modern proponents of the Templars try to show that all the accusations against the order were false, we are certain that in fact they *were* guilty of some of the charges levelled against them. Whilst it is likely that the lowliest amongst the Templar servants and sergeants-at-arms considered themselves to be perfectly normal Catholic believers, it has to be remembered that the Knights Templar were a creation of the Star Families, whose basic beliefs would certainly have been heretical in the eyes of the 14th-century Catholic Church – not least their veneration of John the Baptist above Jesus. It is therefore highly likely that knights, officers and leaders of the Templars adhered to the Ebionite form of Christianity and that their religious practices within the confines of Templar presbyteries reflected the fact.

This is borne out by some of the evidence that was supposed to have been collected by the inquisitors and torturers. For example, the Templars were said to have worshiped a mysterious bearded head, which they called 'Baphomet'. It has been claimed that this word is a corruption of 'Mahomet', a form of Muhammad, and that the Templars' accusers suspected them of covert sympathy with Islam. However, when an ancient Jewish code known as the Atbash Cipher is applied to it, the name Baphomet becomes *Sophia*, meaning 'wisdom', an important concept in Star Family belief (*see* pages 62–3). It was suggested at the time that this 'bearded head' actually represented John the Baptist and this would certainly make sense. The Star Families considered John to have had equal status with Jesus, and perhaps to have been even more important since he came before Jesus in the line of Davidic prophets around whom their beliefs were based.

Much later, in fact as recently as the 19th century, the Catholic Church attacked Freemasonry as the definite and absolute counterpart of 'Templarism'. St John was also important to Freemasons and in a papal allocution (solemn address), Pope Pius IX (1846–78) linked both the Masons and Templars to the 'Johannites', or ancient followers of the Baptist. The pope declared:

> The Johannites ascribed to Saint John the Baptist the foundation of their Secret Church, and the Grand Pontiffs of the Sect assumed the title of *Christos*,[2] *Anointed*, or *Consecrated*, and claimed to have succeeded one another from Saint John by an uninterrupted succession of pontifical powers. He who, at the period of the foundation of the Order of the Temple [Templars], claimed these imaginary prerogatives, was named Theoclet; he knew Hugues de Payens, he installed him into the Mysteries and hopes of his pretended church, he seduced him by the notions of Sovereign Priesthood and Supreme royalty, and finally designated him as his successor.

This may well represent proof that the Catholic Church had known all along what the real beliefs of the Templars were and that the Templars had adopted a definite Johannite stance in their secret doctrines and practices.

Suggestions that the Templars had spat or stamped upon crucifixes were almost certainly exaggerated, but one piece of evidence is very telling. A young French Templar, whilst on trial, reported being instructed by an older brother. The senior Templar had held a crucifix before him and had said, 'Do not have too much faith in this – it is too new!' In terms of Star Family beliefs this would also make sense. The Star Families did not repudiate the importance or significance of Jesus, but rejected the Church's teaching that Jesus was 'the' Christ, the *sole* Messiah. They also rejected the idea of his virgin birth and resurrection – it is likely that the senior officer's words alluded to these relatively 'new' doctrines of the official Church. As far as the Star Families were concerned, their lineage went back thousands of years prior to both John the Baptist and Jesus, both of whom were simply 'servants' to a cause and not the cause itself.

As to the accusation that the Templars performed a perverted sacrament and altered the ceremony of mass, the Templars could well have been guilty as charged in terms of established Catholic doctrine. We have no way of knowing what ceremonies took place behind the closed doors of Templar churches and presbyteries, but we do know that any form of sacrament or mass that did not accord absolutely with Roman practices would have been considered heretical.

The Templars were finally dissolved by the pope in 1312. There was some dispute about what should happen to all the property of the Templars and it was decided that since it would be impossible to return gifts and donations granted to the order over almost two centuries, all Templar property should pass to the Knights of St John, who were not under suspicion. Philip IV simply kept much of what the Templars had once owned in France – in order, he said, to defray the costs of their detention and trials.

Philip had personally triumphed but the condemnation of the order was not universal. England was tardy when it came to investigating the Templars and in the event only found some members guilty of the heretical belief that their Master could grant them absolution for sin. In some areas, such as Portugal, Spain, Germany, Cyprus and most of Italy, the Templars were declared innocent. The Portuguese Templars simply reformed under the name 'Knights of Christ' and carried on much as before. In fact, the pope, while giving in to pressure on him to dissolve the Templars, refused to declare the order as a whole guilty of heresy. He believed that there was not enough evidence to prove that the order's beliefs – as opposed to what a number of its members had been accused of – were fundamentally heretical. He was supported in this view by the failure of other countries – apart from France – to condemn the Templars wholesale, and indeed perhaps they had been more careful in their investigations in other countries than had been the case in France.

The Templars in Scotland

Scotland was in a peculiar position during the persecution of the Templars since its king, Robert the Bruce, and in practice his whole nation, were at the time outside the influence of Rome. In order to gain the Scottish throne Robert had murdered a rival, John Comyn, in 1306, with the result that the pope had excommunicated both Robert and his kingdom.

The Templars were not tried in Scotland, though upon being received back into the Church after 1320, King Robert did have to at least pay lip service to the pope's wishes. However, by this time some years had elapsed and Templars in Scotland could easily have taken up new roles within society. It is unlikely, as some authors suggest, that the entire Templar fleet that disappeared from La Rochelle sailed to Scotland. There is no report of this having happened. In any case the English patrolled the seaways between France and Britain and could surely not have missed an entire flotilla of Templar ships on their way north.

Nevertheless there are persistent rumours that Templar Knights fought for the Scots against the English at the battle of Bannockburn in 1314. Whilst there is no definitive proof that this was the case it is certainly not out of the question. Scottish Templars may have reasoned that they had absolutely nothing to lose by supporting the Scottish king especially since, by this time, England had followed the pope's ruling and had arrested Templar Knights and seized their land. This may have led the Templars to see England as their enemy. Certainly, to avoid the same fate as their brethren further south, it was in their interest to prevent the extension of English power into Scotland.

Another motive may have been an act of tribute to their last Grand Master, for the Scottish victory at Bannockburn came only two months after Jacques de Molay had been burnt to death in Paris. The Grand Master and one of his senior colleagues, called upon to confess their guilt publicly, had made a dramatic recantation of their earlier 'confessions'. King Philip IV was so furious that he had both men burnt at the stake the very same day. (Interestingly, de Molay denied most of the charges levelled against the Templars but made no mention of the main accusation, denying the divinity of Jesus Christ.)

The Aftermath: Switzerland

Back in France, King Philip IV had managed to destroy, in a few short years, everything the Star Families had so carefully created across centuries. His mishandling of Flanders led to a near total destruction of its industrial infrastructure, which meant that little or no woollen cloth was reaching the Champagne Fairs. Not that this mattered much because the Fairs were already beginning to decline, also largely thanks to Philip and his policies. Without the Jews and the Templars, lines of credit broke down and with the addition of the lack of woollen cloth arriving from the north, the Fairs drew fewer and fewer traders.

Strangely enough, within a year of Jacques de Molay's execution in Paris and the Scots' supposed acceptance of Templar support against the English, an event of significance was taking place well to the east of the French royal domains. A few years earlier, the three small Alpine states of Uri, Schwyz and Unterwalden had jointly declared their independence of their overlords, the imperial house of Habsburg. These territories bordered the economically important St Gotthard Pass through the Alps, an area that the Habsburgs prized. In order to put down the three states, Duke Leopold I of Austria, brother of Duke Louis IV of Bavaria, set out for the region in November 1315, with an army of around 5,000 men, intent upon putting paid to any thought of self-determination in the region. His forces and those of the confederation of three states met at the battle of Morgarten, which took place on 15 November 1315.

Leopold marched his troops to a position from where he hoped to surprise the combined forces of Uri, Schwyz and Unterwalden, planning to attack them from the south via Lake Aegeri and the Morgarten Pass. The confederates were expecting an attack from the east and had built significant ramparts. However, someone, usually referred to as 'the Knight of Huenenburg' warned the peasants to 'watch out on St Otmar's Day' at the Morgarten. As a result the confederates were ready and waiting. They ambushed the Habsburg forces in the mountain pass, causing a rout and securing a great victory that shook the Habsburgs to their core. As with Bannockburn, there are persistent legends that white-mantled knights assisted in the victory.

The three original states each became 'cantons' in the independent republic of Switzerland, officially called the Swiss Confederation and Europe's oldest democratic state. As in the United States, the original states were eventually joined by other regions. Switzerland has been and remains one of the strangest and least understood countries in the world. In fact for most of its history it has not been a country at all, but rather a confederacy of very separate regions that merely co-operated in their mutual defence. Defended against mighty neighbours principally by its Alpine position, Switzerland survived against almost insurmountable odds. It has several different languages and could easily have been torn apart by the bitter wars of religion in Europe that followed the Reformation in the 16th century. Despite its large Catholic population, it was to relatively tolerant Switzerland that early proponents of Protestantism travelled to seek safety – men such as John Calvin, who introduced his own brand of Protestantism into Geneva.

Little is known about the inner workings of the historical Swiss state and the country remains a great enigma. Despite producing some of the fiercest and most respected fighters for centuries (generally employed as mercenaries) it has steadfastly maintained a neutrality that has spanned centuries.

Switzerland is justifiably famous for its banking. This extends far back in time and private bankers existed in Switzerland before the 15th century, at which time the Florentine ruler Cosimo de Medici set up a banking house in Basle. The 'private' bankers of Switzerland were wholesalers, brokers and forwarding agents. Their real speciality was in credit transactions, but their very existence is something of an enigma because they appeared from nowhere in the 14th century. This may represent further proof that escaping French Templars sought refuge in the Alps, where they continued to do what they had been doing for the previous two centuries. Switzerland is famous for its almost fanatical secrecy, which of course one would expect if its origins lay with a heretical religious order that had been abandoned and destroyed by the Church.

The more one looks at Switzerland, the greater its Templar and ultimately Star Family credentials seem to be. Whilst maintaining its almost fierce neutrality, Switzerland has done much to promote world peace and it was of course the founding state of the Red Cross, which still carries the same symbol as that used by the Templars. (The Swiss flag itself, a white cross on a red background, is a reversed version of the Templar emblem.) Switzerland does not have a particularly good historical record when it comes to the treatment of Jews living within its boundaries, but strangely enough expulsions and persecutions of Jews did not commence until the middle of the 14th century. Up until that point the Swiss cantons had a very large population of Jews, who lived in harmony with their neighbours. Basle had one of the largest communities in Europe, who were mainly from France and Germany in origin. Bern, St Gall, Zurich, Schaffhausen, Diessenhofen and Lucerne all acquired Jewish communities in the 13th century and the vast majority of the Jews in Switzerland were engaged in banking – just as they had been in Champagne.

In some respects the sort of business taking place in the cantons was similar to that which had taken place at the Champagne Fairs. The use of credit had become common amongst merchants, who increasingly chose to avoid carrying their wealth and goods around Europe as they once had done. Nevertheless, Switzerland lay on important trade routes through the Alps and its refusal, almost from the start, to allow itself to become involved in international alliances that must ultimately lead to wars and invasions made it popular as a place for European merchants passing through to deposit some of their financial reserves. They could be as certain as was possible at this period that their money would remain safe.

In addition to its financial heart Switzerland was one of the first countries of Europe to establish a large and profitable textile industry, which seems to have begun to gain ground at the start of the 14th century. This trade included linen but was centred on wool – which of course was always one of the chief concerns of both the Cistercians and the Templars. As with Britain, Switzerland's ultimate commercial wealth sprang from the back of its sheep, but unlike Britain it remained an inward-looking state, suspicious of its neighbours and refusing, at any price, to sacrifice its sense of freedom and the distinct nature of its many parts.

In short, Switzerland gives every impression of a state that ultimately owes its existence to the Templar Knights who fled there, as we have seen, probably some time before the attack on the order orchestrated by Philip IV. Since Alan Butler and Stephen Dafoe first made this suggestion in the late 1990s, the idea has proliferated amongst Templar researchers and now seems to be generally accepted as an explanation for the disappearance of the majority of Templars from France. It appears that in fact fewer than ten per cent of the Templar personnel previously thought to have been in France at the start of the 14th century actually fell foul of Philip IV's attack.

Having studied all the momentous events inspired by those controlling Champagne from the end of the 11th century, it is not difficult to identify an obvious strategy, one that that lasted for several centuries. The method of the Star Family leaders in Champagne was to use 'ordinary' agencies to produce 'extraordinary' results. The prosecution of the First Crusade with the capture of the Holy Land and key trading routes; the creation of the Cistercian order and that of the Knights Templar; the building of a sound industrial base in Flanders; and the creation of the Champagne Fairs cannot be seen as isolated phenomena. The common objective of all these strategies, no matter how they appear in isolation, was economic in nature. They benefited not only Champagne but drew the whole of Europe and areas beyond into a new sort of relationship, brought about by a vast increase in international trade.

Both the Cistercians and the Templars were supposed to be religious institutions and yet in the case of each it can be seen that their ultimate result owed far more to politics and economics than to Christianity. Taken together, the decisions smack of the presence of a far-sighted and very influential agency with a specific remit – to erode the power of the feudal state in general and of the Catholic Church in particular. To deny this and to insist that all the events inspired from within Champagne across three centuries were unrelated and entirely coincidental seems to us to blindly ignore tangible and persuasive evidence.

The sudden appearance of Switzerland, at exactly the same time as the Templars were outlawed and Star Family influence in Champagne became impossible under French rule, is yet another indication of the existence of a 'rationale'. Switzerland and its important trade routes, together with its close proximity to the new banking and commercial centres developing in northern Italy, offered a secure base of operation for the Star Families. Safe within the Alps, sitting at the very heart of what would become the most secretive state the world has ever known, the Star Family rulers could bide their time and gradually retrench.

The destruction of the Templars may or may not have seemed to be a terrible setback as far as the Star Families were concerned. The genie of trade had been let out of the bottle and a dozen King Philips could not put it back. All he and his tame pope succeeded in doing was to cut off the head of the Hydra. Others grew in its place. Trade routes rapidly shifted away from Champagne, because the Star Families could no longer control what happened there. Switzerland was a much safer option, with its natural security created by the mountains that comprised its topography. After all, a few hundred peasants had destroyed an entire army of 5,000 armed knights at Morgarten. Nobody lost sight of this fact and Switzerland was never invaded again until the reign of Napoleon Bonaparte – the contemplation of disaster was simply too great. In addition Switzerland quickly made itself useful to all its neighbour states and eventually to those far beyond. Because of its avowed neutrality it had no allies and no enemies. Amidst the vicissitudes of European fortunes it was a citadel of confidence. During three centuries of actions the Star Families had learned a very important rule: it is not the person with the military power who ultimately rules the world, but the one who holds the purse strings.

As the 14th century came to an end Europe was on the brink of a revolution that had started with the First Crusade and the conquest of the Near East. Trade continued, fortunes were made and lost and nation states rose and fell. In northern Italy experiments in democracy were taking place and these were born not of kings or fighting barons but rather of merchants and the bankers who supported them. But if the muscle of the New Jerusalem was to be found in the Swiss Alps, its heart lay far to the west in that place where the sacred treasures found by the Templars in Jerusalem were kept safe. Yet another set of peculiar circumstances allowed the Star Families to make a permanent home for their treasures. This would be created by the dynasty of priests that had protected Star Family interests all along. The New Jerusalem in its manifestation in stone would be built by the St Clairs, the priests of the Holy Shining Light. The next Shekinah would be viewed by these priest not from the bare stone platform in Jerusalem – but from the side of a green Scottish glen.

CHAPTER 8

The New Temple of the Shekinah

The Holy Shekinah had last appeared out of the zodiac sign of Sagittarius in the year 8BC, the time at which Solomon's secret priesthood, the leaders of the Star Families, had looked for the Messiah to arrive and to drive what they saw as the forces of darkness from their land (see Chapter 2). The Shekinah had appeared as predicted and in its wake had arisen the leaders and prophets of the Jerusalem Church (John the Baptist, Jesus and James) but the expected New Jerusalem had not arrived. On the contrary, the Jewish nation had suffered an unprecedented calamity at the hands of the Romans.

As we have seen, however, the Star Families survived. In the centuries that followed they and their particular form of Essene-inspired Judaism had grown and flourished, to become a virtually unseen but potent rival to the Pauline Roman Catholicism that they had always hated so much. The years between the First Crusade and the period of Cistercian and Templar greatness had been a high point for the power and influence of the Star Families. And then all had been brought to nothing through the loss of the last toehold in the Holy Land, the actions of Philip IV of France and the reign of Pope Clement V. It is no surprise, therefore, that the Star

Families looked to the next Shekinah to herald a revival in their fortunes. Following the previous pattern of Shekinah appearances, we would expect it to arrive exactly 1,440 years after 8BC, in other words in 1432. But anyone expecting it then would have been disappointed, for in that year the Shekinah did not appear.

The skilled astronomers of the Star Families almost certainly knew quite some time in advance that the Shekinah was not going to appear this time around. Knowledge of astronomy was increasing in the 15th century, and Arab astronomers, notably Ibn al-Shatir (1304–75), had developed mathematical techniques for predicting the movement of the planets more accurately. Their work would most likely have been transmitted to the Star Families via Spain and the Star Family court of Navarre.

The reason for the Shekinah's non-appearance was simple. Over thousands of years all cyclical patterns alter, one near-imperceptible step at a time. The solar system is a wonderful clock and Venus is an amazing minute-hand to the clock, but there is no such thing as the perfect repetition of an astral cycle. The particular cycle of Mercury and Venus that had led to the appearance of the Shekinah at the time of the building of Solomon's Temple and the expected arrival of the Messiah was already thousands of years old. Watching the Shekinah cycle, speeded up, on a planetarium, it is possible to see that, event by event, across a staggering length of time, Mercury and Venus gradually drop back towards the Sun, until eventually they are so close that they converge with the Sun's disc and the Shekinah can no longer be distinguished. This is what happened in 1432.

The New Shekinah

But what Venus takes away, she gives back in other ways. Using their astrolabes and the mathematical techniques they had learned across centuries, mainly from Arab sources, the Star Family astronomers would have been able to establish a *new* pattern of Shekinah appearances. This new Shekinah would not manifest itself on the winter solstice, as the old one had done, but on the autumn equinox.

Because of the peculiarities of the Earth's orbit around the Sun, when seen from any point on the Earth's surface, the Sun appears to rise and set in different positions on the horizon as each year advances. In the northern hemisphere the Sun rises south of east in winter and north of east in summer – producing our seasons. The extreme points of rising and setting occur at opposite ends of the year. Midwinter comes when the Sun rises south of east on 21 December, whilst midsummer occurs when the Sun rises north of east on 21 June. These are known as the midwinter and midsummer solstices (solstice literally means 'sun standstill', because to the naked eye the Sun appears to pause as it ends its north-south or south-north journey and begins to travel in the opposite direction). The solstices were of the most potent importance to our most ancient ancestors.

Midway between the solstices are the equinoxes. These happen when the Sun is exactly halfway on its journey from south to north or north to south. Spring equinox occurs around 21 March and autumn equinox around 21 September. On these two days each year the Sun rises exactly due east and sets exactly due west and day and night are of equal length (equinox means 'equal night [and day]').

The solstices and the equinoxes are known as the four 'stations' or 'corners' of the year and they have been recognized, studied and even worshipped for almost as long as humanity has raised its collective head to the sky in wonder and curiosity.

The Holy Shekinah that had been of supreme importance to the Jews and their ancestors had appeared at the winter solstice – a time of solemn importance and some dread to all ancient humans. Our remote ancestors would have watched anxiously to ensure that the Sun did not keep travelling southwards at dawn beyond the expected solstice. If it did, the weather would grow ever colder and all life would eventually end in relentless frosts and mountains of snow. From a very early date, great ceremonies took place across the northern hemisphere, ensuring that the right procedures were undertaken to convince the gods to send the Sun north again, so that spring would return and nature be reborn.

Such ceremonies also took place at the other corners of the year. Those that were practised at the summer solstice would have been mainly joyful affairs, with the promise of nature's bounty at hand but also a little apprehension in case the Sun continued its march north, bringing greater heat that would parch and eventually kill the crops. The equinoxes were also highly significant. The one at spring was a time of gratitude, with the knowledge that the darkest days were now over and that the longer days were at hand. The autumn equinox brought gratitude for the bounty of harvest but with a strong sense of sacrifice and the knowledge of the inevitable darkening days ahead.

In different cultures across the planet the ceremonies held at the corners of the year would have varied greatly but offerings of gifts to the gods, or to whatever hidden power was deemed responsible, would have been common, and in some cultures these would have included animal and even human sacrifice. Everything possible had to be done to propitiate the gods, the better to ensure that the expected patterns continued, allowing human life to go on.

It is worth bearing all this in mind when we consider the reaction of the Star Family astronomers when, casting their planetary calculations into the future, they saw a new Shekinah pattern emerging centred not on the midwinter solstice, but on the autumn equinox. The first autumn equinox Shekinah would take place on 21 September 1456. Perhaps this promised a new start, and it certainly was not without biblical significance. The Bible records that the two great Temples of Jerusalem – the first built by Solomon and the second by Zerubbabel after the Babylonian captivity (and later restored and embellished by Herod) had both been dedicated at the time of the autumn equinox. We are told in the case of Solomon's Temple:

> Solomon assembled the elders of Israel, and all the heads of
> the tribes, the chief of the fathers of the children of Israel,
> unto King Solomon in Jerusalem, that they might bring up
> the Ark of the covenant of the LORD out of the city of David,
> which is Zion. And all the men of Israel assembled themselves
> unto King Solomon at the feast in the month Ethanim, which
> is the seventh month.[1]

The lunar month of Ethanim is now known as Tishri in the Hebrew calendar.[2] Although it is the seventh month of the civil year it is the start of the religious year and therefore a time of significant feasts and holidays. The most important of these is the Feast of Tabernacles, which begins on the 15th day of Tishri. This feast is, in effect, a harvest festival.

For the ancient Jews, and indeed all agrarian-based societies, the autumn equinox marked the great harvest, when nature's summer flourish gave way to the grains and fruits that would sustain them through the long, dark days of winter. The tall, golden ears of corn, together with the fruits of the trees and bushes were absolutely essential to their survival. This largesse could be taken away at any time, perhaps as a result of a cold spring, violent summer storms or generally unseasonable conditions. To those who recognized the capricious and unpredictable nature of God's grace the right form of worship and the greatest show of gratitude might ensure that the harvest would be brought in safely.

At the heart of the autumn celebration, for most belief systems, was the concept of sacrifice – giving back some of the rewards received. Nature (for which read the Goddess and the Earth) had, with her own body, raised her offspring, which would be ruthlessly cut down by humanity for its own needs. The concept of the growing and sacrificed Corn God (*see* Chapter 3) is so old it is impossible to know where and when it began. But like so much else from primitive religion it was never quite forgotten. We have already shown that even Jesus, either in fact or fable, had deliberately associated himself with the sacrificed Corn God in his speech and actions at the Last Supper (*see* pages 65–6). The mystery religions of Demeter and Mithras also had significant celebrations around the autumn equinox that spoke of death and rebirth.

The Sinclairs of Rosslyn

For the new Shekinah to fall at this time of the year was, therefore, highly significant. Certainly, the importance of the autumn equinox Shekinah of 1456 was not lost on one group of Star Family priests. These were the St Clairs (or Sinclairs) – the priests of the Holy Shining Light. They had been present in Scotland since shortly before Duke William of Normandy had invaded England in 1066. At that time the hopes of the Saxons rested upon a displaced Saxon prince known as Edgar Atheling. Edgar had fled to Scotland after leading a rebellion against William in 1068 and after some time in Hungary his sister Margaret had followed him there. Margaret had married King Malcolm III of Scotland and so become queen. We know that the St Clairs were present at the Scottish court at least as early as this because one of them, William 'the Seemly', was Margaret's cupbearer and was given extensive lands including some in Midlothian. He had previously shared Margaret's brief exile in Hungary and was clearly one of her favourites.

From this point on, the Sinclairs (we will use the modern spelling from now on) were never far from the Scottish court. With a combination of good diplomacy, judicial marriages and unswerving loyalty, they maintained their position through the vicissitudes of Scottish history, often being richer than the king himself. Always staying clear of political subterfuge and baronial infighting, the Sinclairs amassed titles and honours and eventually gained control of the important islands of Orkney and Shetland by the latter part of the 14th century. By the mid-1440s William Sinclair, third *jarl* of Orkney (*jarl* means 'earl' or 'prince' in Norse, then the main language of those islands), was an indispensable ally of King James II of Scotland. Amongst his titles William was also Lord High Admiral of Scotland and in 1454 he was elevated to the rank of Lord Chancellor of Scotland – effectively the king's second-in-command.

William Sinclair's family seat was Rosslyn (or Roslin) Castle in Midlothian, close to the seat of royal power, and it is there that the next key episode in the history of Solomon's priesthood unfolds. As we have seen, the documents found by the first Templar Knights under the ruined Temple of Jerusalem back in the 12th century had been brought to Scotland, possibly as early as 1128, where they were probably kept in the new Tironensian abbey of Kelso before being transferred in 1140 to a safer location, the Tironensian abbey at Kilwinning (*see* Chapter 6). Just over two centuries later they moved again, this time to Rosslyn Castle, about ten miles south of Edinburgh on a promontory above the River Esk.

A castle of some sort had existed on the site since the early 12th century, but the building that still stands in part today was not begun until *c*. 1304. The castle was much enlarged and modified when William Sinclair, earl of Roslin, came into his titles in 1417.

We are now certain that the precious documents from below the Temple of Jerusalem were brought from Kilwinning to Rosslyn Castle shortly before 1447. The first, albeit circumstantial, evidence comes from a record of a fire that broke out at the castle in that year:

About this time [1447] there was a fire in the square keep [of Rosslyn Castle] by occasion of which the occupants were forced to flee the building. The Prince's [Earl Sinclair's] chaplain, seeing this, and remembering all of his master's writings, passed to the head of the dungeon where they all were, and threw out four great trunks where they were. The news of the fire coming to the Prince through the lamentable cries of the ladies and gentlewomen, and the sight thereof coming to his view in the place where he stood upon Colledge [sic] Hill, he was sorry for nothing but the loss of his Charters and other writings; but when the chaplain who had saved himself by coming down the bell rope tied to a beam, declared how his Charters and Writts [sic] were all saved, he became cheerful and went to recomfort his Princess and the Ladys [sic].[3]

It seems very strange that a man such as William, earl of Roslin and *jarl* of Orkney, a person known for his kind disposition and generosity, should be more concerned for a few legal documents than he was for his own wife or the other occupants of the castle. On the other hand one could understand his grief if he had thought, for a terrible, brief moment, that the sacred documents entrusted to him by the Star Families were in danger of being destroyed. After all, they were holy and absolutely irreplaceable.

The scrolls had been in peril on a number of occasions since the Temple of Jerusalem had been burned to the ground in AD70 above the deep tunnels where the documents lay. Once removed from their hiding places by the Knights Templar they were at risk of discovery and destruction. The sea voyage from the Holy Land to Scotland must have been a worrying time, as ships not infrequently came to grief crossing the Bay of Biscay or navigating the coastline up the Irish Sea. The time that they were uprooted again and taken across southern Scotland was another period of vulnerability – which the fire in the castle had demonstrated.

But this time the scrolls had travelled to their final destination. William Sinclair would ensure that they would remain safe within the walls of a Temple of the New Jerusalem that he was to erect at Rosslyn.

The 'Third Temple'

This new structure was to be built out of the same stone as the Jerusalem Temple, almost a quarter of a world away but on the same geological seam of rock. It was to be as faithful a copy of the Herodian second Temple as it was possible to create. Below ground, reproducing the Temple was not a problem because Earl William Sinclair possessed the Knights Templars' account of their excavation. Above ground, all that was still understood of the original Temple related to a section of the west wall that had survived the destruction wrought by the army of Titus in AD70. The earl's men reconstructed this partial west wall and then built the main body of the new Temple using a ground plan that was known to be accurate from the subterranean bases of the destroyed walls. However, the main part of the Rosslyn structure had to be new and they created an original design that was a brilliant interpretation of Ezekiel's vision of the New Jerusalem described at the time of the destruction of the first Jerusalem Temple, that of King Solomon, by the Babylonians.

Earl William did not choose local builders. He selected stonemasons from the guilds in Europe – groups that still used the rituals given to them by the Knights Templar during the great cathedral-building period of the 12th century. These men held their rituals in the so-called crypt in the lower level of Rosslyn, which was completed before the main body of the building.

On a high promontory, just two minutes walk from the castle; the construction of this very special building began. According to tradition, Earl William had commenced excavations for the subterranean chambers and the foundations of the building as early as 1440. But the first stone of the new home for the Templar treasures could not be put in place until the day on which the Shekinah would return – and now it had been calculated that this would take place on 21 September 1456.

Of course, Earl William could tell no one outside his immediate Star Family circle that he was rebuilding the ancient Temple of the Jews. For the benefit of the world at large the new edifice was to be called 'The Church of St Matthew'. Today it is known as Rosslyn Chapel.

Solomon had employed the skills of Hiram Abif to construct his legendary Temple, and now Earl William also needed skills far beyond his own to complete his own masterpiece in stone. The man he had by his

Plate 1 *(above)* Clairvaux Abbey, Champagne, the headquarters of St Bernard of Clairvaux

Plate 2 *(below)* Rosslyn Chapel as it appeared in 1917

Plate 3 *(above)* The ruins of the former St Matthew's Chapel, now standing in a cemetery close to the present Rosslyn Chapel

Plate 4 *(below left)* Contemporary picture of St Bernard of Clairvaux, now to be seen in the treasury of Troyes Cathedral, together with relics of St Bernard's skeleton

Plate 5 *(below right)* Troyes Cathedral in Champagne, France. Troyes was the headquarters of the Star Families from the 11th to the 14th century.

Plate 6 *(above)* The East Window of Rosslyn Chapel with the light box clearly shown in the point of the arch

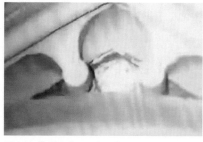

Plate 7 *(below)* The interior of the Rosslyn light box is highly reflective, as is demonstrated here when a high-powered torch was shone into the aperture.

Plate 8 *(left)* A five-pointed star or pentacle, carved into the fabric of a church in Yorkshire, England. This 15th-century example proves conclusively that the pentacle was often used as a Christian symbol.

Plate 9 *(above)* Is this a representation in stone of the Holy Shekinah in her guise as an angel?

Plate 10 *(left)* This carving from Rosslyn Chapel is said to depict a Masonic-style initiation, at a time before Freemasonry even existed!

Plate 11 *(right)* Examples of botanical carving within Rosslyn Chapel. Depicted here is some form of aloe or cactus.

Plate 12 *(below)* The South Porch of Rosslyn Chapel

Plate 13 *(above)* A very rare carving from Rosslyn – this one depicting a Green Woman

Plate 14 *(left)* A carving of the Green Man from the exterior of Rosslyn Chapel

Plate 15 *(left)* The Earl's Pillar or Master's Pillar from Rosslyn Chapel

Plate 16 *(below left)* A hideous Green Man from the exterior of Rosslyn Chapel

Plate 17 *(below right)* The so-called Apprentice Pillar in Rosslyn Chapel

Plate 18 *(above)* The famous three pillars of Rosslyn Chapel

Plate 19 *(below)* The Seven Virtues from a carving in Rosslyn Chapel

Plate 20 *(above)* The town crest of Halifax in England, showing the head of John the Baptist and the Agnus Dei with Templar flag and St John's staff, depicted on the gates of the Piece Hall

Plate 21 *(below)* The view to the east from Rosslyn Chapel

side when Rosslyn Chapel was being created was Sir Gilbert Haye. Born *c.* 1405, Haye was the son of an illustrious Scots family that, like the Sinclairs, had always been close to the seat of Scottish power. Haye was educated at the new university of St Andrews, where he proved himself a brilliant scholar. By 1428 he was in France, probably originally as an emissary of the Scots king, and he remained there until 1456, becoming chief librarian to the king of France and building up a collection of books that would rival those of Florence and the Vatican. Haye was a superb linguist who spoke and read no fewer than 16 languages – a great asset with the many foreign-tongued craftsmen brought in to build the new Temple.

Haye lived in France during one of its most colourful periods and he knew and supported the shortlived teenage firebrand, Joan of Arc. He became a personal friend of the heir to the throne, Prince Charles, and was a principal guest when Charles was crowned King Charles VII of France in 1429. Immediately after the coronation, the new king personally knighted Haye.

And then in 1456, at the age of 52, at the peak of his prestige and fortune in France, Haye took the surprising step of leaving the French court and his life's work in his beloved library in order to return to the isolated castle of Rosslyn in Scotland. With little warning he had given up a high position at one of the great courts of Europe in order, so history tells us, to take up the lowly post of tutor to the sons of Earl William Sinclair.

This does not ring true. We believe that Haye had a most important reason to join Earl William. It is our view that his mission was to be the new Hiram Abif – a role that Haye must have considered to outshine any other.

There are more surprises. Earl William had remained high in the estimation of successive Scottish kings throughout his whole adult life and in 1452 he had added the role of Constable of Scotland – effectively commander of the military – to his other titles and offices. And yet early in 1456, the same year that Haye left the court in Paris, the earl also resigned the high positions he had held at the royal court in Edinburgh to concentrate on his new project.

Historian Barbara E Crawford was perplexed by this apparently inexplicable disappearance from court and she wondered if the earl had argued with King James II and fallen out of royal favour.[4] But the available evidence does not support this theory, because William remained high in the king's affection. As late as 1455, he had received the prestigious and important lands and title of Caithness and had been assisting the king in his struggles with the often-rebellious Douglas clan.

Then in June 1456 the Scots king put his signature to a document that would grant the village of Roslin the status of a burgh, or borough. (The village, like the earldom, is generally 'Roslin' although the chapel is referred to by the alternative spelling Rosslyn.) Henceforth it would be able to hold a Saturday market and an annual fair and would enjoy all the privileges of burgh status. It was at this time that Earl William abandoned the village of Roslin that had stood across the glen to the east of the castle and began to build an entirely new community to the west.

All of these events lead us to believe that although some accounts state that Rosslyn 'Chapel' was commenced in 1440, actual building above the ground did not commence until 1456. The earl needed a workforce of skilled craftsmen and they and their families would have to be housed – hence the new village and its new civic status. The date of 1456 for the new village is a sure indication that no large force of workers was present at the chapel site before this time. In all probability work undertaken prior to 1456 comprised the digging of the network of tunnels and chambers that lie far beneath the chapel and the preparation of the building's foundations.

The world at large was told that Rosslyn Chapel was going to be a 'collegiate' church. This was not the same as a normal parish church. Collegiate churches had originally been institutions of learning and a committee of men known as 'secular canons' or 'canons irregular' administered them. Like monasteries, collegiate churches owned their own property, usually outlying farms. These lands were rented out and the proceeds were what funded the church.

Collegiate churches remained distinct from parish churches in one other important respect. Parish churches fell under the jurisdiction of a local bishop. To the priest of the parish church the local bishop was his direct and absolute superior, but this was not the case with collegiates. Permission to build a collegiate church had to come directly from the pope and once completed they lay outside of the control or influence of the normal Church hierarchy. In 1456 the pontiff was the enfeebled and indecisive Pope Callistus III but the real power behind the papal throne was

Cardinal Aeneas Sylvius Piccolomini. Piccolomini, who would himself become Pope Pius II in 1458, was known to Earl William and a friend to the Star Families – he may even have been a Star Family member himself.

Earl William Sinclair needed his new 'chapel' to be a collegiate for two reasons. Firstly, it was going to be a very strange sort of church – and in fact, as we shall see, it was not really a church at all. Second, he did not want the local Church hierarchy interfering with his plans or even looking too closely at what he was actually doing.

From first to last Rosslyn Chapel was designed to be a repository for the documents discovered in Jerusalem in the 12th century. But it was also much more. It was nothing less than a copy of the ruined Herodian Temple of Jerusalem taken from the accounts of the first Templar Knights who had dug below the rubble. To create such a structure was fraught with difficulties – not so much in terms of its construction, but rather regarding what the finished building would look like and the reaction it would elicit. Earl William and Sir Gilbert Haye must have thought long and hard about the potential problem of the reception of such an unusual building. There were bound to be uncomfortable questions. Between them the two men came up with a solution so clever it verges on genius.

An Act of Concealment

It was first necessary to make it known that the finished church would be a fairly conventional building of the period. Like many churches, it would contain a 'lady chapel' (a chapel dedicated to the Virgin) at the east end, beyond which would be a north and south transept and then a nave running to the west.

Members of the Church hierarchy were shown the plans for the completed collegiate church, which would be rather splendid yet basically not much different to others around the country. Official visitors might even have been taken on a tour of the foundations that were laid in trenches that threaded across the hillside from the large-scale west wall of the partly built 'lady chapel'. These foundations were simply piles of stone that looked as though they were the beginning of the promised collegiate church.

In the event, no complete collegiate church was ever built. When the 'lady chapel' was finished all work suddenly stopped. Today, the standard explanation is that the Sinclairs must have run out of money or interest, but we believe this to be incorrect. We are certain that there was *never any intention to build anything more than the 'lady chapel'*.

The plans for a large, conventional church were nothing but a smoke-screen devised by Sinclair and Haye. John Wade, a good friend of Chris Knight, is a Greek and Latin scholar as well as a full member of the premier Masonic lodge of research known as Quatuor Coronati. Wade was originally convinced that Rosslyn had been intended to be nothing more than a conventional collegiate church. John and Chris met just after John had returned from a visit to Rosslyn and John stated that he was persuaded by the collegiate argument. The reason for this conviction was that scanners had detected some parts of the foundations of the intended church.

Chris pointed out that *dummy* foundations would have been essential in order to convince those in authority that the building would eventually look just like a normal cruciform church. In fact there can be no doubt that these are false foundations. The proof came from a source of the very highest standing in the form of Jack Miller, Head of Studies in Geology at Cambridge University and a Fellow of the Geological Society.

Visiting Rosslyn with Chris, Miller had pointed out that the large, oversized west wall of Rosslyn, assumed to be part of the unfinished collegiate church, was not correctly tied into the fabric of the main building. Any attempt to build further would have resulted in the collapse of the entire structure.

Miller said: 'Well, there is only one possibility – and I can tell you that you are correct. That wall is a folly.'

In his view there was no doubt that the builders never intended to build one inch further than they did. The quality of design and workmanship was too good for this failure to tie in the stone to have been some colossal mistake.

It was Miller who first drew Chris's attention to the nature of the stone used in the project. As a geologist, he was qualified to state categorically that it was from the same stratum as that used for the Jerusalem Temple. Further, to confirm the impossibility of the 'collegiate theory' he stated that the large west wall was not an unfinished section of some large structure, but a deliberate copy of a ruin. He said, 'If the builders had stopped work because they had run out of money or just got fed up, they would have left nice square-edged stonework, but these stones have been deliberately worked to appear damaged – just like a ruin. The stones haven't weathered like that… they were cut to look like a ruined wall.'

Over the years Chris has taken several academics to Rosslyn and all have found it a very strange place. Professor Philip Davies, a world-class authority on the Dead Sea Scrolls and early Judaism, was amazed at what he saw. After looking around the building he stated that it appeared to him to be a *Jewish* building rather than a church of any kind. He felt the west wall was very Herodian in style.

Professor Jim Charlesworth, another Dead Sea Scrolls scholar from Princeton University and the Albright Professor of Archaeology in Jerusalem, agreed, stating: 'This is not a Christian building.' He also pointed out that the west wall was entirely Herodian in design and that the designers had gone to great lengths to imitate the ruins in Jerusalem using especially crafted versions of what are known as 'robbed stones'. As well as being an academic, Charlesworth is an ordained clergyman, and he cancelled his planned attendance at the Sunday morning service, saying that it was inappropriate to hold a Christian service in this obviously Jewish building!

Professor Charlesworth has spent many years looking for missing Dead Sea Scrolls that are known once to have existed and he agreed that there was a very high probability that they were under Rosslyn. He spent some considerable time putting together a world-class team of archaeologists to conduct an excavation, but so far the trustees of Rosslyn have not (to our knowledge) responded, despite a promise that the assembled team would be comprised of reputable experts.

There is no doubt that at the time Earl William was building Rosslyn he had to treat it like a church, because if anyone within the hierarchy of the Church had suspected it to be a Jewish-inspired structure he would have forfeited his life very quickly indeed.

A major requisite for any church was its dedication. All churches of the period were dedicated to a saint, an apostle or the Virgin Mary. The candidate in the case of Rosslyn most probably came from Sir Gilbert Haye. It was inspirational, relevant to the Star Family beliefs and offered a plausible reason for the very specific geographical orientation of the building (since it had to face the light of the Shekinah).

Since the very start of Christianity it had been specific policy in the West that churches should, wherever possible, be built so that their altars pointed east – supposedly towards Jerusalem. To most people east was a relative term, meaning that part of the horizon where the Sun rose each morning. When churches were planned an observation would be made at first light on the feast day of the proposed saint to whom the church would be dedicated. For example, if the dedication was to St Edmund, the English martyr, the day in question would be 6 November. The point on the eastern horizon at which the sun rises on 6 November would be considered 'east' for that particular church and the whole orientation of the building would be laid out accordingly.

Even now, it is entirely possible with old Scottish, English and Welsh churches to calculate the probable original dedication of the church simply by taking a compass reading and comparing it to a book of saints days. Whilst the local topology of a particular site will affect the time the Sun's first rays appear, the alignment of the north and south walls will identify one or two days in the year and therefore the dedication to one or other of the saints associated with those days.

In the case of the building at Rosslyn, it was vitally important that the building face almost exactly due east, in order to replicate the situation of the Temple in Jerusalem.

This effectively meant that the dedication of Rosslyn Chapel could only be to a saint whose feast day fell on either the spring or the autumn equinox, because these are the only times of year at which the Sun rises due east. The Earl and Gilbert Haye had the perfect candidate in the form of St Matthew.

The Church of Matthew

There is something very strange about St Matthew's day as far as the Western Church is concerned. Documents from the very early Church, probably dating back to *c.* AD200, testify that Matthew died on 16 November and indeed the Eastern Orthodox Church still celebrates his feast on this day. However, in the West, as far back as we can trace and certainly as long ago as the days of the Church historian Bede (AD672–735), St Matthew's day has been celebrated on 21 September – the day of the autumn equinox. How and why this state of affairs came about remains a mystery.

St Matthew turned out to be a perfect dedicatee for a host of other reasons as well as his feast day. In Church tradition, St Matthew was one of the first disciples of Jesus. The New Testament tells us that he had been a publican, or tax gatherer, a profession hated by most Jews during the time of the Roman occupation – and yet Jesus had called and accepted him. Although he is not mentioned extensively in the gospels as they stand today, St Matthew was reported as being at Jesus' empty tomb with Jesus' mother and Mary Magdalene, and Matthew the disciple has traditionally been identified with Matthew the gospel writer. His gospel was the only version of the story of Jesus on which the Ebionites relied: it had originally been written in either Hebrew or Aramaic and had not contained any reference to the nativity of Jesus. In addition, the original gospel of Matthew had painted John the Baptist far more favourably than either the later, much altered, Greek version or the other gospels.

Symbols of the Hidden Treasure

In 1996 Chris accidentally overlaid two acetate sheets on an overhead projector and discovered that the plan of Rosslyn Chapel is identical to that of the subterranean walls of Herod's Temple. They matched like a hand fitting into a glove. Further investigations by Chris showed that inherent in the ground plan of Rosslyn Chapel were two distinctive features that were very Freemasonic in nature. The first of these was a 'Triple Tau', a symbol composed of three 'tau crosses' (a *tau* cross, from the Greek name for the letter T, simply looks like a capital T and T is also the last letter of the Hebrew alphabet.) The symbol is said in Freemasonry to be the 'jewel' of the Royal Arch degree and among other things it is said to signify *Templum Hierosolymae* (the Temple of Jerusalem); *Clavis ad Thesaurum* (the key to a treasure);*Theca ubi res pretiosa deponitur* (a place where a precious thing is concealed); or *Res ipsa pretiosa* – (the precious thing itself).

This Masonic ritual, which nobody understands today, appears to unlock the secret of Rosslyn. The Temple of Jerusalem, the key to a treasure, a place where a precious thing is concealed, and the precious thing itself – Rosslyn is all these things!

It is as though Earl William Sinclair had created this ritual to be passed on down the generations as the eventual key to understanding Rosslyn. And that is likely to be exactly the case because the first Grand Master Mason of Freemasonry was a descendant of the builder of Rosslyn – and he too was called William St Clair. The ritual of the Royal Arch, the fourth degree of Freemasonry, describes the excavation of the ruined Temple in Jerusalem, with Freemasons being figuratively lowered down on ropes to investigate concealed chambers below the Temple to recover ancient documents. The Triple Tau has specific Freemasonic relevance to the Jerusalem Temple and as Chris demonstrated, it is formed on the ground plan of Rosslyn by lines connecting the eight easternmost pillars of the chapel.

Chris went on to realize that the only missing symbol in the chapel was that of Solomon's Seal, or the Star of David. In the old Royal Arch degree, Solomon's Seal was described in the following manner:

> The Companion's Jewel of the Royal Arch is the double
> triangle, sometimes called the Seal of Solomon, within a circle
> of gold; at the bottom is a scroll bearing the words *Nil nisi*
> *clavis deest* – Nothing is wanting but the Key – and on the
> circle appears the legend *Si tatlia jungere possis sit tibi scire*
> *posse* – If thou canst comprehend these things, thou knowest
> enough.

Chris has already detailed elsewhere[5] how he drew a line through the bottom pillars of the Triple Tau, set a pair of compasses to the width of the building on the plan, and described an arc out from each wall. The two arcs intersected exactly between the most westerly pillars to form an equilateral triangle. He then drew another line across the width of the building between the second two pillars from the west entrance and described two further arcs in an easterly direction; they intersected right in the centre of the central pillar of the Triple Tau, forming a perfect Seal of Solomon. The two pillars inside the symbol were placed at the precise crossing point of the lines of the star.[6]

Ground Plan of Rosslyn Chapel

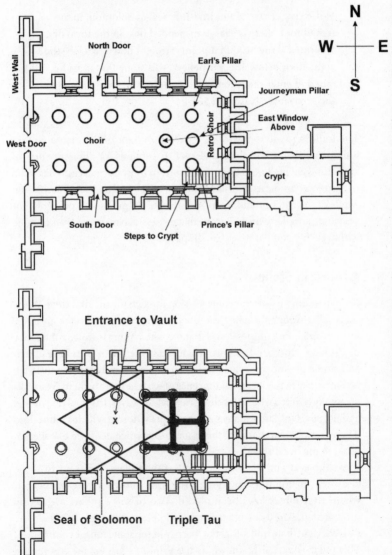

Figure 9 Ground plan of Rosslyn Chapel showing the Triple Tau and Seal of Solomon

Further, as Chris has already observed,

> At the very centre of this invisible Seal of Solomon, in the
> arched roof, there is a large suspended boss in the form of a
> decorated arrowhead that points straight down to a keystone
> in the floor below. It is, we believe, this stone that must be
> raised to enter the reconstructed vaults of Herod's Temple
> and recover the Nasorean Scrolls.[7]

The building is loosely Gothic in style, though unlike many Gothic
buildings it has a barrel-vaulted roof. It contains 32 different sorts of
arch, but what really sets Rosslyn apart from most normal churches is the
tremendous amount of ornamentation that is to be found across the
whole of the exterior and interior of the building. There is probably not
a building anywhere else in Europe that possesses so many carvings in stone
within such a comparatively small space.

A Forest in Stone

It is fascinating to watch people visiting Rosslyn for the first time. When
they walk through the gate from the path outside and into the grounds,
most people's first impression is that the whole thing is smaller than they
might have expected. But once inside, and when their eyes have grown
accustomed to the somewhat dark interior, they stand utterly transfixed,
trying to take in the sheer magnificence of what lies before them. The walls
are totally covered with naturalistic carvings of leaves, fruits, plant tendrils
and flowers. Only after many visits and a great deal of self-discipline does
it become apparent that all of this stone foliage emanates from one specific
point in the building.

At the east end of Rosslyn, three stone pillars, different to those
elsewhere in the building, guard the area known as the retrochoir,
where altar tables have been placed. Two of these pillars are highly
ornamented, whilst the other is relatively plain in design. It is from the
extreme right-hand pillar that the journey of the stone foliage commences.
This pillar is variously known as the Prince's Pillar or the Apprentice
Pillar. At its base are a number of dragons and above them the pillar

becomes what looks like the trunk of a very stylized tree, around which entwine a number of large but delicately carved vines. These twist around the pillar up its entire length until, at the capital, they break out into a profusion of stone branches and foliage, extending across much of the available space of the room.

In amongst this stone foliage, on boss ends or peering out from recesses, there are dozens of the representations of the Green Man, an ancient piece of Celtic imagery that is a human face either covered with branches and tendrils or else which is entirely composed of them. There are well over 100 examples of the Green Man in the building and the number is growing all the time as new examples are recognized.

But the Green Men are not alone. The chapel also contains literally dozens of carvings of angels. Around half of these carry scrolls or books, some have flamboyant hairstyles and all are wonderfully and expertly represented. In the east end particularly there are representations of peasants, lords, kings, musicians and fantastic creatures – all of which obviously had a very particular meaning to those who created the structure but which seem to represent a hopeless, confusing puzzle to the modern visitor.

Secrets of the Apprentice Pillar

As stated above, the ornate pillar from which the carved foliage derives is known as the Apprentice Pillar. The standard story given to visitors concerns the master mason of Rosslyn, who having been given the commission of creating this fabulous pillar, felt it necessary to travel to Rome, either to gain inspiration or to view a very similar pillar in the Eternal City. Only on his return would he feel himself able to tackle such a demanding and wonderful creation. Whilst he was away, his apprentice decided to undertake the carving himself and it was complete by the time the master mason returned. He was so stunned at the beauty of the apprentice's skill that he flew into an uncontrollable rage and taking a hammer he struck the apprentice on the head, killing him instantly. It is said that one of the faces close to the roof-line, not far from the pillar, shows a representation of the apprentice, with a wound on his head.

This story seems to be a garbled and inaccurate counterpart to the tale of Hiram Abif (*see* Chapter 1) but as Alan Butler and local investigator John Ritchie were to discover, the truth of the Apprentice Pillar is even more fantastic than that.

Alan and John Ritchie were co-operating on a book entitled *Rosslyn Revealed*, which they planned be the most thorough investigation of Rosslyn 'Chapel', its history, and the meaning of its carvings, that had yet been written. As to the truth behind the Apprentice Pillar, they discovered this within a corpus of writings of early theologians known as 'the Ante-Nicene Fathers', so called because they wrote prior to the Council of Nicaea in 325 (*see* Chapter 3). This great body of literature includes most of those important Church traditions that are not actually present in scripture. For example, it is generally accepted that the mother of the Virgin Mary was called Anne, but there is nothing in the gospels to suggest this. Rather it is to be found in the works of the Ante-Nicene Fathers, as well as various popular non-canonical scriptures. Other Christian traditions are enshrined in their works, as are accounts of the lives of the apostles after the death of Jesus, stories of innumerable saints, and sermons from some of the earliest Church fathers.

While investigating why St Matthew had been chosen as the patron saint for the supposed church at Rosslyn, Alan and John came across a fascinating story detailing the fabulous events surrounding the martyrdom of St Matthew and the events that immediately preceded it.

Written by an unknown author and most probably created around AD200, this is a fanciful tale that relates the journey of St Matthew to a city called Myrna. This is likely to have been a place in Asia Minor, present-day Turkey. The story suggests that Matthew was engaged in a 40-day fast in the vicinity of Myrna when a heavenly child approached him. He took the visitor to be an angel and perhaps one of the children who had been killed by King Herod. But it was Jesus, manifesting himself in the form of a child. After a long discussion the Jesus-child gave Matthew a staff and instructed him to place it in the ground on a high piece of land overlooking the church in Myrna.

This Matthew did, and what followed surprised both him and the inhabitants of the city. No sooner had the staff touched the ground than it began to grow, until it formed the trunk of a great tree. Around the trunk there were spirals of vines and from its branches leaves and fruits of every possible sort appeared. At the top of the tree was a beehive that sent honey cascading down to the inhabitants below and at the base of the tree a lake developed, in which swam innumerable creatures.

Because of the details of the story and the way they matched so well the carvings to be seen in Rosslyn, there was no doubt in the mind of either Alan or John that St Matthew's adventures in Myrna had been used as a model for the Apprentice Pillar and the mass of stone vegetation that springs from it. Everything in the Matthew story is present at Rosslyn, even down to the reference to a beehive. One of the pinnacles, high up on the roof, has been deliberately hollowed out by the masons to allow access to wild bees. They thrived there for centuries and locals used to say that in summer honey dripped down the walls of the building.

The accuracy of the story was further borne out with the rediscovery of an etching or woodcut of Rosslyn Castle. Its date is unknown but bearing in mind the complete state of the castle in the picture, it must have been created before the mid-1600s, because at that time the castle was extensively damaged as a consequence of English Civil War. The picture shows the eastern elevation of the castle, in front of which stands a mysterious character in robes, with a staff in his left hand. Beyond the staff is the tree that figures in the story. In recent times nobody had understood the meaning of this character in the castle foreground on this drawing, but it seems highly likely that this is a representation of the story of St Matthew.

As Alan and John Ritchie suggested in *Rosslyn Revealed*, any visiting Church dignitary of the 15th century, stunned by the sheer profusion and complexity of the carvings in Rosslyn, would doubtless have wanted to know what it all meant. Once reminded of the legend of St Matthew and his exploits in Myrna, it would appear that everything was in order and that this building merely recreated, if a little ostentatiously, the paradise on earth that sprang from St Matthew's divine staff.

To us, however, this goes nowhere near to explaining the sheer multiplicity of images pecked out in stone within Rosslyn, but it would doubtless have sufficed for a bishop or cardinal, convinced as he undoubtedly would have been that Earl William was a true son of the Church and a great patron of religious art.

Many carvings at Rosslyn are claimed to have a Freemasonic connection,

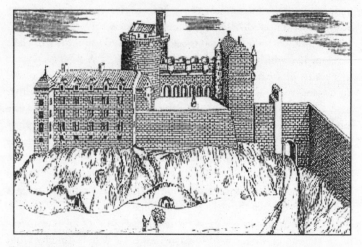

Figure 10 Drawing of Rosslyn Castle showing St Matthew in foreground with his staff and tree. The cave entrance behind St Matthew could well be intended to represent the passage that connects Rosslyn Castle to Rosslyn Chapel.

but most of the supposed associations seem spurious. However, one carving does depict what today would be recognized as a candidate going through his First Degree ritual. The candidate is a young, clean-shaven man, blindfolded and kneeling with a noose around his neck. The free end of the noose is being held by a bearded man who is standing behind and appears to be dressed in the costume of a Knight Templar. The kneeling man's feet are in the form of a square and he is holding a book in his left hand. In front of him stand two pillars. The number of correspondences between this carving and the modern Masonic ritual are simply too numerous to be coincidental.

Other carvings seem to have been inspired by a drawing known as *The Heavenly Jerusalem*. The surviving example was created *c.* 1120 by one Lambert de St Omer and is housed in Ghent University library. Chris Knight's earlier investigations had led him to believe that the drawing of the Heavenly Jerusalem was a copy of one of the documents originally found by the Templars beneath the Temple Mount in Jerusalem. The copy, Chris logically assumed, had been made when Hugues de Payen's second-in-command, Geoffroi de St Omer, had taken some of the material from Jerusalem to be interpreted by an aged scholar from his own town, St Omer, in France. This scholar, Lambert, was an accomplished linguist and spent much of his life compiling the world's first encyclopaedia, which remained incomplete at his death.

Our conclusions were that the carvings in Rosslyn were not copied from Lambert's version of *The Heavenly Jerusalem* but rather from the original document, from which Lambert had made his hastily produced copy – and which eventually found its way to Rosslyn along with the other Essene documents. The drawing of the Holy Jerusalem carries iconography, for example squares and compasses, that would be instantly recognizable even to a modern Freemason, and its themes lie at the very heart of Freemasonic ritual and practice – especially those associated with the Royal Arch degree.

In conclusion, therefore, while the carvings close to the Apprentice Pillar, which should now more properly be called St Matthew's Pillar, could all have been easily explained away as representations of the city of Myrna in the St Matthew story, they are in fact closely related to the historical Jerusalem and its ancient Temple.

Rosslyn and the Kabbalah

The arrangement of the three most important Pillars in Rosslyn Chapel, namely the Apprentice Pillar, the Journeyman Pillar and the Master's Pillar, also betray another medieval obsession, and one that also has its root in the ancient Jewish esoteric Jewish tradition called the Kabbalah. It is a subject that would have lain very close to the heart of Star Family priests.

The Kabbalah became a near-obsession among Christian intellectuals and philosophers in medieval times, though its origins lie exclusively in Judaism. The word Kabbalah itself, which has many variant spellings, lies at the heart of esoteric Judaic worship and belief, though it did not make an official appearance until the 14th century – more or less contemporarily with the building of Rosslyn Chapel.

The Kabbalah consists of two specific works, along with countless commentaries and explanations. These are the Zohar (the 'Book of

Splendour', or 'Light') and the Sepher Yetzirah (roughly, the 'Book of Formation'). Of the two, the Sepher Yetzirah is almost certainly the oldest in its written form, most likely having been produced by the Jewish mystic Rabbi Akiba *c*. AD100. The Zohar, though possibly as old as the Sepher Yetzirah in its oral form, was not committed to writing until the 14th century, having supposedly been collected and transcribed by another rabbi, this one a Spaniard by the name of Moses de Leon.

It is most likely that the philosophical and spiritual ideas that lie at the heart of the Kabbalah are indeed ancient in nature, not least because in parts they bear striking similarities to aspects of other very old religions, such as Hinduism. The Kabbalah arises out of a very great need somehow to 'define' the inexplicable. The God of Judaism is a very remote character. Even to utter his sacred name was and remains blasphemous, most likely because to do so is to 'personalize' the deity and thereby to belittle both him and his position in the universe. The Kabbalah makes it abundantly clear that God is so elevated, so untouchable and indefinable that any attempt to approach him directly is doomed to failure.

Put simply, the Kabbalah suggests that the only path to God is via his emissaries – a series of spiritual entities known as *Sefirot* (singular *Sefirah*). Humans might not be in a position either to know or to communicate with the Godhead, but the Sefirot are. The Sefirot, who might best be described as a form of angel, are usually shown arranged upon a geometric pattern with three vertical lines and many connecting pathways. This is invariably referred to as the 'Kabbalistic Tree of Life' (*see* Figure 11).

Each Sefirah represents a different aspect of the divinity. By knowing and understanding all the Sefirot, and by following the pathways that connect one Sefirah to another, it becomes possible for mere human beings to achieve at least a glimpse of the divine.

The Kabbalah also offers advice on how best to follow God's laws and thereby to live a virtuous and happy life. Nevertheless, the subject remains fiercely complicated, not least because it is suffused with linguistic codes, all of which are based on the letters of the Hebrew alphabet. Each Sefirah relates to a Hebrew letter and the Kabbalah also contains aspects of numerology.

It can be seen from the picture of the Kabbalistic Tree that all the pathways between the Sefirot ultimately originate from the Sefirah that

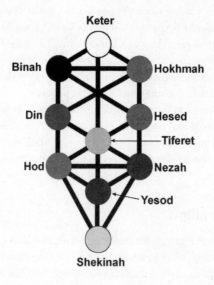

Figure 11 The Kabbalistic Tree of Life. Each of the globes represents a Sefirah. These are connected by pathways (*see* main text).

occupies the lowest and most central position, and it can also be observed that this Sefirah is called *Shekinah*. Although all Sefirot are interdependent and so no Sefirah can be considered more or less important than the others, all of them are ultimately approached in meditation and prayer via the Shekinah. The importance of this to the ancient pre-Judaic priesthood of Solomon and to their successors in Star Families has become eminently clear from the preceding chapters.

In the Kabbalah, the Shekinah becomes much more important than even its astronomical manifestation as the conjunction of the planets Mercury and Venus. Rather it represents the conduit through which communion with spiritual agencies, and ultimately with God, is achieved.

Almost as soon as the Kabbalah appeared in its written form it fascinated not only Jewish mystics and scholars, but also Christian ones. In reality it was almost certainly known and examined much earlier than the 14th century, even among some supposed Christians. There is a persistent suggestion that St Bernard of Clairvaux (*see* Chapter 5) had Kabbalistic scholars within his abbey of Clairvaux in Champagne and schools of Kabbalistic thought are assumed to have existed in the city of Troyes and certainly in cities further south in France and in pre-Inquisition Spain, where Judaism had a long and illustrious history.

Whilst there can now be no definitive proof that knowledge of the Kabbalah played any direct part in the design or construction of Rosslyn Chapel, the possibility becomes much more likely when one examines the Chapel and its design in the context of another specific aspect of Freemasonry.

The Three Pillars

Freemasonry is replete with symbols and pictures and some of the most important among these are 'tracing boards'. Seen in all lodges, tracing boards represent pictures or icons and each tracing board has significance for a particular aspect or degree of Freemasonry. Tracing boards undoubtedly originated in the workshops of stonemasons. Often literally traced out in chalk on the square paving slabs of the workshop floor, these were scale drawings of planned constructions. In Freemasonry the chalk drawings eventually became painted cloths laid on the floor of the Masonic Temple and ultimately pictures that were hung on the walls.

One very interesting tracing board is that which relates specifically to the First Degree of Freemasonry (*see* Figure 12). All tracing boards carry messages, which are usually relayed to the rising apprentice Freemason as he follows the various paths of the Craft, though it is quite possible that some of the messages contained within them are now misunderstood or unknown, even to those who are supposed to be 'in the know'.

The tracing board associated with the First Degree consists of three pillars, each of a different classical order of architecture (Ionic, Doric and Corinthian). Each has a name and a compass position and all three allegorically relate to specific attributes to which the would-be Freemason is expected to aspire.

The pillar on the left is known as 'Strength', hence the letter S that appears on its base. That on the right is known as 'Beauty' and carries the letter B,

Figure 12 The tracing board associated with the First Degree of Freemasonry

whilst the central pillar with its W, is called 'Wisdom'. The three female figures arrayed on the ladder that leads up the central pillar are said to represent the three Virtues of Faith, Hope and Love.

It has long been pointed out that there are striking parallels between the three pillars of the First Degree tracing board and the three pillars of the Kabbalistic Tree. At least since the 19th century both supporters and opponents of Freemasonry have suggested that there are strong aspects of Kabbalism at the heart of Freemasonic practice and that this tracing board illustrates that fact.

However, what does not seem to have been recognized before is that the three pillars on the First Degree tracing board almost certainly have their origin in the three pillars at the east end of Rosslyn Chapel. This was made all the more likely by the rediscovery of the Rosslyn Chapel light box (*see below*) and by the fact that, as we will show, Freemasonry as we know it owes its very existence to the Chapel.

The three pillars of Freemasonry are known as Strength, Beauty and Wisdom, while those of the Kabbalah are called Mercy, Severity and Mildness. Their Kabbalistic attributes are strikingly similar to those in the Freemasonic explanations and a connection cannot be doubted. It follows, therefore, that the instigators of Freemasonry knew the 'real' story behind the three pillars of Rosslyn and were aware of their Kabbalistic heritage. However, to have openly admitted such a Jewish connection in the 15th century would have led to persecution at the hands of the Church. For this reason Freemasons gave the pillars different names and biographies in order to protect their real heritage as the three pillars of the Kabbalistic Tree of Life. It seems certain that today all knowledge of these matters has been lost, even among the highest-ranking Freemasons.

Over the entrance to the crypt, and therefore in the same general location as the carvings that resemble the drawing of the Holy Jerusalem, are the only words carved into the fabric of the interior of Rosslyn Chapel. These are in medieval Latin and in translation they read 'Wine is strong, a king is stronger, women are stronger still, but the truth conquers all.'

This might sound like a strange sentence but it is also used in Freemasonic ritual. It appears in a degree called 'The Order of the Knights of the Red Cross of Babylon', which is closely associated with the Holy Royal Arch degree. As we noted in Chapter 1, the words come from the Book of

Esdras (1 Esdras), a non-canonical work that was known in the 1st century AD, and refer to an event during the Jewish captivity in Babylon. The Masonic degree consists of three dramas that tell of incidents drawn from the biblical Book of Ezra chapters 1-6,[8] 1 Esdras chapters 2–7 and Josephus' *Antiquities of the Jews* book 11, chapters 1–4. And what is the subject of the degree? Nothing less than the rebuilding of the Temple of Jerusalem.

The ritual opens with the most senior Freemason, called the Most Excellent Chief, asking a question: 'Excellent Senior Warden, what is the hour?'

The reply is: 'The hour of rebuilding the Temple.'

The ritual goes on to tell how the phrase 'Wine is strong, a king is stronger, women are stronger still, but the truth conquers all' was the answer to a riddle set by the Babylonian King Darius during the Jewish captivity. Zerubbabel, the leader of the Jews, correctly answered the riddle and was allowed to return to Jerusalem, with his people, to rebuild the Temple. In addition the king promised to give back to them the treasure stolen by the Babylonians from the Temple.

So, the only words carved into the stone of Rosslyn are those that permit the rebuilding of Yahweh's Temple. What greater proof could be necessary of what Earl William Sinclair was doing?

The Underground Vault

A further connection between Solomon's Temple, Freemasonry and Rosslyn is the recent discovery, directly beneath the Seal of Solomon, of an underground vault with a long subterranean tunnel leading to the castle. The 14th degree of the Ancient and Accepted Scottish Rite of Freemasonry, which is called 'The Grand Elect, Perfect and Sublime Mason', describes just such a subterranean passage that connected King Solomon's Temple with his palace in Jerusalem. The ritual includes the words:

> King Solomon builded a secret vault, the approach to which was through eight other vaults, all underground, and to which a long and narrow passage led from the palace. The ninth arch or vault was immediately under the holy of holies of the Temple. In that apartment King Solomon held his private conferences with King Hiram and Hiram Abif.

Niven Sinclair, a businessman who has devoted a large part of his life and personal wealth to the study of Rosslyn, told Chris Knight that in 1997 a number of men, including Niven himself, had excavated beneath Rosslyn and found the chamber and the huge underground passageway that leads to the castle, which is several hundred yards away.

The relative positions and topology of Rosslyn Chapel and Castle are as close as one can get to that of Solomon's Temple and the king's palace in Jerusalem. Both tunnels lead more or less due south and drop down a valley.

No one knows whether Solomon's Temple, at least as described in the Bible in all its fabulous magnificence, ever really existed. But we can be certain that Earl William Sinclair thought it did, and he obviously knew of its secret design. The chances of it being mere coincidence that the special features of Rosslyn – which are so utterly unique amongst 'churches' – match detailed descriptions found in Masonic ritual are virtually zero. Put this together with a number of known facts and we must surely have a 100 per cent certain link between ancient Jerusalem, Rosslyn and Freemasonry. Let us summarize the main points:

1　The only inscription in Rosslyn is a phrase which, according to a legend that is at least 2,000 years old, was the key to the rebuilding of the Jerusalem Temple.

2　A Masonic degree that calls its members 'The Order of the Knights of the Red Cross' (that is, the Knights Templar) describes itself as being concerned with the rebuilding of the Jerusalem Temple, and quotes the very same phrase that appears in Rosslyn.

3　Words used in the rituals of another important Masonic degree give meaning to symbolic features found in Rosslyn, for example:

　　'*The Temple of Jerusalem*';
　　'*The key to a treasure*';
　　'*A place were a precious thing is concealed*';
　　'*The precious thing itself*';
　　'*Nothing is wanting but the Key;*'
　　'*If though canst comprehend these things, thou knowest enough*'.

4　Freemasonic ritual also describes a secret feature of King

Solomon's Temple. This was a chamber under the holy of holies that was connected to the king's palace. Rosslyn has this exact feature connecting it to the castle.

5 Rosslyn is the *only* medieval 'chapel' known to have a secret underground chamber that is connected by a large tunnel to a nearby castle.

6 The west wall of Rosslyn is demonstrably a folly and the foundations for the collegiate church are fake; yet the design of the west wall is obviously and deliberately a copy of the Herodian Temple.

7 The stone used to build Rosslyn is from the same seam of rock as the Herodian Temple in Jerusalem.

8 Rosslyn is indeed a hoax – it is not, and never was, a church. Yet so many people still insist that it is, against a wave of evidence and academic opinion to the contrary.

But there is still more for this fabulous building to reveal.

The Light Box

Another recent discovery, again made by Alan Butler and John Ritchie, confirms the importance of Rosslyn in terms of its geographical setting and also the astronomical knowledge of its creators. Thanks to information supplied by one of John's cousins, who is a staff member at the 'chapel', John and Alan were alerted to a strange piece of apparent 'decoration' that can be seen outside the building, above the point of the large east window. On further investigation this turned out to be a discovery of major importance, because it is no mere piece of ornamentation but a sophisticated and deliberately created tube which is designed to allow light from any bright object on the horizon to pass through it and into the interior of the building.

This tube, or light box, is pentagonal in shape but is set within a pyramid. The tube is lined with some sort of highly reflective material that is so efficient that when a powerful lamp is shone into it, the reflection is almost blinding. It is also clear that at the internal end of the tube there is some sort of red-glass filter because when a light shines through the light box from the exterior of the building, the resulting light inside the building is blood red.

Being at the very centre of the east end of the building, the light box points at the distant horizon. So, for example, when the Sun rises exactly due east at the time of the spring and autumn equinoxes, as soon as it has cleared the horizon the full intensity of its light passes down the tube and into the interior. This can only work because the orientation of Rosslyn is 'exactly' east-west.

But it isn't just the Sun that rises due east at the time of the equinoxes, so do the planets Mercury and Venus. Figure 14 is a chart from a computer planetarium. It shows the eastern horizon, as seen from Rosslyn, as it would have appeared about an hour before dawn on 21 September 1456.

The curved line along the bottom of the picture represents the horizon and the letter 'E' stands for due east. Mercury and Venus stand side by side and with the naked eye their combined light would have seemed to converge. Of course the Chapel was only *commenced* on the day of this event, but once the light box was completed it would capture events such as this and send their light into the body of Rosslyn.

Venus on its own would be bright enough to illuminate the interior through the light box, because the tube is mirrored on the inside and so

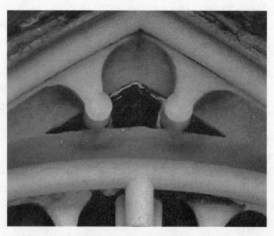

Figure 13 Exterior view of the light box at the east end of Rosslyn

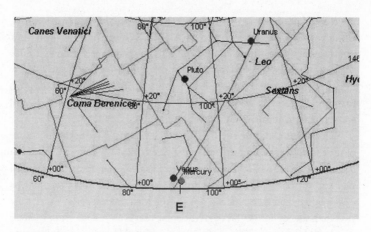

Figure 14 Astronomical chart showing the Holy Shekinah that occurred on 21 September 1456 (St Matthew's Day)

efficiently transmits any light that falls within it. However, this would only be possible on occasions when Venus was very close to the Sun as the morning star during the equinoxes. When far from the Sun, and rising well ahead of it, Venus would rise north of east and it would then travel to the south as it rose in the sky. This would put it beyond the scope of the light box.

There are occasions other than the equinoxes when Venus would cast its light through the light box, but in the 15th century it would have taken the skill of an extremely competent astronomer to work out when this would happen. As an example, the Sun will illuminate the light box on St Matthew's Day 2007, and although at that time Venus will be a bright morning star, it will not itself appear in the light box until 48 days later, on 8 November at 3.05 a.m.. It will then reappear in the light box exactly eight years later, on 8 November 2015, and on the same day every eight years into the distant future.

With patience it would be possible to build up a picture of Venus' appearances in the light box at any time, and once these had been established the patterns could be written down, kept and consulted whenever necessary. The true Shekinah, i.e. the conjunction of Mercury and Venus just prior to dawn, would be a very rare phenomenon in the light box.

THE HIRAM KEY REVISITED

What is particularly interesting is the fact that the stonework in this window only dates back to the mid-1800s. Whilst the new stonework undoubtedly reproduces an original light box in that window, it does suggest that there were still people around in the 19th century who knew the importance and purpose of the light box. This is the first indication that the Star Families may have survived into relatively recent times – and are probably still active to this day.

Earl William Sinclair and Sir Gilbert Haye must have been well aware of the discrepancies that existed in the calendar of their day. Way back in Roman times, Julius Caesar had introduced a new calendar so that the civil year and the celestial year would run in harmony. The Julian calendar, as it was called, had a year of 365 days and added one extra day every four years to make up for the fact that the solar year is about 365 and a quarter days long. However, while a great improvement, this was not quite accurate enough, because the year is in fact very fractionally less than 365.25 days. Consequently, the solar year slipped behind the calendar by one whole day every 128 years. By the period of the building of Rosslyn, the discrepancy between the civil calendar and the celestial calendar was around nine days. As a result, when Rosslyn was commenced, St Matthew's Day and the day of the autumn equinox did not coincide as they should. There were already calls for a change to the civil calendar in the 15th century, and Rosslyn was specifically built in the knowledge that these would be implemented sooner or later. The new Gregorian calendar, decreed by Pope Gregory XIII in 1582, adjusted the old discrepancies and came into use almost at once in Catholic countries. But it was only gradually accepted elsewhere, and in Protestant Scotland the new calendar was not implemented until 1752, so St Matthew's Day and the day of the autumn equinox never coincided at Rosslyn until this date.

Rosslyn is one of the wonders of British and indeed European architecture and it stands alone because there is nothing quite like it anywhere else in the world. The only logical conclusion to draw from the available evidence is that it is a monument to the beliefs of the Star Families, who recreated, high on the side of a beautiful Scottish glen, as faithful a reproduction as they could of the building that was of pivotal importance to their beliefs – the Jerusalem Temple. The so-called 'chapel' was a deliberate beacon to those who 'knew' but it could easily have spelled disaster both for the Sinclairs and the buried documents if the Catholic Church had learned of its true significance and purpose. It was therefore crucial that the secrets built into Rosslyn did not become common knowledge.

Rosslyn was considered to be the Temple of the New Jerusalem that would house the precious scrolls removed from beneath the Herodian Temple by the Knights Templar. It was important to William Sinclair that the intellectual 'keys' to the building would be transmitted across the generations, truly and faithfully by people who would not understand the cipher themselves.

To this end Sinclair added new rituals to the original rites of the Star Families and the Knights Templar. He associated this with the overriding metaphor of building in stone that was embodied in the guilds of operative stonemasons that had been structured by the Templars. A number of generations later, another William Sinclair was to become the first Grand Master Mason of Scotland – a title that became hereditary from that time onwards.

The secrets of the Temple of the New Jerusalem were intact and awaiting a future time to be awakened. The Star Family group that had became the St Clairs or Sinclairs of Scotland had chosen their name well. 'St Clair of Rosslyn' means in Gaelic 'ancient knowledge passed down the generations'.[9] Of course St Clair was originally a Latin-inspired French name but its double association in its Gaelic form is especially interesting in the Scottish context.

Earl William Sinclair was a man of genius. Rosslyn was the 'hardware' and Freemasonry carried the 'software'. All that was required was to bring them together and run the program.

CHAPTER 9

The Holy Secret

It took a sizeable workforce many years to create Rosslyn. Its wonderful array of Gothic arches and the stunning carvings that cover its walls, inside and out, required artisans of the very best quality – an array of experts who could almost certainly not be found nearby. The majority of those who built and adorned Rosslyn would have to have been enticed from across Europe and contemporary records show that Earl William Sinclair not only created homes for his workers in the new village of Roslin but that he also offered extraordinarily high wages.

But the reason that William went so far for his workers was not just because of their skills – it was because these men still practised the initiation rituals given to them by the long-defunct Order of the Knights Templar. Any skilled stonemason might have ensured that the structure would be built but that would not make certain that the secrets lying at its very heart would not become immediate public knowledge.

For many years before the stonemasons arrived, a group of Star Family operatives had dug deep below the site of the new Temple. The dramatic episode of the trunks of documents rescued from the fire in Rosslyn Castle in 1447 (*see* page 145) indicates that the Essene scrolls were not buried at that time. But nine years later, in 1456, the site was ready for the laying of the foundation stone. It may or may not be coincidental that the process of re-concealing the scrolls took nine years, exactly the time that the

Knights Templar took to extract them from under the ruined Jerusalem Temple over three centuries previously.

Ever since Chris Knight put forward his argument that there are Essene scrolls below Rosslyn,[1] almost everybody has envisaged that they will be found in a subterranean, rock-hewn vault behind an armoured door accessed by some hidden staircase. Nothing could be further from the truth.

William Sinclair's masterpiece is built on some 130 feet of sand.[2] The intention can only have been to return each scroll to a point that corresponded to its original resting place below the ruined Jerusalem Temple. The Knights Templar will have kept records of where each document was found, which would correspond to the descriptions given in the Copper Scroll.

The Mystery of Oak Island

At this point it is worth digressing from our story to consider a small island off the coast of Nova Scotia (which means 'New Scotland') in eastern Canada. The 140-acre Oak Island is just a few miles from the city of Halifax (now a Regional Municipality), which shares its name with the town in Yorkshire already discussed in reference to St John the Baptist (*see* page 119). It is also the next sailing stop south of the city of St Johns – named after the Baptist.

Oak Island is suspected of being the location of the treasure of the Knights Templar, whose fleet escaped from the French harbour of La Rochelle on the night before King Philip IV of France sprung his trap to capture the Templar order. The theory appears to be not without substance.

The mystery of Oak Island began with excavations carried out in 1795, when a young man called Daniel McGinnis and two friends found a ship's tackle hanging from a tree branch and a nearby depression in the ground. They dug down a couple of feet and discovered a level of carefully laid flagstones, which had no apparent purpose on an island that had never been inhabited. They dug further into the sand and at 10 feet came across a platform made from oak and as they continued in their strenuous investigation they uncovered further platforms at 20 and then 30 feet.

A few years later a company called the Onslow Syndicate was formed by a number of local businessmen to fund further exploration on the basis that they might have stumbled across a cache of hidden pirate treasure. The oak platforms continued to be found until, at the 90-foot level, the diggers came to an inscribed stone with a code etched upon it. They deduced from this code that the treasure was just another 40 feet below. However, the code may have been a false clue leading them into a booby trap, because the shaft was quickly filled with seawater that was to prevent further excavation for another 200 years.

It became clear that a series of flood tunnels had been dug from coves on both sides of the island. To date, only a single gold chain, a pair of iron scissors and a piece of illegible parchment have been found despite the millions of dollars that have been invested in excavations – and five people have lost their lives.

Whether or not the discoveries on Oak Island date back to the Templars or are later, they bear the hallmark of a similar technology to that used by the Templars and this in turn may give us a clue to what could be expected beneath Rosslyn. Like Oak Island, Rosslyn's secrets are deposited deep in sand – and booby-traps can reasonably be expected for those that have not understood the ciphers built into Masonic ritual.

The work conducted underground in those nine years prior to 1456 was complex and the tunnel connected to Rosslyn Castle must have been quite a feat of engineering.

Sinclair's Secret Guild

When it came to erecting the main 'chapel' building, Earl Sinclair needed labourers, rough stone dressers and stonemasons, as well as artists, because at one time all of the carvings of Rosslyn were picked out in vibrant colours. If the documents were to remain safe in their new resting place beneath, and he and his own family were not to fall foul of the same forces that had destroyed the Templars, Sinclair simply had to devise some way of keeping his workers bound in. Once again he called on the knowledge and resources of Sir Gilbert Haye. Gilbert had written many books and translated many more. He was an expert on chivalry, kingship, philosophy and science, but he had also studied something else that would prove to be of paramount importance – he had investigated and written extensively on craft guilds.

The concept of guilds goes so far back in time that historians find it difficult to say for certain when they first appeared. Originally there were different sorts of guilds, some religious, others social and still more created for mutual economic reasons, but all of them represented groups of individuals who came together of their own volition in a common cause. Merchants' guilds developed very early in Britain (at least as early as *c.* 1090). These were generally based in a specific location, for example Bristol, Canterbury or London, and were associations whose primary intention was to safeguard all trade in a particular location for those who belonged to the guild.

This made sense as far as law and order were concerned because the merchants' guilds were self-regulating. They were as interested in the moral and law-abiding aspects of trade as they were in profit. Every member of a local merchants' guild paid an annual sum and this went toward supporting the families of ill or deceased members and educating their children. By acting and negotiating in concert, merchants' guilds could safeguard their own interests and ensure the fairness and honesty of their members.

Craft guilds were very similar in nature to the merchants' guilds and are probably just as old. One of the earliest and most significant craft guilds was that of the stonemasons, the existence of which appears to date back to the time of King Athelstan of England (ruled 924–939).

It was obviously in the interests of those involved in a particular trade to remain as exclusive as possible. By gathering together in a tightly knit association they could regulate their craft and maintain the exclusivity that ensured future work. A guild was both a trade union and a trade federation because it was important to everyone concerned. Young men who entered a specific trade were invariably the sons of others already engaged in the same work. They were 'fostered' out to a master, who was not only responsible for teaching them the trade but also for their moral and spiritual well-being.

After a protracted, indentured, apprenticeship, the young man would eventually gain the status of 'journeyman'. Then, following a requisite period, an interview by his peers and usually also a specifically designed ceremony, the journeyman became a master of his trade and could set up business in his own right.

Stoneworking, above all crafts, was next to godliness. Whilst the general view in medieval times was that working in stone was just another craft, the families that produced the Knights Templar knew differently. Since the Stone Age, astronomers – those who understood the workings of the heavens – had been the priests and these holy men instructed how to build in stone. All prehistoric stone structures were made either for observing and measuring the world given by the gods or for purposes linked with death and the afterlife. Structures such as Maes Howe in Scotland, Newgrange in Ireland, Bryn Celli Ddu in Wales or Avebury in England were celestial observatories that changed the way people live.

So advanced were these astronomer-priest-stonemasons that more than 5,000 years ago they created a system of measurement based on a precise international unit of measurement obtained from observing the rotation of the Earth in relation to Venus. Alexander Thom, the professor of engineering at Oxford University who first identified its existence, called this unit the 'megalithic yard' and its $1/40$th subdivision a 'megalithic inch'. So exact was the megalithic yard that it was determined to a fraction of the width of a human hair.

What is far more surprising is that the Star Families appear to have been aware of this Stone Age measuring system. The pound weight, first introduced at the Champagne Fairs (*see* page 114), is defined by the amount of grain held by a cube with sides of 4 x 4 x 4 Megalithic inches. When filled with water, the same cube holds precisely one imperial pint!

From the moment that the Knights Templar had recovered their lost scrolls in 1118 they had started to take control of the guilds of stonemasons by giving them ancient rituals of initiation that had not been used since the time of Christ. When Herod the Great had first financed the rebuilding of the Jerusalem Temple in 19BC, only stonemason-priests were allowed to build the holy structure. No fewer than 10,000 of them were employed over the 90 years of building, and each must have undergone a ritual to permit him to work at his appropriate grade. From the 12th century onwards, Europe's finest stonemasons were sharing these ancient rituals.

This new Star Family institution functioned in more or less the same way as its ancient predecessor. Those joining either the Cistercians or the Templars in their earliest and most glorious days knew nothing of the existence of the Star Families or of the unique and peculiar beliefs that lay at the heart of their calling. And that is the way it stayed for perhaps 90 per cent of Cistercian monks and Templar knights throughout their entire lives. Only the chosen few, intelligent men who rose through the ranks to occupy positions of authority, would ever be introduced to the 'inner secrets' of either order. These would be men who were loyal and had proven themselves capable of safeguarding lesser secrets that in fact were probably of no real importance. Prospective candidates for higher initiation would be closely monitored, maybe across decades, before they were made party to anything truly important.

The skilled workers who were brought to Rosslyn were already initiated in these Templar-given rituals and they were used to protecting secrets, so Sinclair and Haye could be certain that those of Rosslyn would never become common knowledge. But now the earl grafted a whole range of additional ceremonies onto the rituals of his stonemasons – oaths and regulations that turned a craft association into a fraternity that was very much deeper and even more secretive. In this fraternity lie the roots of what would later become known as Freemasonry.

Masonic Degrees and Rituals

The modern First Degree of Freemasonry almost certainly dates back to Old Testament times, while the Third Degree is many thousands of years old and its key elements of resurrection beneath the light of Venus are undoubtedly pre-Canaanite in origin. Amongst the new degrees that were created was the all-important Holy Royal Arch. As already discussed (*see* page 167) this degree is concerned with rebuilding the Holy Temple and describes how excavations of the site of the ruined Temple led to the discovery of documents that held great secret knowledge.

As we have noted, the degree contains the figurative 'keys' that announce the beginning of the process necessary to unlock the secrets of Rosslyn. It also tells how Solomon's Temple was constructed to allow the light of the Shekinah to enter – possibly secrets that were found in the Essene scrolls:

Bezaleel was the inspired workman of the Holy Tabernacle, which he built to house the Ark of the Covenant and to allow the light of the Divine Shekinah to shine upon it. His design afterwards became the model of King Solomon's Temple, and conforms to a pattern delivered on Mount Horeb by God to Moses, who afterwards became the Grand Master of the Lodge of Israel...

This favour was signalled to the brethren by the appearance in the East of the Divine Shekinah, which represents the Glory of God appearing on Mount Sinai at the deliverance of the Sacred Law.

Later in the same rite, mention is made of the fact that the shining of the Shekinah is not necessarily a regular or predictable event. The ritual warns that God can remove this sign of his favour, if he chooses:

At the consecration of the Holy Tabernacle, and afterwards at the dedication of the Temple of the Lord by King Solomon, the Divine Shekinah descended so its light shone upon the Ark or Mercy seat as it stood in the holy of holies, covered by the wings of the Cherubim, where it appeared for several generations, until the Israelites proved unfaithful to the Most High. And so may the light of Masonry be removed from all who prove unfaithful to their God!

As extra protection, initiates of Earl Sinclair's fraternity were prevailed upon to take binding oaths. Until very recently, Freemasons would repeat the same sort of oaths that were created for Rosslyn – with threats of terrible penalties involving body parts being ripped open or cut off if they did not protect these secrets. Of course, modern Freemasons understand that this is nothing but ritual – a symbolic threat – but the same may not have been the case in 15th-century Scotland. Those were violent times and powerful men such as Earl Sinclair did not simply *represent* the law in their domains, they *were* the law.

The rituals, practices and iconography used by the fraternity of Rosslyn are probably not greatly different from the earliest known forms used in

Freemasonry. Following the usual practices of the guild, initiates – which in this case almost certainly meant anyone involved in the project of building Rosslyn – were inducted as apprentices, eventually rising to the rank of journeyman and then master mason.

It stands to reason that everyone involved in the project must have been inducted because some of the most closely guarded secrets, for example the location of the subterranean vault, would have been known to the simplest and least educated of the labourers. The earl's aim therefore was to create a private 'club' in which all those involved were members at one level or another.

In many respects Rosslyn can be considered to be the first Freemasonic lodge, because it will have included 'non-operatives' in the rituals – members who, like most modern Masons, who were not literally stone-masons. Not least among such men were Earl William and Sir Gilbert Haye.

When Rosslyn was finished and the scrolls safely returned to their new 'Temple of Jerusalem', the second and third generation of workers left to find building work elsewhere. And they took their rituals with them.

Like modern Freemasons they would have relied on signs and symbols – special handshakes, special phrases and gestures – so that one member could immediately recognize another.

Membership of this first Freemasonic lodge would have brought significant benefits. If any brother was injured or fell ill, his family would be supported and his children educated and trained in the craft of stone-masonry. These alone would have been significant incentives in an age where security of any sort was distinctly lacking. Members were well housed and became part of a close community – further strengthening the bonds of secrecy that surrounded the mysterious structure of Rosslyn. And so the tradition grew and was maintained during the entire period that construction was taking place.

It seems quite possible that this was all that Freemasonry was ever intended to be at the start, simply a means of ensuring confidentiality through the creation of a somewhat secretive, self-help fraternity, backed by one of the richest men in Scotland. Only with the passing of time and a change in circumstances did the situation alter. The Star Families would soon face a new threat, and paradoxically it was one that they had partly brought about themselves. Not long after Rosslyn was completed, events in Christendom took an entirely unexpected turn. What happened would change everything – and would give rise to Freemasonry proper.

Meanwhile, however, Earl William Sinclair died in 1482 and was succeeded as lord of Rosslyn by Oliver, a son from his second marriage. His other major title, earl of Caithness, went to William, another of his sons. At the old earl's death Rosslyn was not quite complete.

Reports from the period show that Rosslyn Chapel was used by the Sinclairs and the inhabitants of the village of Roslin throughout much of the first half of the 16th century. It is suggested that the Sinclair family held their own services not in the building itself, but rather in the crypt. This is approached by a steep flight of steps leading down from the right side (south) of the Apprentice Pillar. The crypt had its own altar and we can only guess at the nature of the services that took place there in the decades following the completion of this new Temple of Jerusalem.

Unusually for a supposed church, Rosslyn once had shutters that could be closed over all of the lower windows of the building. It has been suggested that this was because the windows in question were never glazed but this is not the case. Very early photographs from the 1840s show the building to be in a generally bad state of repair with some of the windows broken, but the lower windows were definitely glazed. It is true, though, that we cannot know when these earlier windows were put in.

As we have already indicated there are times when the light of the planet Venus would have entered the light box high up above the east window in the early hours of the morning. If ceremonies of a Masonic nature were taking place in the late 15th and early 16th centuries, the shutters would have been necessary in order to keep out the prying eyes of those who were not party to what was taking place. Indeed, shuttering all the windows except for the light box would greatly magnify the effect of Venus shining into building.

Christendom Splits

As Rosslyn was being completed, dark clouds were gathering over Catholic Europe. With the death of the humanist Pope Pius II (Enea Silvio Piccolomini) in 1464, the liberalism and humanism of the preceding 30 years was ruthlessly stamped upon. The humanists, probably backed by the Star Families, struck back. An attempt was made upon the life of the reactionary Pope Paul II in 1468 but the plot failed. Successive popes became ever more aggressive and conservative toward the forces of humanism represented by the Star Families.

Pope Innocent VIII (1484–92) strengthened the Inquisition, popularized the burning of witches and magicians, and advocated a crusade against a peace-loving and harmless Christian sect called the Waldensians. Innocent's successor, Alexander VI (1492–1503) – real name was Rodrigo Borgia – connived and murdered his way to the papacy.

After Alexander VI things went from bad to worse. Spending huge amounts on art treasures and personal luxury, successive popes ran short of money. Practices such as the selling of indulgences, first introduced in the 14th century, were stepped up around the turn of the 16th century by Pope Julius II to fund his rebuilding of St Peter's basilica as the most splendid church in Christendom. An indulgence was literally a fast ticket to heaven. Any Catholic could, for a certain sum of money, purchase their release, or even that of relatives, from the punishments of purgatory. Abuse was widespread, as rich and poor alike were blackmailed with the threat of hellfire by unscrupulous indulgence-sellers. Together with the lucrative running of saintly shrines, the market in supposed relics and a hundred other abuses in the name of the Church, the papacy became in many quarters a byword for corruption and vice.

The result was an inevitable backlash and this was inititated by Martin Luther (1483–1546), a brilliant German Augustinian monk, teacher and theologian, who had been born as the final work was carried out upon Rosslyn. Following a number of sermons against indulgences, in 1517 Luther drew up, in Latin, a list of 95 'theses' on the question of indulgences, calling for a disputation (public debate) on the matter. He wanted to clarify exactly what indulgences could and could not grant, although he did not expressly dispute the power of the pope to grant them. At this stage Luther had no intention to break up the Mother Church, but simply to initiate an urgent debate aimed at reform.

After famously nailing his theses to the door of the castle church in Wittenberg on 31 October 1517, Luther sent a copy to his superior, Archbishop Albrecht of Mainz, with a covering letter expressing his concerns about the traffic in indulgences in Albrecht's archdiocese. While Luther had not directly challenged papal authority, Albrecht quickly forwarded the letter to Rome suggesting that Luther was implicity attacking the pope.

A generation or two earlier this could have remained a local affair in the German Church. But a recent technological innovation – printing – meant that a mass-produced German translation of Luther's theses was being read throughout Germany within two weeks. Within two months Luther's name was known across Catholic Europe.

At first Rome dismissed Luther as 'a drunken German who when sober will change his mind'. Pope Leo X ordered an investigation into Luther's argument, which found that Luther's criticisms did indeed challenge papal authority. Rome declared Luther a heretic.

But Luther did not change his mind, far from it. A combination of growing German support and the hostility of Rome made him more determined. His views became more radical, and he soon denounced the entire Roman Church, from the pope downwards, as materialistic, corrupt, lacking legitimate authority, and the antithesis of the Church founded by Christ (or rather, the one founded by St Paul). The Reformation had begun, and it was to change the religious and political face of Europe.

One by one, beginning in Germany, secular rulers in northern Europe followed Luther in rejecting papal authority, a move that conveniently allowed them to seize Church and monastic assets in the process. The future was beginning to look bleak for many of the old Catholic institutions, including the abbeys. Monastic lands and buildings were seized and the monks turned out into society with small pensions to earn their livings as best they could. One of the probable casualties of this momentous split in Western Christendom was the enigmatic Tironensian order of stonemason monks (*see* Chapter 6), who disappear from history.

The Reformation caused untold problems for the Star Families and their affiliated organizations. To them the Protestant faith was worse than what had existed before. They had spent hundreds of years infiltrating the Church in Rome and the Ebionite-style beliefs of the Jerusalem Church and the Star Families had existed within the Catholic Church for a long time, concealed within the panoply, ceremony and iconography of Catholicism. In comparison Protestantism was spare, austere, unyielding and very committed to the Pauline Church that the Star Families despised so much. Ebionism itself had survived, unseen, within Catholicism like mistletoe on an apple tree but the branches of Protestantism, like the stark white interiors of its churches, offered no possibility of concealment.

Protestantism in its Calvinist form finally became the national religion of Scotland in 1560, when the Scottish Parliament overthrew the doctrine, worship and government of the Roman Catholic Church. To the outside world it looked as though the Sinclairs of Rosslyn were stubbornly sticking to the old Church, even when to do so meant they were in danger of losing their influence, prestige and perhaps, ultimately, even their lives. The reality of the situation was quite different. Like so many Star Family legatees they were stuck between a rock and a hard place. Ebionites generally could not leave the umbrella of one Church where they had at least carved a hidden niche for themselves, to join another that they both found even harder to swallow doctrinally and which had no dark corners to offer them any sort of protection.

Throughout the long years of the wars of religion the Star Families in Scotland kept their heads down and survived as best they could. During the reign of the very Catholic Mary, queen of Scots (1561–68), an angry Protestant mob from Edinburgh broke into Rosslyn. They tore all the statues from their niches around the outside of the building, and then smashed them into thousands of pieces. In all probability they would have done even more damage were it not for the quick thinking of a local man named Cochran, who diverted the mob to the wine cellars of Rosslyn Castle, where they helped themselves to the wine and stole away before soldiers arrived.

Almost miraculously the majority of the carvings within Rosslyn survived, though some show signs of significant wear thanks to the relentless northern winds that blew around the interior for decades once the shutters had rotted and any windows had been broken.

The New Way Forward

The result of the religious wars of the 16th century represented a standoff, with some countries showing all-out support for the reformed Protestantism, whilst others, such as France and Spain, stuck to the Catholic Church. When the dust began to settle the Star Families had to find a way forward. Their determination to build the New Jerusalem and to create God's kingdom on earth remained undiminished but it had become clear that neither branch of the Christian faith in Europe would see their plans maturing.

Of course, most Star Families were obliged to retain some sort of public allegiance to either the Catholic or Protestant faiths, depending where they lived, since only Christianity, of whatever sort, was officially tolerated. But at the same time many Star Family members became supporters of semi-covert subcultures such as the Rosicrucians, a peculiar form of mystic pseudo-Christianity that better represented Star Family beliefs and ideals. They also espoused the rising idea of deism – which accepted the existence of God but did not try to pigeonhole him, and they were party to the rising forces of humanism that they had participated in championing during the 15th century.

In Scotland, the forces of Calvinist Protestantism were so strong and intolerant that any alternative belief was simply not countenanced. There, the only means of expressing Star Family ideals was to do so in complete secrecy, through a secret society. And of course the Scottish Star Families already had just such a society of their own. They had created it for a very specific reason, but it had continued to function even after the construction of Rosslyn and its influence was spreading. In the new religious climate, this secret society would become an organization that allowed individuals to celebrate God in any guise that they preferred. True Freemasonry was about to be born.

The Schaw Statutes

The first documentary evidence for the existence of Freemasonry, which is definitely not directly related to the act of cutting and dressing stone, comes from Scotland in the years 1598 and 1599. Before that there are mentions of Freemasons but it is unclear whether or not these related to operative masons, i.e. masons who were actually employed in the art of building. It is with the Schaw Statutes that true, modern Freemasonry was born.

The central figure at that time was King James VI of Scotland (later James I of England) who was, in all probability, a product of the Star Family-Norman coalition. He was born of a dynasty that came from Norman stock in the form of the influential Stewart (Stuart) and Bruce families. The earliest known member of the house of Stewart was Flaald the Seneschal, an 11th-century Breton noble of Norman descent, while the Bruce family stemmed from Robert de Brus, a Norman knight who came to England with William the Conqueror and was originally granted lands in Yorkshire.

King James appointed William Schaw to the post of Master of the Works of Scotland in the year 1584. Fourteen years later Shaw published a document, or statute, which laid out in full the rules and regulations under which all Freemasons were to act. It is likely that, in the main, Schaw was referring in the first statute to actual cutters and dressers of stone. However, his deliberations did not please everyone and within a year he was forced to convene another meeting that would deal with some of the issues that his first statute had failed to address. Perhaps most telling is the fact that the meeting that led to the second Schaw statute was held on 24 June – the feast of St John the Baptist.

Specifically, the Freemasons of Kilwinning were angry because the first statute made specific mention of lodges in Edinburgh, but not Kilwinning, which its members claimed had precedence over all other lodges on account of its antiquity. Schaw addressed this issue in the second statute, published in 1599. He mentioned Kilwinning by name and admitted its venerable age, stating that the lodge was 'notourlie manifest [commonly known to have appeared] in our awld antient writtings'.

Most notable of all is the fact that the wording of the second Schaw statute seems to take account of the fact that by this time Freemasonry was much more than any ordinary craft guild.

The Scottish-based Star Families knew that they had a great responsibility, as they were the guardians of the Essene documents in their new holy temple that was Rosslyn (*see* Chapter 8). The rituals that Earl William Sinclair had devised to hold and protect the secrets of Rosslyn had been added to the ancient rites past down the generations from the time of Solomon. Now, these rituals would be used on a broader base to bring together all men, whether Catholic or Protestant – or even Jewish.

The records of the Lodge of Scoon [*sic*] and Perth No. 3, which date back to 1598, state that King James VI was made a Freemason on 15 April 1601. Soon afterwards, James decided that he would like to become the Grand Master Mason of Scotland. However, he was politely informed that he could not have this position because it was a hereditary title – held by the Sinclairs of Rosslyn.

In 1603, the news reached Edinburgh that Queen Elizabeth I of England was dead, and had named the king of Scots as her heir. James VI immediately travelled south to London to become King James I of Great Britain – and he took Freemasonry with him.

CHAPTER 10

Brothers All

The enthusiasm for Freemasonry of King James I of England must have quickly caught the imagination of courtiers at the royal palace in Greenwich, near London, where the new monarch spent much of his time (and where, on nearby Blackheath, he is also reputed to have introduced his English subjects to the Scottish game of golf). And despite the absence of lodge records to confirm the presence of the Craft in the city, other sources indicate that it certainly did become popular among professional men across the whole city within a decade or two.

In Scotland surviving lodge records show that increasing numbers of notable figures were joining during the early 1600s.[1] In the lodge of St Andrews in Fife, the members used the game of golf as a cover for their Freemasonic activities. They kept Masonic records when times were good but when there was any negativity towards the Craft, they only kept accounts concerning their strange stick-and-ball game.

Virtually no records of the business conducted by English lodges have survived from the first half of the 17th century, either because they were never kept or because they were destroyed at the time of political diffi-culties caused by the 1715 Jacobite rebellion (*see* page 202). However, the available evidence strongly suggests that exactly the same gentrification process was happening in English Freemasonry, as leading figures increas-ingly entered the Craft.

The Inigo Jones Document

The great architect Sir Christopher Wren was Grand Master of Freemasonry during the second half of the 17th century. But there was another, equally famous, architect who was a member of the Craft from the earliest years of the reign of King James I. His name was Inigo Jones.

Jones was born in 1573 in the vicinity of Smithfield in central London and spent many years studying architecture in Italy before being appointed as the King's Surveyor; a post later held by Christopher Wren. One of Jones' best-known buildings is the Queen's House at Greenwich, built for King James' wife, Queen Anne of Denmark. The king held court at Greenwich and it was a centre for London Freemasonry at the time. It was here that the young architect created a Masonic document now know as 'The Inigo Jones Manuscript' in 1607. This document sets out to describe the ancient nature of Freemasonry:

> GOOD BRETHREN and FELLOWS, Our Purpose is to tell
> you how and in what manner this Worthy Craft of
> MASONRY, was begun; And afterward, how it was kept and
> Encouraged by Worthy KINGS and Princes, and by many
> other Worthy Men.
> AND ALSO to those that be here; We will Charge by the
> Charges that belongeth to Every FREEMASON to keep; FOR
> in good Faith, If they take Good heed to it, it is worth to be
> well kept, FOR MASONRY is a Worthy Craft, and a curious
> SCIENCE, and One of the LIBERAL sciences.
> THE Names of the Seven liberal sciences are these:
> I GRAMMAR, and that teacheth a Man to Speak and write
> truly.
> II RHETORICK and that teacheth a Man to Speak fair, and in
> soft terms.
> III LOGICK, and that teacheth a Man to discern truth from
> falsehood.
> IV ARITHMETICK, which teacheth a Man to Reckon, and
> Count all manner of Numbers.
> V GEOMETRY, and that teacheth a Man the Mete and
> Measure of the Earth, and of all other things; which

SCIENCE is Called MASONRY.
VI MUSICK, which Gives a Man Skill of Singing, teaching
him the ART of Composition; & playing upon Diverse
Instruments, as the ORGAN and HARP methodically.
VII ASTRONOMY, which teacheth a Man to know the Course
of Sun, Moon and Starrs.

The document goes on to recount the passage of this great knowledge from the time of the Flood onwards and describes the building of King Solomon's Temple by Hiram Abif. It continues by telling the story of the rebuilding of the Jerusalem Temple by Zerubbabel and again by Herod. Jones also claims that Masons from Jerusalem travelled to Glastonbury in England in the year AD43.

Patronized by royalty and the Church, Inigo Jones – whose St Paul's Church, Covent Garden, was the first church in the classical style in England – was at the heart of English society from the early years of the reign of King James through to his death in 1652. There can be no doubt, therefore, that the Craft was thriving in London right through the 17th century.

The Road to Civil War

In 1652, when Jones died, Oliver Cromwell had temporarily displaced the monarch with his Commonwealth of England. This had come about through an accumulation of events with ramifications that were to affect Freemasonry for nearly two centuries.

King James I is widely considered to have been one of the most intellectual and learned people ever to sit on the English throne. He continued the patronage of science, literature and the arts begun by Queen Elizabeth I and he was recognized as a talented scholar himself through his (anonymous) treatises such as *The True Law of Free Monarchies* and perhaps the very first piece of anti-smoking propaganda, *A Counterblast to Tobacco*.

The most significant work associated with the king was undoubtedly the new English translation of the Bible that he commissioned, which became known in Authorised Version or the King James Bible. It was begun in 1604 and the first edition appeared seven years later.

The introduction to the King James Bible expresses a public-pleasing hostility to the Catholic Church. One section states:

> **If ... we shall be traduced by Popish Persons at home or abroad, who therefore will malign us because we are poor instruments to make God's holy Truth to be yet more and more known unto the people, whom they desire still to keep in ignorance and darkness...we may rest secure, supported within by the truth and innocency of a good conscience.**

This angry rejection of Catholicism demonstrates a new outlook where 'the people' are seen as having a right to 'knowledge', as opposed to the Catholic view at the time that was based on maintaining control of the faith by not promoting learning outside of the Church itself.

James died on 27 March 1625 and his son became Charles I. Almost immediately the new king made himself unpopular by marrying the 16-year-old French princess Henrietta Maria, a Catholic – causing a fear that the new king would lift restrictions on Catholics and undermine the official establishment of Protestantism. The prosperity that England had enjoyed under the long and generally judicious rule of Elizabeth and James had led to the emergence of a powerful middle class. This was composed of both new landed gentry and of a booming merchant sector, and many of these people became increasingly wary of Charles's policies and attitudes, especially what they suspected were Charles I's absolutist tendencies.

Like his father, Charles believed firmly in a concept known as the 'divine right of kings', in other words that monarchs were chosen by God and so therefore were answerable to no other agency but God. While Charles I professed Anglicanism, his High Church leanings were disliked by the more radical Protestants, who were known as Puritans. At the time the House of Commons was dominated by Puritan merchants and gentry. Conflict with the intransigent Charles was sure to come.

Charles tried to push through unpopular measures and when Parliament resisted, he would simply dissolve it. Several times he ruled alone, breaking long precedent by attempting to raise taxes without parliamentary approval. In 1642 the tensions between king and Parliament erupted into civil war.

The war ended in 1646 with the defeat of Charles, but there were further outbreaks of fighting in 1648. Shortly afterwards Charles I was brought to trial for treason and executed in January 1649. The monarchy was abolished and England was declared a Commonwealth by the leader of the Parliamentary forces, Oliver Cromwell.

The First Recorded Freemasons in England

It was from this momentous period that we have the earliest surviving record, dated 20 May 1641, of the initiation of a Freemason on English soil. On that date Sir Robert Moray was brought into the Craft by fellow Scots in Newcastle during a skirmish into England in support of King Charles (whose unpopular policies sparked a war in Scotland even before the Civil War in England).

This is celebrated as the first induction of a Freemason on English soil, although given that the Freemason King James I had arrived in London in 1603, and that Inigo Jones's document appeared in 1607, it is highly unlikely that Moray was truly the first Freemason to be initiated in England. It is, however the first occasion for which records survive.

The earliest extant record of an Englishman being made a Freemason dates from the Civil War. Elias Ashmole was the king's Controller of Ordinance based in Oxford, the Royalist capital after London fell to the Parliamentary army. In 1646, after the surrender of Oxford, Ashmole travelled north to Warrington, where he was initiated into Freemasonry on 16 October as he records in his diary:

> 4H.30 P.M. I was made a free mason [sic] at Warrington in Lancashire, with Coll: Henry Mainwaring of Karincham in Cheshire.

The names of those were then of the Lodge, Mr Richard Penket: Warden, Mr James Collier, Mr Richard Sankey, Henry Littler, John Ellam, Richard Ellam and Hugh Brewer.

The very next day Ashmole set out for London, the Parliamentary stronghold. This was both a difficult journey – by carriage on miserable roads – and also a dangerous undertaking, since all ex-Royalist officers were banned by law from approaching within 20 miles of the city. Yet his visit was certainly not clandestine, as one source wrote in 1650: 'He [Ashmole] doth make his abode in London notwithstanding the Act of Parliament to the contrary.'[2]

There can be little doubt that Ashmole's strange journey from Oxford to London via the distant town of Warrington was an essential part of a plan. It appears that his only hope of being admitted into the Parliamentarian capital was to become a brother Freemason.

Many people have speculated that Cromwell himself was a Freemason, but no documents exist today to confirm this. However, it is almost certain that many of his senior officers were members of the Craft. For example, Sir Thomas Fairfax, commander of Cromwell's 'New Model Army' was a Freemason and his family seat at Ilkley, Yorkshire, still has its own Masonic Temple dating back to this time.

Ashmole, presumably through his new contacts in the Craft, was permitted to enter London and stay there. A few years after the war, on 17 June 1652, he records a meeting at 'Blackfriers' [sic] with a 'Doctor Wilkins & Mr Wren'. Wren was the astronomer and architect Christopher Wren, who was to go on to rebuild London's churches, including his masterpiece, St Paul's Cathedral, after the Great Fire of 1666. Wren was destined to become the Grand Master of Freemasonry in London.

At the time, Wren was a young don at Wadham College, Oxford, of which Dr John Wilkins, also a Freemason, was the warden, or principal. Wilkins was also Oliver Cromwell's brother-in-law and later became bishop of Chester and a founder member – along with Brother Sir Robert Moray, the man who had become a Mason in Newcastle in 1641 – of the Royal Society.

These were some of the most important people of their day and it appears that Freemasonry was the common denominator. Whilst Ashmole's diary is the first physical record of an Englishman being made a Freemason, there appears to have been a significant Freemasonic infrastructure in place in London, and apparently also in towns like Warrington, well before 1646.

In 1660, the monarchy was restored after the death of Oliver Cromwell in 1658 and the brief rule of his son Richard. The new king, Charles II, returned from exile in Europe with promises of religious toleration and a general pardon for all except those who had signed his father's death sentence.

A New Masonic Society

In November that year, Sir Robert Moray summoned a group of influential scientists and thinkers to a meeting at Gresham College in London. Many of these men were already Masons and others would soon follow suit. The king needed advisors and Moray was determined to gather the best he could find – no matter what their previous allegiance might have been. The result of this meeting was the formation of the Royal Society, the first truly scientific institution in the world.

The nucleus of the Royal Society, calling itself 'The Invisible College', had met informally at Gresham College as early as 1645. Some commentators claim there is no proof that all those who had taken part in the Invisible College were Masons, but from its very first meeting the Royal Society was run on principles taken straight from Freemasonry. Like any Masonic Lodge, the Society had three officiating officers and decided from the outset strictly to avoid discussions of either politics or religion. In addition, the voting system used by members was identical to that used in Freemasonry. Under these circumstances it seems fair to suggest that a large proportion of the Royal Society's members were already Freemasons at its inception.

The people who created the Royal Society were the selfsame individuals to whom the responsibility for rebuilding London after the Great Fire that destroyed two-thirds of the city on 2–3 September 1666. This had started in a baker's shop and had spread rapidly, fanned by strong winds. Some Puritans saw it as retribution from God because of the profligate ways of Charles II and his court, whilst others were simply stunned at the destruction of so large and prosperous a city. The commercial heart of England had gone, including most of its churches.

Upset as they must have been concerning the loss of their own properties in the city, the members of the Royal Society no doubt also saw a great opportunity. When London rose from its ashes it would be a model of Freemasonic aspiration and symbolism.

Wren: England's Master Mason

Chief amongst the members of the Royal Society was Christopher Wren, a man who could turn his hand to anything in the creative sphere. Like

Wren, most of the Freemasonic members of the Royal Society believed that the newly-built London would represent the New Jerusalem in a very real and concrete sense.

The most important building to succumb to the flames of the Great Fire was St Paul's cathedral. St Paul's could have been rebuilt in its old medieval form but Wren, who was commissioned to rebuild it, saw the opportunity to replace it with something totally different.

Wren had been born in East Knowle (East Knoyle), Wiltshire, in 1632, the son of a clergyman. Wren senior was called to duties in London and also Windsor and it was there that the young Christopher Wren made the acquaintance of Charles, the eldest son of King Charles I. The two became firm friends, which would stand Wren in good stead after Charles himself became king.

Wren gradually became an all-round scientist, with a specific interest in astronomy but also a profound knowledge of anatomy and architecture. This was not an age of scientific specialization so his diverse interests are not surprising. However, Wren's butterfly mind in his early years did not go unnoticed. A near contemporary in the Royal Society said of him: 'The diffusion of his abilities is as amazing and frustrating to us as it very possibly was eventually to himself.'[3]

In 1657, three years before the restoration of the monarchy, Wren became Professor of Astronomy at Gresham College, that same institution where the Royal Society would be born a few years later and a place of undoubted Star Family influence. He was a member of the Invisible College that met in the same building on an irregular and unofficial basis. Although generally kept busy with his astronomical and mathematical studies, as early as 1663 Wren showed his skill as an architect when he designed Pembroke College chapel in Cambridge.

Almost immediately after the Great Fire, Wren was appointed Commissioner for the Rebuilding of London. From this point on his workload was phenomenal. He designed no fewer than 51 churches as well as numerous civic and private buildings. Fortunately for London, and despite the immense pressure of work, Wren lived a very long life. The result is that much of the City of London as it now appears is a monument to Wren's perseverance and talent.

Exactly when Wren became a Freemason is uncertain. According to some sources it was as late as 1691, but another Masonic founder of the Royal Society, John Aubrey, claimed that Wren had been a leading Freemason since 1660 and this seems more likely. In fact, when one looks at two of his creations, Wren's Freemasonic credentials become obvious long before 1691. These masterpieces are St Paul's, Cathedral his greatest work, and the Monument, built to commemorate the Great Fire on the approximate spot where it started.

London's New Temple

According to writer Adrian Gilbert,[4] when Wren laid out the plans for the new St Paul's cathedral, he chose to orientate the building eight degrees north of east, which was substantially different from the orientation of the original building. (As we said earlier [see page 152], most British churches were aligned to that part of the eastern horizon where the Sun rose on the day of their dedicatory saint. In the case of London on St Paul's day, 29 January this should have been 30 degrees south of east and not eight degrees north.)

Wren's positioning of St Paul's meant that the west end of the church was in a direct line with the old Temple Church, located in a district that had not been destroyed by the Great Fire. The Temple Church, which still stands, is on the site of the Knights Templar Preceptory for London. Gilbert maintains that Wren took this decision with Jerusalem in mind. The Temple Church in London, like many other Templar churches, is a copy of the Church of the Holy Sepulchre in Jerusalem and its relationship to the new domed St Paul's was the same as the relationship between the Church of the Holy Sepulchre and the Dome of the Rock in Jerusalem.

This having been achieved, it meant that Ludgate Hill on which St Paul's stands – also the site of probably London's oldest pre-Christian Temple – now took on the position of the Temple of Solomon in Jerusalem. There seems little doubt that Wren was quite familiar with the topography of the Holy City and that he was trying to represent it symbolically in the rebuilt London.

A Monument to the Craft

St Paul's was impressive, but from a Freemasonic standpoint the London Monument beats it. Although this was a much smaller undertaking its rich symbolism speaks volumes about London Freemasons of the period and what their beliefs and aspirations actually were.

The Monument stands in Fish Street. It is a very large Doric column, which contains a staircase to allow visitors to climb to its summit. At 202 feet in height, it would have dwarfed almost all the buildings surrounding it when it was finished in 1677. Ostensibly the Monument was just that – a structure specifically built to commemorate the Great Fire. But Wren put into its construction a whole series of coded messages that would only make sense to the elect of the Craft.

The idea of the monument was that its height would be the same as the distance between its base and the baker's shop in Pudding Lane where the fire had started. But why then did Wren choose 202 feet, when it would have been just as simple to round this off to 200 feet? According to Gilbert, the answer lies in the shadow cast by the Monument. London's position on the globe is such that during the summer solstice (21 June) the Sun will cross a line linking the east and west horizons with its zenith (maximum height) twice, once around 9.22am in the east and the second time around 4.43pm in the west. On both occasions the observer will note that the shadow cast by the Monument will be 350 feet. This gives a ratio of $1:\sqrt{3}$ between the height of the Monument and the length of its shadow. Well-versed as Wren was in astronomy and mathematics, he could not have failed to appreciate this fact and this is almost certainly the reason why the Monument had to be 202 feet in height and not a round 200 feet.

This ratio is that of the *vesica piscis* ('fish bladder'), a strange ancient geometrical figure that architects employed time and again to determine the layout of buildings, and particularly churches.

Figure 15 The Vesica Piscis

The *vesica piscis*, also known as the *mandorla* ('almond') is essentially created by the intersection of two spheres and is a figure replete with ancient symbolism. In ancient times it was taken to represent the conjoining of the God and Goddess (probably, at least partly, because it resembles a vagina). It can therefore also be seen as being deeply symbolic of the Shekinah. Certainly it was a symbol replete with mystic overtones and was often associated with the zodiac sign and constellation of Virgo, the Virgin.

Taken on its own we might see the relationship of the shadow of the Monument to its height as being nothing more than a strange coincidence, except for the fact that we have more evidence of the thinking of the men who created the structure. The base of the Monument bears a series of relief friezes. One of these was created by Caius Gabriel Cibber, but it was commissioned by Wren. It shows London as a goddess, but a goddess who is clearly tired and careworn, the sword of justice (one of the symbols of London) about to fall from her grasp. Adrian Gilbert equates this with a verse of the Lamentations of Jeremiah in the Bible: 'How doth the City sit solitary, that was full of people! How she has become as a widow!'[5]

The city described in Lamentations is none other than Jerusalem. On the plaque to the right of the 'goddess' of London we see other goddesses, one of whom is pouring the cornucopia or 'horn of plenty' across the city. The cornucopia is another figure replete with Freemasonic symbolism.

These are all rich symbols of rebirth, which is entirely appropriate in terms of the recreation of the City of London. They would have meant little to the uninitiated, who doubtless took the Monument at face value. But to the new scientists of the age and especially to Freemasons, London was undergoing its own 'third degree' ceremony of death and rebirth.

It appears that Wren originally wanted a statue of a goddess to surmount the Monument but this would have proved to be very expensive. Equally costly (and for some reason in Wren's estimation somewhat confusing) would have been his second suggestion, a phoenix. In the end the committee, at Wren's suggestion, preferred a great urn, with a solar orb emerging from it. It is not surprising that Wren ultimately offered this option because it represents part of the code necessary to work out the *vesica piscis* relationship that exists between the Monument and its shadow at the time of the summer solstice. At the same time it reflects the solar allegory at the heart of Freemasonry.

The same fascination with the movements of the Sun was shown by the Essenes in their desert fastness, 1,600 years prior to the burning of

London and its resurrection. The Essenes, as we have seen, had retained a solar calendar when mainstream Judaism had adopted the lunar one from Babylonia; indeed this determination to maintain the solar heritage of Solomon's special priesthood was a key reason why the Essenes had come into being as a distinct sect in the first place (*see* page 34).

An Age of Enlightenment

After the Civil War and the austerity of the Puritan Commonwealth, the restored monarchy ushered in an age of enlightenment characterized by a tremendous creative spirit. Somewhat belatedly, the revival in classical styles of architecture that had begun in Italy during the Renaissance, flourished in England for the first time during the period. There was, for a short while at least, a feeling of great confidence regarding the future. The old differences of religion appeared to have died down as a slightly uneasy truce between Catholics and Protestants prevailed under the Restoration restored regime monarchy of King Charles II. Trade and business got back to normal and then prospered in the new Restoration age.

The evidence suggests that Freemasonic membership was increasing amongst the rising middle classes and the more radical free-thinkers whose numbers had grown since the Renaissance and Reformation of preceding centuries. It is likely that at this time Freemasonic ritual also received a boost from unexpected influences never envisaged by those who first created it. There was a growing interest in the study of history, and mass printing coupled with an increasing use of English, rather than Latin, for scholarly works brought books to an increasingly educated and informed middle class that sparked a fascination for the mysteries of the past.

Playwrights and poets eulogized a semi-mythical, halcyon period equated with the rise of ancient Greece, characterized by a rural idyll in which people had lived in harmony with nature and natural laws. This fascination with a lost Arcadia led to a renewed interest in the ancient mystery religions of the classical age, particularly those of Demeter and Isis. Intrepid travellers were bringing back tantalizing glimpses of the splendour that had been Babylon and Egypt, whilst Britain's own mysterious past – the time of the semi-mythical druids and the building of the great megalithic monuments such as Stonehenge – also fed into the collective imagination of the later 17th and early 18th centuries. Aspects of this little-understood but nevertheless highly intriguing past found their way into developing Freemasonry.

At Freemasonry's core, though, still lay its original mysteries, put there by the Star Families in order to ensure secrecy regarding issues that were not for public consumption. Above all, Freemasonry still embraced at its heart the imperatives of the Johannite Ebionites, now, since the Reformation, removed from the cloak – and therefore restrictions – of mainstream Christianity. Freemasonry offered a 'different way' and one that could be appreciated by those with an open mind. It suited well the men of science whose rise was marked by the creation of the Royal Society in London. Only those who studied long and hard, taking on board the most mystical aspects of Freemasonry, could ever have understood the jewel that lay at its centre. But Freemasonry represented an important bridge that led from the dogma of established Christianity towards the less spiritually certain destination of science.

By its very nature Freemasonry espoused liberty of conscience, that liberty which was to become a watchword across the world in centuries to come, and it embraced the idea that it was possible for any person to achieve their own personal *gnosis* – knowledge of God, or understanding of the universe, without recourse to pope or preacher.

At the start of the 18th century, people looked at Britain's rising prosperity, boosted by the dawn of the agricultural revolution and the first throes of industrialization, and started to talk openly about a Britain country that really could be 'The New Jerusalem'. Following the twists and turns of a turbulent past, the Star Families – members of which must certainly have moved at the heart of London society – would have been content enough to pursue this goal through Freemasonry, the latest cover for their beliefs and activities. They had at last moved into a position in which they no longer needed the Church, of whatever denomination, at all. This was important, because it kept them above the continuing sectarian vicissitudes of the later Stuart reigns.

A Time of Turmoil

King Charles II had maintained a judicious line in matters of religion. But James, his brother and heir, was a Catholic and following Charles's death in 1685 it was not long before the new king ran into trouble. Among several instantly unpopular acts James II sought to lift penal laws against Catholics and to bring the Anglican Church under strict control. This and other measures brought nationwide discontent and in 1688 James was forced to flee abroad. He was declared to have abdicated the throne and Parliament offered the throne to his Protestant daughter and son-in-law, Mary and William of Orange, the Dutch leader. William was also James II's nephew, and Mary's cousin.

The ousting of James II became known as the 'Glorious Revolution', although in fact it was really a Parliamentary coup d'état in which little blood was spilled (although James's subsequent landing in Ireland led to a tough military campaign in which James was finally defeated in 1690).

William's arrival in Britain, with a force of 15,000 soldiers, was made possible by the actions of a group of men known as the 'Immortal Seven'. These men were mostly aristocrats and at least four of them can be shown to have been Freemasons. The Immortal Seven were certainly backed by a sizeable proportion of the population and it is interesting to note that prominent members of the Royal Society, most notably Sir Isaac Newton, risked their careers and indeed lives by standing up to James II.

King William III (1688–1702) and Queen Mary II (1688–1695) were cousins (both grandchildren of Charles I), and ruled as joint sovereigns. They had no surviving children, so on William's death in 1702 (Mary died in 1695) the throne passed to Mary's sister, Anne. She reigned for 12 years but none of her children – she had no fewer than 18 pregnancies – survived her. The Act of Settlement of 1701 had barred Catholics from the throne, and on Anne's death in 1714 the crown passed to the nearest Protestant male heir, Elector George of Hanover, who was a great-grandson of King James I. With the arrival of King George I, the rule of the Stuarts ended and the Hanoverian age began.

But the exiled Stuarts had not renounced their claim and still had their supporters, known as Jacobites (from *Jacobus*, the Latin for James). In 1715 there was a rising in Scotland in support of James Stuart (the 'Old Pretender'), the son of James II, but this suffered a double defeat by the

Hanoverians in battles at Preston in Lancashire and Sheriffmuir near Stirling. James Stuart fled back into exile in France. The Jacobite leaders, Lords Derwentwater and Kenmure, were publicly beheaded in London. Seven other noblemen involved in the rebellion were executed and others had their estates confiscated, whilst hundreds of their soldiers and supporters were transported to the Caribbean and the American colonies.

Freemasons Under Suspicion

Suddenly things began to become dangerous for the Freemasons. Despite their attempt to remain above sectarian matters, word spread around London that Freemasons were Jacobite sympathizers because of their previous close connection to the Stuart throne. People were aware that Freemasonry had come from Scotland and that it was also very popular in France (*see* Chapter 12); at the same time, no outsiders knew what went on at Masonic meetings, or what the purpose of the society was. Secrecy begets suspicion and suspicion quickly leads to assumed guilt.

Many Freemasons feared any investigation into their activities. Whilst the membership held little regard for the Jacobites, lodges did possess a lot of material on a range of mysteries and other esoteric matters, which could easily be misconstrued as covert paganism – even witchcraft – by anyone with a vested interest in finding fault.

The majority of Freemasons therefore abandoned their lodges and lay low; many publicly disowned their lodges, and lodge after lodge closed down. Even their Grand Master, Sir Christopher Wren, would have nothing more to do with the Craft, at least in public.

Wren had reason to keep his distance. Not only had he become the Grand Master of Freemasonry, he had also been a founding member of the 'Philosopher's Lodge of Druids' back in 1674 and had presided over the 'Mecca Lodge of Druids' in 1675. These were not activities that might be smiled upon if the new regime demanded an official enquiry into the Craft and its leading members.

The Grand Lodge and the Ancient Order of Druids

It was clear to the leading Freemasons of London that if the Craft were to survive it would have to radically adapt itself to the new political realities.

A meeting of six surviving lodges was held at the Goose and Gridiron tavern on Thursday 24 June 1717 – the feast of St John the Baptist, a date that also marked midsummer.

In the event, two lodges decided that it was too dangerous to have such a conspicuous meeting and pulled out. The three lodges that did arrive at the Goose and Gridiron in St Paul's churchyard on the appointed date were from the Apple Tree Tavern in Covent Garden, the Crown Ale House near Drury Street and the Rummer & Grapes Tavern in Channel Row, Westminster. The fourth was the lodge of the Goose and Gridiron itself.

Three of the lodges had just 15 members each, whilst the Rummer & Grapes dominated the day with an impressive 70 members. At the meeting the four London lodges unilaterally formed themselves into a 'Grand Lodge' of London and Westminster. Anthony Sayer was the first Grand Master of the new lodge. The two other most senior members, the wardens of the new order, were Jacob Lamball and Joseph Elliot.

At the new Grand Lodge, Sayer and his leading officers turned to the subject of separating from Masonry certain ideas that they considered did not entirely fit with their reborn order. The next time they all met was just three months later at the Apple Tree tavern in Covent Garden on the day of the autumn equinox. Here they, with many others, inaugurated the 'Ancient Order of Druids' (*Druidh Uileach Braithrearchas*) which became known as the 'British Circle of the Universal Bond'. The man in charge of this meeting was the Irish theologian John Toland, who that day was elected the order's first Grand Master.

Like Freemasonry, the Druids had three grades achieved through initiation. Also in both cases, the central theme of these grades was observational astronomy and, in particular, the movements of the Sun through the year. So it was that in 1717 Freemasonry was reborn on the day of the year that enjoyed the most daylight, whilst the Druid order was reborn on the following autumn equinox – when the day and night were of exactly the same length – St Matthew's Day, which had been so important to the dedication of Rosslyn Chapel.

John Toland remained Grand Master of the Druids until 1722, when he was replaced by William Stukely, who went on to hold the position for 43 years. Stukely is remembered as the man who spent his life investigating the megalithic structures of Stonehenge and Avebury and establishing their alignments with the Sun and the Moon.

Stukely could be forgiven for considering Stonehenge to be like some ancient Masonic Temple. The lodge proceedings take place inside an emblematic version of the Jerusalem Temple, with the master representing the rising Sun in the east, the junior warden in the south to mark the noon and the senior warden in the west to mark the setting Sun. The two pillars of Boaz and Jachin, which stood in the porch of the Jerusalem Temple, are present to indicate the extremes of the Sun on the horizon at the winter and summer solstices. Boaz marks sunrise on midsummer's day and Jachin sunrise on midwinter's day. A bright star is set on the wall between the pillars, rising in the east just before dawn. This is only illuminated very briefly at one crucial point in the Third Degree, when the candidate is resurrected from 'death' to become a master mason. This light was symbolically recreated by the light box above the east window at Rosslyn (*see* Chapter 8).

Hell-Fire Clubs

In 1722, the same year that Stukely became Grand Master of the Druids, Philip, duke of Wharton, became the Grand Master of Freemasonry (by now calling itself the Grand Lodge of England, which acted as an umbrella for many smaller local lodges). But the duke had other, even stranger interests: because he was also the founder of the London Hell-Fire Club. This was an institution that famously promoted excess in all things, including sexual acts, usually conducted publicly amongst its gin-sodden membership.

The practices and philosophies of the various Hell-Fire Clubs that sprang up at this time were the very opposite of those of Freemasonry. Freemasonry taught moderation, the Hell-Fire Clubs promoted excess; Freemasonry bound its members to obey the moral law and to be lawful citizens; the Hell-Fire Clubs encouraged drunkenness, debauchery and a disregard for social convention.

But this link between Freemasonry and the Hell-Fire Clubs was not a casual one. The Dublin Hell-Fire Club was founded by another Mason, Richard Parsons, the first earl of Rosse, and the first Grand Master of Ireland. It seems that despite being the apparent antithesis of Freemasonry, the Hell-Fire Clubs shared many of the same members and leaders.

To this day the United Grand Lodge of England, which considers itself to be world's premier Grand Lodge, states that nothing can be known about Freemasonry prior to 1717. Such group amnesia can be politically advantageous. Unfortunately some of the officials connected with the UGLE today seem actually to have come to believe these obviously disingenuous statements.

'Antients' and 'Moderns'

Some attempts were made in England to preserve the original rituals of Freemasonry. By 1751 the Grand Lodge of England had degenerated significantly. Smaller lodges were leaving the Grand Lodge umbrella at an unprecedented rate, meetings were spasmodic and badly run, often raising Grand Masters who were very young men, chosen for their social rank rather than from their Masonic expertise or moral rectitude. In addition, the Grand Lodge began to exclude lodges of which it did not approve.

Part of the motivation behind such developments was to curry favour with the Hanoverian government by distancing the Craft from accusations of sympathy with the Jacobites. The Jacobites, who had risen once again in 1745–6 in support of Charles Edward Stuart (the 'Young Pretender'), the grandson of James II. But a significant number of Masons deplored these changes and felt that they were undermining true Craft ideals. The result was that in 1751 they broke away and formed their own Grand Lodge, that of the 'Antients' (sic), as opposed to the 'Moderns'.

Basically the Antients believed that the Grand Lodge was gradually perverting Masonic rituals, teaching and symbols. To the Antients, some of what had been lost was of paramount importance. Amongst their complaints was the fact that the Grand Lodge had failed to give due veneration to St John's Day and did not recognize the degree of the Royal Arch, and had generally failed to represent Freemasonry in its established and original form.

It is important to note that the Antients enjoyed much patronage from Ireland and Scotland and so its members may have been closer to the source of Freemasonry than their 'Modern' counterparts. They were led by a Hebrew-speaking Irishman called Lawrence Dermott.

The split lasted for 60 years, until the Moderns threatened the Antients with prosecution under The Unlawful Societies Act of 1799, which the Moderns had pushed for. But the forced reunification did at least ensure that the most important elements of the ancient knowledge at the heart of Freemasonry were restored to the Craft following the changes of the Moderns.

Freemasonry reached its greatest popularity in Britain at exactly the same time as the British Empire was being created. The development of the empire was in no small way due to those first Freemasons who had served King Charles II as the embryonic Royal Society. A primary purpose of the meetings of the Royal Society at its start was to find ways to improve the Royal Navy. Without doubt the Royal Navy proved to be the key to Britain's imperial expansion and it was the means by which it defeated its European rivals, especially France, in the 18th and early 19th centuries.

Blake's Jerusalem

As the 18th century draws to a close, let us return for a moment to the Order of Druids, that new organization with distinctly Masonic overtones. In 1796, the Druids chose a new Grand Master: William Blake, one of the most remarkable creative personalities of this, or indeed any other period of English history. Blake's membership of the Druid order is well known, but there is little doubt that he was also a Freemason, since many of his most famous paintings display such powerful Masonic imagery. He is equally noted as a poet, and perhaps he is best remembered for the poem *Jerusalem*:

> And did those feet in ancient time
> Walk upon England's mountains green?
> And was the holy Lamb of God
> On England's pleasant pastures seen?
> And did the countenance divine
> Shine forth upon our clouded hills?

And was Jerusalem builded here
Among these dark satanic mills?

Bring me my bow of burning gold!
Bring me my arrows of desire!
Bring me my spear! O clouds, unfold!
Bring me my chariot of fire!
I will not cease from mental fight,
Nor shall my sword sleep in my hand,
Till we have built Jerusalem
In England's green and pleasant land.

This shows that even decades after Freemasonry was formalized in London there was still a very definite desire to follow the Star Family plan that had been in place since at least the 11th century – the same plan that Earl William Sinclair had tried to follow in Scotland in the 15th century.

At the time Freemasonry was developing and growing in Britain, many Britons were travelling to distant lands and establishing colonies, most of which would eventually become nation-states in their own right. These colonists took Freemasonry with them and this worldwide proliferation of the Craft was one of the most important steps towards the world we know today.

CHAPTER 11

The New World and the New Jerusalem

It is impossible to know precisely when Freemasonry first arrived in the North American continent, since records do not survive from before 1717. No doubt the Craft appeared early, possibly before the founding by the Pilgrim Fathers of the Plymouth Colony in Massachusetts in 1620. There may even have been Freemasons among the founders of the very first English colony, Jamestown in Virginia, in 1607. The first Freemasons to arrive in the New World would probably have been settlers from Scotland who formed Masonic lodges, but if so there is no extant record of them. Surprisingly, the earliest known mention of Freemasonry at all in the American colonies is found in a document written in 1730 – well after the forming of Grand Lodges in England and Ireland – by a 24-year-old Bostonian named Benjamin Franklin. It testifies to the fact that several Masonic lodges already existed in the colonies before that time.

Early American lodges were made up of men who simply got together to conduct the strange rituals they had learned from the men who had gone before them. At that time there was no structure to the way that lodges sprang up. Then news came from London that American Freemasons were now considered to be 'irregular'. They were told that they were not proper

Freemasons unless they had a warrant from a self-appointed governing body, such as the Grand Lodge in London.

The first so-called 'regular' lodge in North America was St John's Lodge of Boston, warranted from London in 1733, and soon others sprang up warranted by the Grand Lodge of Ireland. Many of these lodges in the American colonies were instigated by British army officers, which led to a proliferation of permanent lodges amongst soldiers in camp and local businessmen. From this period on, warrants were granted for provincial Grand Lodges in the colonies and the Craft began to grow rapidly, particularly in the major towns along the Atlantic seaboard.

Revolt in the Colonies

The causes that fuelled the tensions between the American colonies and their British overlords are well known. From a British perspective it was quite simple: the colonies in America cost money to garrison and defend, and there seemed to be no reason why the colonists should not contribute towards these costs. Consequently a series of very unpopular taxes were imposed on the colonies, which the locals saw as being inherently unfair.

To the colonists it appeared that London wished them to have no control over their own affairs. After all it was they who cleared the wilderness, who fought off the Indians and the French, who built the villages that became towns and the towns that grew into cities. And yet they were not allowed to infringe British monopolies by selling their own produce and were forced to buy almost everything they needed from British importers, at vastly inflated prices. Matters came to a head on 16 December 1773, with the 'Boston Tea Party', when colonists dumped three shiploads of British tea into Boston harbour in protest at British duties on tea imports. The duties had been imposed by the British Parliament but not approved by colonial legislatures. The cry 'No taxation without representation' became widespread. By 1775 the dispute between Britain and its colonies had become an armed struggle, and the American War of Independence had begun.

There is no doubt that the protagonists of the Boston Tea Party were Freemasons from the nearby St Andrews Lodge, which met over a tavern called the Green Dragon. This was the true start of Freemasonic-led resistance against British rule in North America. Despite the protestations of some historians it can be amply demonstrated that almost every key stage in the ensuing conflict between the rebellious colonies and Britain was largely arranged and prosecuted by Freemasons.

There could be several reasons for this. For example, whilst the British regiments opposing the colonists were ruled by established forms of discipline and rank structure, the colonists at first enjoyed no such cohesion. They were a disparate group, allied only by their united opposition to aspects of British rule and devoid of any basic organization. As such they were hardly likely to fare well against a well-trained and extremely disciplined occupying army.

The various settlements on the North American seaboard also lacked any essential cohesion, so that whilst a particularly large community, such as Boston, might feel resentment over unjust treatment by Britain, there was no real structure through which Boston might co-operate with its neighbouring towns and cities to create an organized resistance.

In fact, just about the only pretension of organization amongst the colonists throughout the whole area – and specifically amongst the male colonists – was to be found in the rapidly growing and ever more popular Freemasonry. Within the ranks of the lodges, which invariably met in taverns where lodge members were often plied with strong drink, it was easy for radical speakers to whip up the disaffection that was genuinely felt in places such as Boston. The Boston Tea Party, led by the massed ranks of the Freemasons from St Andrew's Lodge, demonstrated the result.

The Cry of Liberty

There can be little doubt that it was ultimately the Star Families, already (like the Washingtons) present in the colonies, who took the tame 'Georgian' or 'Hanoverian' Freemasonry prevalent in the infant United States and turned it into something quite different. After centuries of struggle in Europe to fend off the worst excesses of religion and repressive government, the Star Families surely saw in America a genuine opportunity to build the New Jerusalem that had eluded them for so long. Their rallying cry was 'Liberty' and this is very telling.

Liberty literally means 'the power to act, believe or express oneself in a manner of one's own choosing' and 'freedom from repression or slavery'. But 'liberty' has a historical background that betrays the reason for its deliberate use in the American colonies.

The word liberty comes from the Latin word *libertas*. This concept was personified as 'Libertas', an ancient Roman goddess who was particularly revered by slaves who had achieved their freedom. The attributes assigned to her were taken partly from an even earlier Etruscan deity called Feronia, the goddess of the dawn. This might give us a clue as to what Liberty really represented to the Star Family priests who lay at the heart of developing American Freemasonry. In Kabbalism, that most revered and ancient symbol, the Shekinah, occupied a pivotal position at the base of the 'Tree of Life' (*see* Chapter 8). In addition to being the visible astronomical manifestation that had lain at the heart of early Israelite belief, Shekinah was also considered to be both the 'bride of God' and the 'angel of justice and liberty'. To those who really knew, therefore, Liberty was simply another name for the Shekinah – whose first and most important promise was a true and lasting community between Man and God. But as Liberty, the Shekinah also became much more, because she was cleverly turned into a concept that could be embraced by even the least sophisticated or religious members of society.

It can be shown that many of those who rose to prominence to lead the American colonists in the long and difficult struggle against Britain were *not* overtly religious – at least not in the historical Christian sense of the word. Their utterances demonstrate clearly that though they may have retained a deep and abiding belief in the Deity, they were dead set against any concept of an ordered or established Church with any part to play in the running of civil society as the Anglican Church had in England. The words of the First Amendment to the United States Constitution, signed in June 1789, make the leaders' position clear:

> The civil rights of none shall be abridged on account of religious belief or worship, nor shall any national religion be established, nor shall the full and equal rights of conscience be in any manner, or on any pretence, infringed.

George Washington, a senior Freemason who served first as commander-in-chief of the American forces against the British, and then as the new nation's first president, said that, 'Every man ought to be protected in worshipping the Deity according to the dictates of his own conscience.'

Meanwhile another Freemason, Benjamin Franklin, who played an important part in both the American and the French Revolutions, had written to a friend:

> When a Religion is good, I conceive it will support itself; and when it does not support itself, and God does not take care to support it so that its Professors are obliged to call for help of the Civil Power, it is a sign, I apprehend, of its being a bad one.

And most outspoken of all on the subject was Thomas Jefferson, another leading light in the American struggle for freedom and the United States' third president. Jefferson, who was not a Freemason but was strongly influenced by its values, was at odds with the Roman Catholic Church, which always demanded conformity, and once said:

> Is uniformity attainable? Millions of innocent men, women, and children, since the introduction of Christianity, have been burnt, tortured, fined, imprisoned; yet we have not advanced one inch towards uniformity. What has been the effect of coercion? To make one half the world fools and the other half hypocrites. To support roguery and error all over the earth.

These are not the words of atheists. In one way or another all three of these men showed themselves to be 'believers', though it is clear that *what* they believed was at odds with orthodox Christianity. Whilst Thomas Jefferson took a personal decision not to join a lodge, there is no doubt at all that both George Washington and Benjamin Franklin enthusiastically embraced the Craft, as did several of those who signed the Declaration of Independence from Britain in 1776 and the historically even more significant United States Constitution in 1787.

Of the 56 men who signed the Declaration of Independence on 4 July

1776, many are believed to have been Freemasons, and the following are documented members of the Craft:

William Ellery	First Lodge of Boston
William Hooper	Hanover Lodge, Masonborough, NC
Benjamin Franklin	Grand Master of Pennsylvania
John Hancock	St Andrew's Lodge, Boston
Joseph Hewes	Visited Unanimity Lodge No. 7
Thomas McKean	Visited Perseverance Lodge, Harrisburg, PA
Robert Treat Paine	Massachusetts Grand Lodge
Richard Stockton	St John's Lodge, Princeton
George Walton	Solomon's Lodge No. 1
William Whipple	St John's Lodge, Portsmouth, NH

Of the 40 signatories to the US Constitution, 15 were, or became Freemasons. A further 13 men may have been Freemasons but documentary evidence is not available.

Grand Master Franklin

Amongst these Benjamin Franklin stands supreme. Franklin (1706–90), the Grand Master of Pennsylvania, was a complex man and a true polymath. He was a leading printer, scientist, inventor, political philosopher and diplomat – as well as being a Masonic Grand Master and a confirmed hedonist.

As a leading figure of the Enlightenment, Franklin gained the recognition of scientists and intellectuals across Europe. With his frequent visits to London and Paris he gained the new nation credibility in the minds of European statesmen. A diplomatic genius, Franklin was almost universally admired among the French when he was the American minister to Paris, and was a major figure in the development of positive Franco-American relations. There can be no doubt that his success in securing French military and financial aid was the foundation of the American victory over the British.

A noted linguist, fluent in five languages, Franklin was also famous for his scientific work, including his discoveries and theories regarding electricity as well as his development of the medical catheter, swimfins (flippers), and bifocals. Besides being a statesman and a scientist he was a philanthropist and also, by all accounts, a philanderer. Franklin may have had high ideals, but he was also very human. He had a number of extra-marital liaisons, including one that produced his illegitimate son William Franklin, who later became the colonial governor of New Jersey. It is also frequently claimed that he attended the London Hell-Fire Club where he indulged in drunken orgies.

Freemasonry and the Forging of the Nation

The American War lasted from 1775 until 1783, but even when the British had been defeated, the job of the revolutionaries was far from finished. The men who had led the colonists to military victory now had to weld the 13 disparate states into a nation. The core commanders in the struggle had been Freemasons and there is a wealth of evidence to confirm that what they desired was a state run on Freemasonic principles. Indeed, Freemasonry and its icons still lie so close to the reins of power in the US that the presence of the Craft cannot be denied.

Some of the most important actions of these men, who are known as the Founding Fathers, betray not only a Freemasonic allegiance but an understanding of surviving Star Family imperatives. A good example of this comes in the date on which the first delegates chose to sign the US Constitution. The Declaration of Independence, in 1776, was essentially a means of uniting the colonists behind a single and unambiguous war aim – ending British rule and establishing a new state. But the precise nature of the new state was another matter, and deciding this had to wait until after the more pressing business of winning the war.

The new United States of America could not truly become a function-ing republic until it had a constitution, and the signing of this crucial document did not take place until 1787. Delegates had been elected from all the states and had come together in Philadelphia, the US capital before the founding of Washington, DC, in May of 1787. By this time it had become clear that the loose confederation of states that had existed throughout the struggle against Britain was no longer enough. If the United States was to become a reality it needed a more centralized government and that is what the delegates in Philadelphia created.

The discussions went on for many weeks and the document was ready for signing by the beginning of September, but there is good evidence that its ratification was delayed until Monday, 17 September. This was a day that for centuries had been put aside by the Church as being sacred to the Virgin Mary and is still known as 'the feast of Our Lady of Sorrows'. This commemorates Mary's sorrow for the suffering of her son Jesus, but since it was also considered to be the first day of the autumn harvest, it is of pagan as well as Christian significance. Most Freemasons are unaware that it is also a festival that is enshrined in the Third Degree ceremony of Freemasonry.

An icon regularly used in association with the Third Degree ceremony is usually referred to as 'The Beautiful Virgin of the Third Degree' (see Figure 16).

There are many versions of this icon. All are more or less the same and the explanation given to Freemasons is that it represents a beautiful virgin weeping for the loss of Hiram Abif, the semi-mythical builder of Solomon's Temple (see Chapter 1). The broken column in front of her represents his epitaph and the figure behind is that of Father Time. But its association with Hiram Abif, builder of Solomon's Temple, is tenuous to say the least. There is no woman associated with Hiram's story, either in the Bible or in popular myth, and to those who understand, the icon betrays its true significance in other terms.

The version of the Beautiful Virgin shown in Figure 16 is of particular interest because it carries astronomical information that these days is not generally included. This information represents a date, because the zodiac sign immediately in front of the young woman is that of Virgo, which in astrological terms is occupied by the Sun between late August and late September.

In a religious context this has always been a pivotal time of year. The days approaching the autumn equinox on 21 September when the Sun passes from the zodiac sign of Virgo into Libra, have been revered by humanity for thousands of years and were linked with the death and rebirth of the Corn God. Those who created the icon of the Beautiful Virgin of the Third Degree can hardly have been ignorant as to its significance.

The figure of the virgin is a conglomeration of the ancient goddesses Isis and Demeter. Isis, of Egyptian origin, grieved for her murdered

Figure 16 A late 19th-century representation of *The Beautiful Virgin of the Third Degree*[1]

husband Osiris, whose coffin she had found trapped in the trunk of a tamarisk tree that had been made into a pillar to support the palace of Biblos. This pillar in its broken form is to be seen in the icon. The Greek goddess Demeter also mourned at the onset of autumn because it was at this time that her daughter, Persephone, was forced to leave the world of daylight and travel to the dark underworld of Hades, where she was obliged to spend each winter (*see* Chapter 3). It was in September, too, that Demeter's association with the god Dionysus was remembered. Dionysus, the god of vegetation, was ritually killed and eaten in September – the god is yet another representative of the dying and reborn Corn God myth, to which Jesus is also connected.

Every year in ancient times a great celebration had taken place in Greece. This was known as the Great Mystery of Demeter. Worshippers came from all over the known world to take part in the mystery, which for every adherent included a ritual ceremony of death and rebirth very similar to the one that takes place in the raising of a Freemason to the Third Degree.

The Mystery of Demeter began on 17 September when sacrifices were made to Demeter in Athens, before the assembled devotees made their way to her shrine at nearby Eleusis for the rite itself. 17 September is the date on which the feast of Our Lady of Sorrows is celebrated – and on which the US Constitution was signed in 1787.

It is also worth recalling that this part of September was of pivotal importance to the building of Rosslyn Chapel, because it was on 21 September 1456 – also St Matthew's day – that the cornerstone of the building was laid.

In fact this whole pivotal week in September is now enshrined in American law as of specific significance. In 2001 President George W Bush enacted a request first made by Congress as long ago as 1952, and signed a law declaring the period between September 17 and 23 to be known as 'Constitution Week'. This is precisely the time period covered by the ancient mystery rites of Demeter and marks the period during which the Sun passes from the zodiac sign of Virgo to that of Libra. Virgo is the zodiac sign of sacrifice and servitude, whilst the following sign of Libra is associated with justice, equality and freedom.

On the day chosen for the signing of the US Constitution, the planets Mercury and Venus were both rising before the Sun. In addition, the Sun, together with Mercury and Venus, were all occupying the zodiac sign of Virgo. In 1787, September 17 fell on a Monday. On the following Sunday, 23 September something of momentous importance would take place: the planets Mercury and Venus came together before dawn to form the sacred Shekinah – on exactly the same day that the final sacred rite had been undertaken in the ancient Demeter celebrations.

If the reader sees in this little more than a bizarre coincidence, then we should look at another pivotal event in the birth of the infant United States. This was the laying of the cornerstone of the Capitol in Washington, DC. There is no building in the whole of the US that better represents the ideal of self-rule and democracy than the Capitol. It is in this building that the elected representatives of the United States meet to propose, discuss and institute federal statutes. It is not surprising therefore that its creation was considered to be of monumental importance by George Washington and his fellow Freemasons in the US leadership. To demonstrate this, the whole cornerstone ceremony, from beginning to end, was openly Freemasonic in nature. The event took place on Wednesday 18 September 1793. On that day the Sun was nearing the end of its journey through Virgo. Both Mercury and Venus rose before the Sun as morning stars and as the cornerstone was laid at 11am, Venus, now invisible in the full light of the Sun, stood directly overhead. This is a newspaper account of the event:

> On Wednesday one of the grandest Masonic processions took place for the purpose of laying the cornerstone of the Capitol of the United States. About 10 o'clock, Lodge 9 of Maryland was visited by Lodge 22 of Virginia, with all their officers and Regalia. Directly afterwards appeared, on the Southern banks of the Grand River Potowmack, one of the finest companies of Volunteer Artillery that hath lately been seen, parading to receive the President of the United States, who shortly came in sight with his suite, to whom the Artillery paid their military honors. His Excellency and suite crossed the Potowmack, and was received in Maryland by the officers and brethren of No.22 Virginia, and No.9 Maryland, whom the President headed, and preceded by a band of music; the rear brought up by the Alexandria Volunteer Artillery, with grand solemnity of march, proceeded to the President's square, in the city of Washington, where they were met and saluted by No.14 [lodge], of the city of Washington, in all their elegant badges and clothing.[2]
>
> The procession then marched two abreast in the greatest solemn dignity, with music playing, drums beating, colors flying, and spectators rejoicing, from the President's square to the Capitol in the city of Washington, where the Grand Marshal ordered a halt, and directed each file in the procession to incline two steps, one to the right, and one to the left, and face each other,

which formed an hollow oblong square, through which the Grand Sword Bearer led the van, followed by the Grand Master P. T. on the left, the President of the United States in the center, and the Worshipful Master of No.22 Virginia on the right; all the other orders that composed the procession advanced in the reverse of their order of march from the President's square to the south-east corner of the Capitol, and the artillery filed off to a destined ground to display their maneuvers and discharge their cannon; the President of the United States, the Grand Master P. T., and Worshipful Master of No.22 taking their stand to the east of a huge stone, and all the craft forming a circle westward. The cornerstone of the Capitol of the United States was then laid with appropriate Masonic Ceremonies.

At frequent intervals volleys were discharged by the artillery. The ceremony ended in prayer, Masonic 'chaunting honors', and a 15th volley from the artillery.

Once again we find a great Masonic ceremony taking place in that most important of weeks – the seven days from September 17 to 23 and again it is fixed for a time when both Mercury and Venus are morning stars, rising ahead of the Sun.

As Alan Butler was collecting the astronomical information set out here,[3] another book appeared on the other side of the Atlantic, this one researched and written by David Ovason. Quite independently of each other Alan and Ovason, both of whom are well versed in astronomy and astrology, had noted the apparent Freemasonic fascination with astronomy and in particular with the zodiac sign of Virgo. Ovason filled 600 pages with his observations regarding the city of Washington, DC, carefully detailing its most important buildings and streets, demonstrating how important the sign of Virgo had been in their planning and construction.[4]

The very position of Washington betrays this importance because the District of Columbia stands on the dividing line between Maryland and Virginia. Maryland derived its name from Queen Henrietta Maria, the wife of King Charles I, whilst Virginia was named after Queen Elizabeth I, the Virgin Queen. However, this apposition of 'Mary' and the 'Virgin' symbolizes the Christian character most closely associated with the zodiac sign of Virgo and ultimately therefore Demeter, Isis and the Shekinah – 'brides of God'.

Curiously, in the east of Washington across the Potomac River – close to both the White House and the Pentagon – is an area called Rosslyn.

George Washington the Mason

The ultimate choice as to the location of the new federal capital had fallen to President George Washington. Washington gives every impression of being well acquainted not only with Freemasonry but also with the aims and objectives of the Star Families. The symbolic significance of the meeting of Maryland and Virginia at the spot he chose on the Potomac would surely not have been lost on him.

Ultimately the federal capital came to bear Washington's own name and the national banner that flew from its many flagpoles was also his invention. George Washington was descended from an aristocratic family that had first emerged in County Durham, England, around the time of the creation of the Templars. Their estates were initially around Hartburn, on the River Tees, but they later exchanged these for lands on the north bank of the Wear at *Wessyngton* (Washington), from which the family took its surname. They later settled further south, at Sulgrave Manor in the English Midlands. The family had Norman forebears and was almost certainly a Star Family. Following the disbandment of the Templars in 1342, the Washingtons exchanged their earlier coat of arms (a rampant red lion of Jerusalem) for the arms shown below. The background to the shield was originally silver, whilst the crossbars and stars were red. The stars may be an allusion to the Washington's Star Family status.

The arms first arrived in America in 1666 with two brothers, one of whom, Col. John Washington, was George Washington's great-grandfather. George Washington was always said to be

Figure 17 The Washington coat of arms (red stars and bars on a silver field)

ambivalent toward his British aristocratic ancestry but he was neverthe-less careful to retain his family's coat of arms and he used it regularly. When it became necessary for the infant United States to possess a flag of its own there seems little doubt that Washington's coat of arms was the model. Or, at least, the same thinking lay behind the symbolism of both emblems.

The first 'Stars and Stripes' had 13 alternate red and white stripes, rep-resenting the first 13 states, and similarly had 13 stars, which in the case of the flag were white on a blue background. The use of the five-pointed star in particular cannot be seen as coincidental since it was a symbol with deep Freemasonic overtones and, as we have seen, was also significant with regard to Star Family beliefs and their knowledge of the movements of the planet Venus.

The Freemasonic City

Once a site for the new federal capital had been chosen, work went ahead relatively quickly. The design of Washington was initially vouchsafed to a French engineer and designer who had served in the American revolutionary army. His name was Pierre Charles L'Enfant, who was also a leading Freemason. It is suggested, not least by David Ovason, that L'Enfant's Freemasonic beliefs were reflected in the street plan he envisaged for Washington. A good example of this can be seen in the diagram below, which shows L'Enfant's plans for Washington overlaid with the pentacle or five-pointed star, which, via the city's streets, connects some of its most important buildings.

L'Enfant was a fractious and difficult man and walked out on his commission before it was completed. As a result the plans were resurrected by Benjamin Banneker, a self-taught, freed slave who had been one of L'Enfant's former assistants. Banneker was a remarkable man and although L'Enfant had taken all his plans with him at his departure, Banneker was able to reconstruct them from memory. There is no evidence that Banneker was a Freemason (which would have been extremely unlikely at the time because of his racial origins) but it is a known that he was fully conversant with astronomy and he seems to have followed L'Enfant's original plans to the letter.

David Ovason's exhaustive investigation of the streets and buildings

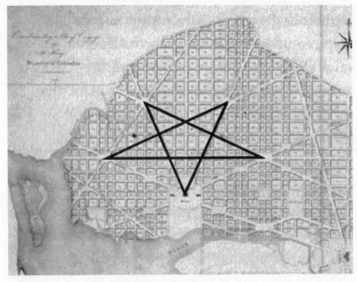

Figure 18 An old street map of Washington with the pentacle superimposed upon it. The bottom point of the star terminates at the White House.

of Washington across nearly 200 years of history demonstrates just how cosmologically aware the city's planners and architects have been. In particular Ovason presents a convincing number of instances in which the zodiac constellation of Virgo has been incorporated into street plans, buildings, friezes, fountains, statues and stained glass. The fact that the latest of his examples date from the 20th century would seem to indicate that the knowledge possessed by those who first constructed America's capital was not lost and that in some way it has been preserved, almost to the present day.

To summarize, Freemasonry was very nearly destroyed after the Hanoverian accession to the British throne but it began to recover and to find its most political expression in the new United States. Nor was it confined to America, because in 1789, less than two years after the signing of the US Constitution – with its ground-breaking opening words, 'We the People' – revolution erupted in France. The French Revolution was in no small part fuelled by Freemasons from America, especially Benjamin Franklin. What is more, there is ample evidence that from beginning to end the revolution was planned and orchestrated under the umbrella of the many powerful Freemasonic lodges that were springing up within French borders. A new world order appeared to be at hand and, though the old agencies of Church and State fought back tenaciously, the Star Families were once again in the ascendancy.

CHAPTER 12

Freemasonry and Revolution

Nobody knows for sure when or how Freemasonry first arrived in France because at the outbreak of the French Revolution the Freemasons gathered together all their documents on the origins of the Craft and took them into safekeeping. These books were subsequently 'liberated' by a Scots Freemason at the end of the Napoleonic Wars, and as the Morrison Collection they now reside in the library of the Grand Lodge of Scotland, where they still await cataloguing. (Chris Knight has viewed several of these papers and many are beautifully handwritten with astronomical charts relating to the tribes of Israel.)

Freemasonry appears to have taken root between 1726 and 1730, but it is possible that Scottish Freemasonry had existed there for some time, given the traditional close relationship between the two countries. The personal guard of the French kings had, for centuries, been partly composed of Scottish soldiers who formed an elite bodyguard that was even more loyal that the French kings' own troops.

According to the Grand Orient of France (the body that represents by far the greatest percentage of modern French Freemasons), the Craft came to France as a result of sailors, particularly those from England, who set up Masonic lodges in ports such as Bordeaux and Dunkerque (Dunkirk). However it arrived, Freemasonry soon took root and flourished.

An Absolutist Regime

Discontent amongst the intelligentsia and ordinary people of France grew steadily as the 18th century progressed. For centuries, French kings had been deeply authoritarian, a trend begun by King Philip IV, that great enemy of the Templars (*see* Chapter 5), around the turn of the 14th century. The situation was not very different to that which existed in England prior to the English Civil War of the 17th century, which had led to the execution of King Charles I. Like the Stuarts in Scotland and England, the French kings held staunchly to the doctrine of 'divine right'. In other words the legitimacy of the king derived directly from God, which meant that no Parliament or other manmade institution could instruct the king what to do. Meanwhile the Church exercised a similar position. Despite the ravages of the Reformation, France remained a deeply Catholic country and in spiritual matters the Church performed a similar role to that of the French kings, who in turn sought to exercise as much control over the French Church as they could (a trend known as Gallicanism).

The king considered himself to be in direct communion with God and so his word was absolute law. He ruled and made laws through a government almost entirely composed of aristocrats. Ordinary citizens – including, to their increasing dissatisfaction, the professional middle classes – had little or no say in this regime.

Until the Revolution of 1789 France remained a virtually feudal state, as it had been since the days of Charlemagne a thousand years before. A parliament of sorts, the Estates General, did exist, but it was rarely called and was a consultative body without legislative powers. It was comprised of representatives of the three 'estates', or social groupings: the first estate, the clergy, represented around 1 per cent of the population; the second estate, the nobility, represented 2 per cent. Finally came the third estate, the people, representing 97 per cent of the population.

The nobility, controlling the country, made certain that they were generally tax exempt, whilst the clergy too paid virtually no taxes. The professional members of the third estate used their education and skills to avoid a heavy tax burden, so it was the poorest people upon whom the greatest weight of taxation fell. For many, taxes left scarcely enough money to buy bread. This position worsened in the later 18th century as poor harvests and financial mismanagement brought the royal government and nation to crisis point.

Many 18th-century French intellectuals looked with interest at the constitutional settlement in Great Britain after the Civil War and the 'Glorious Revolution' of 1688. In Britain, since 1688, it had become unthinkable for a monarch to raise taxes, or indeed rule at all, without the approval of regular Parliaments. Even the peerage was not a closed group, as in France: in Britain, anyone might be elevated to the nobility, whatever their origins. Such social mobility was unheard of in France, where the nobility monopolized all senior echelons of state, from the army to the civil service.

But worst of all, the *ancien regime* was not working. Despite attempts at financial reform, the whole system of feudal and royal taxation was just too dense and complex for minor tinkering to make a difference. France lurched from one financial crisis to another, made worse by costly and unsuccessful wars. As ever, the burden fell on the poorest, whose suffering made an ugly contrast to the profligate living of the nobility. In 1754 Jean-Jacques Rousseau, one of the great *philosophes* (philosophers) whose political ideas influenced the French Revolution, concluded his *Discourse on the Origins and Foundations of Inequality among Men* by saying:

It is manifestly contrary to the law of nature, however defined ... that a handful of people should gorge themselves with superfluities while the hungry multitude goes in want of necessities.

Freemasonry and Revolutionary Ideas

However, it was not the poor labourers or peasants who took up the political and philosophical ideas that sparked off the French Revolution. This is not surprising because the vast majority of French peasants at the time could not even read or write. Education for ordinary people was either rudimentary or nonexistent.

It was among literate and educated professionals that fervour for both

Enlightenment ideas and Freemasonry proliferated. This large and growing group of the third estate are referred to as the *bourgeoisie*, literally 'burghers' – what we might term urban professionals, such as doctors, lawyers, merchants, bankers and academics, men who were most likely to be affected by the ideas of *philosophes* such as Voltaire and Rousseau. Socially, they were the counterparts of the very same class that had overthrown the monarchy and won the Civil War in England and who, in 1776, instigated the American Revolution. They were also much more likely than the peasantry to join the rapidly growing ranks of Freemasons that soon existed across the whole of France but especially in the urban centres.

By 1789 many members of the bourgeoisie seriously resented their effective exclusion from the governance of the nation. Like the instigators of the American Revolution, they were fertile soil in which to plant, via Freemasonry, the ideas of the Star Families. It might be far-fetched to suggest that the French Revolution was 'inspired' by the rising ranks of the Freemasons, but it is not overstating the case to suggest that Freemasonry was a major factor in making revolution possible.

Places where people could meet to discuss political reform were limited in an authoritarian state where one could be arrested, imprisoned or even executed for sedition. However, Freemasonry, with its history of rather alarming oaths and absolute secrecy, offered a fairly safe conduit through which talk of radical reform could take place. And when unrest gave way to genuine revolt in 1789, there is every reason to believe that it was organized at a local and a national level by the growing number of Grand Orient lodges.

If British Freemasonry was eagerly seeking to avoid suspicions of disloyalty to the Hanoverian regime, and had purged itself of any radical or revolutionary tendencies, the same was certainly not the case within the Grand Orient. This is what the present-day Grand Orient has to say on the subject of religious interference in the running of the state. To anyone beginning to understand the power and influence of Star Family thinking it makes interesting reading:

> The Catholic Roman Church wanted to exercise a totalitarian power in its strictest sense, that is to say in all aspects of the civilian, political and economic society, basically where religion had all the power.

Successive desires, albeit rather vague, of political or spiritual liberation, or both together, manifested against this power. In the Middle Ages it was inside the Catholic Church that these movements were born, but they were quickly classed as heretical and rapidly overcome. The idea evolved from the first reformers until the 18th century philosophers, but was still associated with two different ideas of liberation:

– Freedom of ideas taking over little by little from obligatory beliefs;

– A society demanding political liberty.

Against which, the Catholic Church, led by a papacy, holding on [to] a temporal power not even supported by its fundamental texts, preferred to hide behind a complete refusal of all liberation groups. In France, the thousand-year-old allegiance between the King and the Church made religious disputes unavoidable once political disputes had started.[1]

French Freemasonry makes no pretence about its political beliefs and is so vehement about the way it expresses them that it has regularly fallen foul of other Masonic institutions across the world, since in the British model at least, as we have seen, Freemasons scrupulously avoid discussions relating to either religion or politics.

The Cataclysm of 1789

In France, matters came to a head in 1789. In the face of a new financial crisis, coupled with a severe drought and even famine, King Louis XVI called the Estates General in early summer. It was declared that voting would be by estate, not by individual delegate, which meant any reforms proposed by the third estate would almost certainly be blocked by the combined aristocracy and clergy. Events moved quickly. It became obvious to the many prominent Freemasons among the third estate that if the New Jerusalem was ever to arise on French soil, drastic action was necessary.

The members of the third estate therefore broke away and declared themselves to be the 'National Constituent Assembly' – France's only legitimate parliament – and refused to disband. A number of moderate nobles and clergy joined them.

On 14 July 1789, the *bourgeoisie* enlisted the support of the large mass of the population of Paris. In the early hours of the morning an enraged mob broke into the Invalides prison where they found 32,000 muskets, but no ammunition. Rumour spread that powder was stored at the even more infamous Bastille prison. Later that day the Bastille was stormed – an event that has gone down in history as being the real beginning of the French Revolution. King Louis XVI, returning from a day's hunting that same night, wrote one word in his diary for this day: 'Rien' ('Nothing'). When a minister brought the news from Paris, the king asked: 'Is it a revolt?' To which the minister answered, 'No sire, it is a revolution.'

Control of the situation swiftly passed from the hands of the well-meaning but indecisive Louis. There followed a protracted and eventually bloody battle between moderates, known as *Girondins* and the radical intelligentsia known as the *Jacobins*. This group, which included many Freemasons, had begun as the *Club Breton*, which had among its members leading thinkers such as Jean-Paul Marat and Robespierre. It too had been moderate at first but soon became more radical in its demands. It broadened its membership and soon became one of the most powerful institutions in France. At the height of its influence, there were between five and eight thousand chapters throughout France, with a membership estimated at over half a million people.

Perhaps the greatest of the Jacobin leaders was Georges-Jacques Danton, a lawyer from Champagne who practised in Paris. Like most of his contemporaries at the Jacobin Club he was also a leading Freemason, with a particular allegiance to the Nine Sisters Lodge in Paris, which had been named after the constellation of stars more regularly called the Pleiades. This now little-known and very peculiar Masonic lodge had offered significant encouragement to the American Revolution and done much to engender its French counterpart.

The Nine Sisters Lodge had been the brainchild of Jerome Lalande, who would go on to become one of France's most famous astronomers and mathematicians. The lodge was created in March 1776 with the avowed intention of providing a place of study for Masonic scientists, intellectuals and artists. Some of the greatest French thinkers of the age were members of the lodge, including Voltaire, who became a Freemason late in life, joining the Nine Sisters Lodge on Tuesday 7 April 1778. The climax of the ceremony came when a visiting American Brother, Benjamin Franklin of Philadelphia, handed Voltaire the Masonic apron, which the great Claude Helvetius, a Swiss philosopher and Freemason (1715–71), had worn before him. Voltaire raised the apron to his aged lips and kissed it.

In flagrant disregard of its Masonic undertakings to the Grand Lodge of France, the Nine Sisters Lodge did much to promote the American uprising and the War of Independence that followed it. Nine Sisters members openly supported the American revolutionaries and the richer amongst them gave large sums of money to support the war against British rule. In May 1779 Franklin was elected Grand Master of the Nine Sisters Lodge and was able to influence the French government to declare war on Britain and thereafter to offer open military support to the infant United States.

The Nine Sisters Lodge appears to have been obsessed with trying to understand the origins of Freemasonry, which it believed to be of great antiquity. Many talks were given by respected members of the Academy of Sciences and other august bodies, explaining how Freemasonry encapsulated important myths and traditions from Egyptian, Greek and Roman literature. Such talks took place during two major cultural assemblies held in 1779 and some of them led to published works.

To a great extent, once it had begun, the French Revolution took on the form of an unstoppable juggernaut. By 1792, with the king now deposed and imprisoned, the Jacobins were in charge of a republican regime that was, however, far from the democratic ideal of the United States. For the next several months, the euphemistically named 'Committee of Public Safety' sent hundreds of aristocrats, clergy and political opponents to the guillotine in what has become known as the 'Reign of Terror'. King Louis XVI was executed on 21 January 1793, and his queen followed later the same year.

Power seesawed backward and forward between different groups and there were times during which the most fervent and violent of the original revolutionaries themselves became the target of the increasing terror that rocked the country. Thus when Danton's faction split from Robespierre, the latter succeeded in seeing Danton guillotined before himself falling foul of yet another faction. But no matter where the true power lay in Paris one fact was certain: the absolute power of the monarchy and the Church had been destroyed and – notwithstanding the rise of Napoleon, which was welcomed as an end to the chaos and arbitrary rule of the revolution-aries – neither would ever again be allowed to wield the same power as before 1789.

The cry of liberty that had been raised across the infant United States was shouted even louder in France. In both countries 'liberty' was much more than a simple byword – as we have seen (*see* page 212), it also had a physical manifestation.

By order of the revolutionary government of France, Christianity was officially abandoned as the state religion in November 1793. In order to make the point, a beautiful young actress by the name of Mlle Malliard was brought to the cathedral of Notre Dame (Our Lady) in Paris on 10 December. There she was dressed in classical robes and seated on the high altar of the cathedral. What followed was an improvised ceremony in which the 'goddess' of the Revolution lit a candle, known as the light of reason. The form of this young woman became known as the 'Goddess of Reason', a direct counterpart of the goddess Liberty in the United States. For a time the cathedral became known as the Temple of Reason.

It is interesting to remember that America's most famous image of Liberty – the Goddess of Reason – actually came from France, and that it was entirely Masonic in inspiration. This is, of course, the Statue of Liberty that graces New York harbour. The statue, which was paid for from public subscriptions in France and offered as a gift to the United States on its centenary, was completed and dedicated in October 1886. A plaque at its base makes it clear that, though paid for by the French people as a whole, the Statue of Liberty was actually a gift from the Grand Orient Freemasons of France. This huge statue carries a torch that represents the same candle lit by Mlle Malliard in Notre Dame cathedral back in 1793.

It would be impossible to prove that the French Revolution was orches-trated by any single agency, but Freemasonry appears to have been at the heart of this maelstrom of events. However, as different factions fell and rose in Paris not only did many of the leading Freemasons, who had pushed for an overthrow of royal and Church power, end up with their own heads on the guillotine, but Freemasonry itself was also banned and purged by the Revolutionary government for a time. Nonetheless, the Catholic Church did and still does blame Freemasonry for the events that took place in France from 1789 and it is as a result of these events that the Church began to fight tenaciously against the very existence of Freemasonry.

Church versus Craft

Successive popes were of the opinion that the French Revolution was merely one manifestation of a desire on the part of Freemasonry to destroy the power base of the Church. Rome's deliberate and concerted attack on the Craft culminated in a strange document published by Pope Pius IX in 1860. This was the *Alta Vendita* and, if genuine, it substantiates our observations regarding the surviving Star Families and how they used every possible institution to gain their ultimate objectives.

Before we look at the document itself, let us examine some of the historical background. Although Pius IX made it public, the document had allegedly come into the hands of his predecessor, Pope Gregory XVI. Gregory has not gone down in history as the most intelligent or liberal holder of the high office to which he was elevated in February 1831. True, he did not have a particularly auspicious start to his pontificate, for no sooner had he assumed the papal throne than a major uprising took place in Italy. The Papal States themselves – for in those days the pope was also a temporal monarch, governing a vast swathe of central and northwest Italy – were temporarily captured by a confederacy of rebels who declared a 'Provisional Government' for the whole region. Only by appealing to Catholic Austria did Gregory finally manage to drive the revolutionaries out of northern Italy.

The new pope, whose birth name was Bartolomeo Cappellari, had chosen the name Gregory after Gregory XV, a 17th-century pope who had been prominent in the founding of a Church movement called *Propaganda Fidei* ('For the Propagation of the Faith') that sought to introduce Roman Catholicism to newly discovered territories.

Gregory XVI was a conservative and a staunch opponent of liberalism of any sort. His reign came at a time of momentous upheaval, not only within Italy, but also across much of Europe. The legacy of the French Revolution and the following Napoleonic era was still fresh in the minds of many, and revolutionary movements for democratic change were almost always arising in one part of Europe or another. In July 1830, the year before Gregory's election, France had again been rocked by the overthrow of King Charles X, ending the Bourbon monarchy restored after the defeat of Napoleon in favour of the more liberal regime of King Louis Philippe. It was in this atmosphere of political upheaval and civil disturbance that Gregory looked unfavourably on any organization or institution that seemed to ferment unrest or republicanism.

The Carbonari

One such organization, which was actually losing its appeal by the time Gregory came to the papacy, was known as the *Carbonari*. The origins of this clearly Masonic-style institution are unknown. The Carbonari first appeared in either France or Italy around the end of the 18th century, but did not begin to display any real power until around 1814 in Italy. It appears to have been a deliberate imitation of Freemasonry. The word Carbonari means 'charcoal burners' and whilst conventional Freemasonry bases its rites, history and ceremonies upon the craft of stonemasonry, the Carbonari had similar practices but in this case dedicated to the profession of making charcoal.

The Carbonari were funded by middle-class intellectuals, most of whom were natural supporters of the revolution that had taken place in France some decades earlier. It is possible that the Carbonari came about as a result of the Masonic influence among Napoleon's troops, who had occupied large areas of Western Europe including Italy. What is not in any doubt is that members of the Carbonari saw a close association between their own practices and objectives and those of Freemasonry, to such an extent that any Master Mason could attend meetings of the Carbonari, where they were considered to be full and absolute members.

In the highly complicated political disturbances that beset Italy during the latter part of the 18th century and the first half of the 19th century, it was assumed that unrest was constantly being fomented by the Carbonari, but to what extent this was the case is not really known because members of the Carbonari were as subject to oaths of secrecy as their Freemasonic counterparts.

Membership of the Carbonari took on a very similar form to that of Freemasonry. In place of lodges the Carbonari had *vendite* (singular *vendita*) the name for a place where coal was sold. Their lodges were known as *baracche* (singular *baracca*), the Italian for hut, and the mother lodge of all the Carbonari was known as the Alta Vendita ('High Lodge'), the Carbonari version of the Masonic 'Grand Lodge'. Deputies from all *vendite* attended the Alta Vendita

The Carbonari were split into two classes, apprentices and masters, again very similar to the degrees of Freemasonry. Recognition came through specific forms of handshake and by way of particular signals, known only to the Carbonari. In fact the only major way in which the Carbonari differed from Freemasonry lay in the fact that it displayed a nominal Christian element within its rituals.[2] Most Carbonari were, at least nominally, Roman Catholics

The organization showed a specific reverence for a saint by the name of Theobald. At first there did not seem to be anything especially significant about St Theobald, but as we dug a little deeper, something very surprising came to light. We learned that Theobald had been born in the early 11th century in Provins, Champagne. This in itself would be an interesting connection, but Theobald was not the child of just any family. According to tradition his father was Arnoul, count of Champagne and a direct ancestor of counts Hugues and Theobald II (Thibaud) of Champagne. As we have seen (*see* Chapter 6), the counts of Champagne headed one of the most prominent Star Families in northern Europe.

Further investigation showed that the saint's most likely year of birth was 1017. Raised for a military career, he quit his martial way of life in his late teens and with his father's permission took up the life of a hermit. He lived in various places and travelled a good deal but in the end he settled in Salanigo, Italy. There he lived an ever more isolated existence though in 1066, close to his death, he became a monk in the Camaldolese Order, who wore white habits similar to the later Cistercians.

Exactly why St Theobald was adopted as the patron saint of charcoal burners is not known but it may be as simple as the fact that he lived such an isolated existence, as charcoal burners were also obliged to do by dint of their own profession.

Despite their supposed Catholic leanings and their reverence for St Theobald, the Carbonari were always at odds with the Church. It was said that at their meetings they related a version of Christ's passion that to the Church was blasphemous.

What is most interesting about the events relating to the Carbonari that took place during the papacy of Gregory XVI is that the organization had, apparently at least, disappeared by the time he came to occupy the papal throne. It was rumoured that the Carbonari had taken part in the 1830 revolution in France, but that was almost the last that history heard of them until three decades later when the *Alta Vendita*, a document purporting to contain instructions for a Carbonari-led overthrow of Church power, was made public by Gregory's successor, Pope Pius IX. Gregory is alleged to have first got hold of the document, but why he himself had not published it himself is not known. But one fact is certain: by 1860 the Carbonari had disappeared from the historical record.

The Alta Vendita Document

Where the document sprang from remains a mystery. Pope Gregory had apparently left instructions that its source was to be carefully guarded. He claimed to know personally some of those involved in its creation and perhaps his secrecy was an attempt to shield specific individuals. It also has to be said that the document, which is still known as the *Alta Vendita*, could conceivably be a forgery, dreamed up by Gregory himself or one of his papal officials – and this possibility cannot be ignored. There were, and are, many clever men in the papal hierarchy. However, bearing in mind the events we had seen unfolding in Western Europe from as early as the 11th century, and convinced as we were by the knowledge that specific groups of people had kept up a consistent though clandestine attack on the Catholic Church, to us the *Alta Vendita* has the ring of truth. Here is the passage of the *Alta Vendita* that proved to be most explosive.

Our Ultimate End is that of Voltaire and of the French

Revolution – the final destruction of Catholicism and even of the Christian idea…

The pope, whoever he is, will never come to the secret societies; it is up to the secret societies to take the first step toward the Church, with the aim of conquering both of them.[3]

The task that we are going to undertake is not the work of a day, or of a month, or of a year; it may last several years, perhaps a century; but in our ranks the soldier dies and the struggle goes on.

We do not intend to win the popes to our cause, to make them neophytes of our principles, propagators of our ideas. That would be a ridiculous dream; and if events turn out in some way, if cardinals or prelates, for example, of their own free will or by surprise, should enter into a part of our secrets, this is not at all an incentive for desiring their elevation to the See of Peter. That elevation would ruin us. Ambition alone would have led them to apostasy, the requirements of power would force them to sacrifice us. What we must ask for, what we should look for and wait for, as the Jews wait for the Messiah, is a pope according to our needs …

With that we shall march more securely towards the assault on the Church than with the pamphlets of our brethren in France and even the gold of England. Do you want to know the reason for this? It is that with this, in order to shatter the high rock on which God has built His Church, we no longer need Hannibalian vinegar, or need gunpowder, or even need our arms. We have the little finger of the successor of Peter [the pope] engaged in the ploy, and this little finger is as good, for this crusade, as all the Urban IIs and all the Saint Bernards in Christendom.

We have no doubt that we will arrive at this supreme end of our efforts. But when? But how? The unknown is not yet revealed. Nevertheless, as nothing should turn us aside from the plan drawn up, and on the contrary everything should tend to this, as if as early as tomorrow success were going to

crown the work that is barely sketched, we wish, in this
instruction, which will remain secret for the mere initiates, to
give the officials in the charge of the supreme Vendita, some
advice that they should instil in all the brethren, in the form
of instruction or of a memorandum ...

Now then, to assure ourselves a pope of the required
dimensions, it is a question first of shaping ... for this pope, a
generation worthy of the reign we are dreaming of. Leave old
people and those of a mature age aside; go to the youth, and if
it is possible, even to the children ... You will contrive for
yourselves, at little cost, a reputation as good Catholics and
pure patriots.

This reputation will put access to our doctrines into the
midst of the young clergy, as well as deeply into the monasteries. In a few years, by the force of things, this young clergy
will have overrun all the functions; they will form the
sovereign's council, they will be called to choose a pontiff
who should reign. And this pontiff, like most of his contemporaries, will be necessarily more or less imbued with the
Italian and humanitarian principles that we are going to
begin to put into circulation. It is a small grain of black
mustard that we are entrusting to the ground; but the
sunshine of justice will develop it up to the highest power,
and you will see one day what a rich harvest this small seed
will produce.

In the path that we are laying out for our brethren, there are
found great obstacles to conquer, difficulties of more than
one kind to master. They will triumph over them by
experience and by clear-sightedness; but the goal is so
splendid that it is important to put all the sails to the wind in
order to reach it. You want to revolutionize Italy, look for the
pope whose portrait we have just drawn. You wish to establish
the reign of the chosen ones on the throne of the prostitute of
Babylon, let the clergy march under your standard, always
believing that they are marching under the banner of the

apostolic keys. You intend to make the last vestige of tyrants and the oppressors disappear; lay your snares like Simon Bar-Jona [St Peter]; lay them in the sacristies, the seminaries, and the monasteries rather than at the bottom of the sea: and if you do not hurry, we promise you a catch more miraculous than his. The fisher of fish became the fisher of men; you will bring friends around the apostolic chair. You will have preached a revolution in tiara and in cope, marching with the cross and the banner, a revolution that will need to be only a little bit urged on to set fire to the four corners of the world.[4]

Several factors regarding the *Alta Vendita* captured our attention. First and foremost had to be the method by which the Carbonari – assuming the document to be genuine – suggested the Catholic Church might ultimately be defeated. There was to be no war and no direct confrontation because with the correct strategy armed attacks would prove to be quite unnecessary. The way to defeat Roman Catholicism, believed the leaders of the *Alta Vendita*, was by destroying the power of the Church from the inside. Young devotees of the Carbonari would be sent to seminaries where they would train for and gain holy orders. They would maintain their Carbonari sympathies and would gradually rise through the ranks of the priesthood, becoming bishops, cardinals and perhaps, one day, even popes.

The document specifically refers to Rome as being the 'Prostitute of Babylon'. This is an allusion to the Bible, specifically the Book of Revelation. In chapter 17 the author is confronted by a woman sitting on a scarlet coloured beast with seven heads. She is referred to as the 'prostitute' or 'whore of Babylon', and the writer of Revelation leaves us in no doubt that she is intended to represent Rome, which was famously built on seven hills. The woman is dressed in purple and scarlet – the colours worn by Roman emperors (and later cardinals and popes), and on her forehead is written 'Mystery, Babylon the Great, the Mother of Harlots and Abominations of the Earth'. We are told that this woman was drunk with the blood of the saints and martyrs and the writer finishes the chapter by suggesting that 'the woman which thou sawest is that great city, which reigneth over the kings of the earth'.[5]

This city, suggests the author, with all its wickedness and evil, will have to fall from power before the real kingdom of God can be made manifest on earth and the New Jerusalem be built.

Of specific relevance in the *Alta Vendita* is paragraph five of the above extract, in which the authors suggest that force of arms is not the right approach to destroying the Catholic Church but rather that the little finger of 'the successor of Peter' (the pope) will be enough to win the battle. The paragraph finishes by suggesting: 'this little finger is as good, for this crusade, as all the Urban IIs and all the Saint Bernards in Christendom.'

It is particularly interesting that the authors of the *Alta Vendita* should use these two specific names. Both these men, as we saw in Chapters 4 and 6, were of Champagne aristocratic extraction and each has figured significantly in our story so far. Pope Urban II, originally Odo of Lagery, was the pope who called for the First Crusade at the end of the 11th century (*see* Chapter 4) whilst St Bernard (St Bernard of Clairvaux), probably contributed more to the redirection of the power of the Catholic Church and the transformation of society than any individual who has ever lived (*see* Chapter 5). Yet in the mind of pious Catholics neither of these individuals would be considered in the least radical or anti-Catholic. Both are deeply venerated. Urban II is 'blessed' which means he is halfway to being a saint, whilst Bernard of Clairvaux is not only a much admired saint but is also considered one of the great 'doctors' (teachers) of the Church.

There are two distinctly different ways in which to read this particular section of the *Alta Vendita*. On the one hand the author could be invoking Urban II and St Bernard because they were two of the most venerated men who had served the Church. However, it seems far more likely to us that whoever wrote the *Alta Vendita* fully knew that both Urban and Bernard were members of a fraternity, the objectives of which was to completely reform Roman Catholicism, or even destroy it altogether.

We have demonstrated in earlier chapters how these two men, in their respective ways, were contributing to a diminution of the power of Rome, Urban by supplanting Rome in importance by Jerusalem and the Holy Land, and Bernard by promoting the Cistercian Order, which both directly and indirectly brought about a steady but certain change within society – shifting power towards the masses through the development of industry and trade.

Pius IX and the Freemasons

We have to ask ourselves why, at a time when the Carbonari had in fact effectively ceased to exist, Pope Pius IX and his predecessor Gregory XVI were so obsessed with a document such as the *Alta Vendita*. The answer is not difficult to find. Gregory XVI was one of the most radically conservative popes of his era and so therefore could be expected to jump at any excuse to attack free thinking and liberalism. Pius IX was, at first, a liberally inclined individual, but this was not to remain the case throughout his long papacy.

It was during the reign of Pius IX that the extensive Papal States, land ruled directly by the pope for centuries, finally fell to the forces of Italian unification. Paradoxically, Pius partly had himself to blame for this state of affairs. He had begun his papacy in 1846 determined to put right what he saw as the mistakes of his predecessor. He fought strenuously for human rights and for political freedom of expression and many other leaders throughout the various independent states of Italy followed suit. But instead of quelling the unrest, this policy simply led to an even greater cry for political freedom and for the unification of Italy. The latter came about, whilst Pius IX was still pope, in 1861, under the leadership of King Victor Emmanuel of the house of Savoy – a leading Star Family in the region of southern France and northern Italy. On Pius IX fell the humiliation of losing the Papal States and of becoming the temporal ruler of only a tiny part of Rome itself – the Vatican.

These events hardened the pope's attitudes. There is no doubt that Pius IX turned bitter and suspicious as he saw his own moderate beliefs and actions backfiring. Nor is it any surprise that the date at which Pius chose to release the transcript of the *Alta Vendita* was 1860, at a time when the unification of Italy was imminent and the loss of the Papal States seemed inevitable. Pius was by this stage absolutely mistrustful of all secret societies and of the Freemasons in particular, who he was sure had contributed to his own troubles and those of the Church. In all probability he had no direct evidence of the intentions of Freemasons with regard to Italian uni-fication, but what he did possess was the document left to him by Gregory XVI. This may not have been an open admission of Freemasonic deter-mination to destroy the Catholic Church but, being concerned with the quasi-Freemasonic Carbonari, it was the next best thing.

This is almost certainly why the *Alta Vendita* appeared precisely when it did, and it caused a sensation amongst Catholics. If it is genuine, and in our view it probably is, it represents a plot, if not on behalf of Freemasons then certainly by a closely associated body, to infiltrate and ultimately destroy not just the Roman Catholic Church but, as the *Alta Vendita* itself suggests, 'even of the Christian idea'.

Some groups today insist that Freemasonry is a dangerous and destructive force opposed to Christianity. We see no reason to support such ideas but it seems that other, perhaps related or pseudo-Masonic bodies may have had an intention of undermining the power of the Church – and maybe even Christianity itself. The appearance of the *Alta Vendita* and the reaction it elicited from the Roman Catholic Church at its highest level strongly points to a silent war against the Church from the 11th century.

There are many groups around the world today that jump on the evidence of the *Alta Vendita* as positive proof that Freemasonry stands as part of a deliberate and longstanding plot to alter the world and to create what is generally referred to as the 'New World Order'. On the internet there is a proliferation of sites dedicated specifically to raising the public's awareness of Masonic 'conspiracies'.

The Illuminati

Few of the internet sites in question could be described as rational. Many indeed are little short of paranoid hysteria, often virulently anti-Semitic as well as anti-Masonic in character. Among their numerous unfounded claims is the idea that underpinning Freemasonry is a mysterious and dark agency known as the *Illuminati*. The Illuminati are generally described by the Masonic conspiracy theorists in terms that make them appear to be 'black magicians' or 'Satanists' and there is barely a negative twist or turn in the history of the world over the last couple of centuries that is not laid at their door by one conspiracy theorist or another.

Even if we dismiss the wilder claims of the conspiracy websites about the sinister nature and role of the Illuminati, it is nonetheless worth examining any possible connection between them and the Freemasons. For us, the genuine existence of the Illuminati might also add weight to our own findings regarding the Star Families.

It is now generally accepted that the Illuminati were founded in 1776 by Adam Weishaupt, professor of canon law at Ingolstadt University in Bavaria, Germany. In fact there is no doubt or confusion about this because Weishaupt specifically named his new organization 'The Order of the Illuminati'. However, before we look more closely at Weishaupt, his aims, objectives and actions, we need to recognize that the word Illuminati itself was not his invention since it had existed for many centuries.

The Amalricians

Illuminati simply means 'enlightened ones', having a very similar meaning to the term 'Gnostic', one possessing *gnosis*, enlightened wisdom or knowledge. Although there may have been groups of a truly ancient origin who used the name, its first recognized appearance comes *c.* AD1200 with the followers of a French theologian by the name of Amalric of Bena (Amaury de Bène). Born at Bène near Chartres, France, Amalric taught at the University of Paris and, probably because of his very unusual beliefs, he soon attracted a significant group of followers. After his death they became known as 'Amalricians' but they often referred to themselves as the 'Illuminati'. It is interesting to note that although Amalric was forced by the Church to recant his views, on pain of death, his followers continued to preach his doctrines. Their base of operations was – this may come as little surprise – Champagne.

Amalric believed that philosophy and religion are essentially the same thing. This was not a new concept at the time and much of Amalric's thinking came from an earlier Irish theologian and philosopher, Johannes Scotus Eriugena (*c.* 815–77). What Eriugena passed to Amalric through his writings was a Neoplatonic slant on orthodox Christianity.

The Neoplatonists had originated in 3rd-century Alexandria, in Egypt, where they followed the teachings of the ancient Greek philosopher Plato. However, their beliefs were suffused with elements of Judaism and Christian mysticism. Neoplatonism suggests that there is a single source from which all existence derives and that the individual soul of any person can be mystically united with this primary source.

At the centre of Amalric's teaching lay the belief that God is everything and that the person who remains in the love of God is incapable of committing any sin. This was a dangerous view as far as the Church authorities were concerned since they wanted to keep complete control over what was, and what was not a sin. Such ideas would lead to independent thought, and had to be nipped in the bud. In 1204 the University of Paris condemned Amalric's teachings as heretical and Rome upheld this verdict. Amalric was forced to recant and was lucky to escape with his life.

After Amalric's death c. 1205–7 his followers went further with their heretical beliefs. They declared that God had revealed himself, and would do so again, in a threefold manifestation. There had been, the Amalricians asserted, the age of the Father and the age of the Son. What was to come was the age of the Holy Spirit, which began with God manifesting as Amalric himself. Some of the Amalricians took their master's words too literally and interpreted them to mean that they could do absolutely *anything* they desired, freed from the possibility of divine retribution. In 1209 some of them were burned at the stake, along with Amalric's exhumed corpse. Amalric was formally condemned by the Lateran Council in 1215.

Nevertheless, Amalric was among the first Western thinkers since ancient times to draw extensively on Neoplatonist Greek philosophy. In doing so he provided a very important precedent as far as the future development of European political and religious thinking were concerned.

It is somewhat difficult to differentiate between the Neoplatonist slant of Amalric and the attitude of roughly contemporary Christian mystics such as St Bernard of Clairvaux. St Bernard once described God as being 'height and breadth and depth and width'. His apparently mystical view of Christianity suggested that profane science could not be studied except as a contribution to the spiritual life. The major difference between Bernard and Amalric is that Bernard at least appeared to toe the party line, in that his personal faith was never diametrically at odds with Church teaching. Bernard always took his inspiration from biblical sources, even if some of these were as confusing, obscure and apparently unchristian as the Song of Songs. St Bernard was also in a unique and very strong political position. He had no real fear of successive popes because he was responsible for some of them being in power.

The Church repudiated and even attempted to destroy all those who espoused outright Neoplatonism. The whole concept seemed far too radical for an organization with no place for personal choice or freedom.

Civil authorities agreed, because all rulers in medieval Europe were despotic in nature and any form of free expression, let alone democracy, was unheard of.

Christianity was not alone in being somewhat influenced by Neoplatonic thought. It also had a marked bearing on the beliefs of a significant number of Muslims, partly in Sufism, the mystic aspect of Islam. This fact was not unknown to Adam Weishaupt because his own Illuminati was founded along Sufi lines – so much so that he was accused, even within his own lifetime of being a covert Muslim.

Amalrician communities continued, at first openly and then in secret, across many frontiers but especially in Champagne, and continued well into the 14th century. Their beliefs had a profound bearing on other communities, such as the Beghards of Cologne. Amalric also impressed a man whose name is still well known in religious circles. Born Johannes Eckhart von Hochheim, this Dominican monk, better known as Meister Eckhart, also espoused Neoplatonist views.

Adam Weishaupt

After we lose sight of the Amalricians and associated cults, in the 14th century, the term Illuminati disappeared from common usage and did not emerge again until the 18th century. How much Adam Weishaupt had in common with the Brethren of the Free Spirit and the other groups they inspired is open to conjecture but there is little doubt that he was aware of their legacy, as well as of the similar strands within Islam.

Adam Weishaupt was born on 6 February 1748, to a Jewish family who had converted to Christianity, and was educated in Jesuit schools throughout his childhood. Because he showed great promise, particularly as a linguist, the local Church authorities had him earmarked for the priesthood, and in particular for missionary work. Adam disagreed and used his education in a very different way. Because of good family contacts, together with his own talent, he accepted a professorship in canon law at the University of Ingolstadt. This infuriated local Church leaders because it was the first time such a post had been offered to a layperson.

Weishaupt had a strong interest in history but also studied philosophy. He had a fertile mind and showed a particular fascination for ancient Egypt, about which very little of a specific nature was known at the time.

In 1771, when Weishaupt was still only 23, he decided to create what he specifically intended to be a secret society. Its aims would be to transform the human race and to abolish all spiritual and temporal powers. In organizing what he very soon came to call the 'Illuminati', Weishaupt borrowed from many different sources and it took him five years to work out fully his intended strategy.

There would be three distinct classes of members in the Illuminati. The lowest would be composed of 'novices', 'minervals' and 'lesser illuminati'. Next came two denominations of 'Scottish knights'; and the highest class was reserved for two grades of priests known as 'priest and regent' and 'magus and king'. All of this, especially the 'Scottish knights', demonstrates that Weishaupt was borrowing heavily from Freemasonry.

It is something of a puzzle how the Illuminati ever managed to gain ground because its laws of secrecy were almost fanatical. No member knew who his superiors really were. Neither were new recruits told anything specific about when the Illuminati had commenced or who lay behind it. Aspirants were merely given to understand that the Illuminati traced its origins to very ancient times and that its members included people high in society and the Church. A pledge of absolute secrecy was obtained from anyone interested in becoming 'illumined' and absolute obedience was demanded from all.

There were five known intentions of the Illuminati, which were as follows:

1 The abolition of monarchies and all ordered governments
2 The abolition of all private property and inheritances
3 An end to patriotism and nationalism
4 The abolition of family life and marriage, together with a commitment to ensure children were educated in a communal manner
5 An end to all organized religion

He was certainly a long way ahead of Karl Marx, and history would prove that his ideas had about as much chance of succeeding in the longer-term.

Weishaupt seems to have believed that almost any action that furthered the intentions of the Illuminati were justified, and since he did not recognize the legitimacy of any form of established government he did not feel himself hampered by any law. He appears to have been an early advocate of the later maxim adopted by communists, that 'the end justifies the means'. Despite this, Weishaupt does not seem to have been a cruel or uncaring man by nature. He once said that 'sin is only that which is hurtful' and in this attitude he does seem to have had much in common with the followers of Amalric, who came to believe that sin, of itself, did not exist and was merely a description of wrong actions.

Weishaupt was a fervent disciple of the French thinker Jean-Jacques Rousseau and like him looked towards a world freed from the constraints of Church and State in which all humanity would exist in a universal community with nature. Once again there are great parallels here between Weishaupt's own philosophy and that of the Amalricians. During his education Weishaupt had come to detest Catholicism, and in particular the Jesuits – though he admired their organization and was not beyond using some of their structural principles for the Illuminati.

Each month the lowliest amongst the Illuminati, known as the 'minervals' would meet for a dose of indoctrination. They were well schooled in the philosophy of enlightenment, though they remained in ignorance of the true identities of their teachers since everyone in the organization used a pseudonym. In the case of Adam Weishaupt it was 'Spartacus', the name of the leader of the slaves' revolt against Rome in 73BC. All the time both the minervals and their mentors would cast around for new members and the organization soon began to take on an international nature. The minervals remained largely ignorant of the ultimate intention of the Illuminati until they had achieved a higher status in the organization. Upon reaching this more elevated level they would learn the words of 'Spartacus':

> Princes and Nations shall disappear from off the face of the earth! Yes, a time shall come when man shall acknowledge no other law but the great book of nature; this revelation shall be the work of Secret Societies and that is one of our grand mysteries.

Surprisingly enough, the Illuminati flourished for a time and had representatives in most Western European countries. A deliberate policy from its earliest days was to infiltrate Masonic lodges, where it was estimated that the richest source of new recruits would be found. A co-conspirator of Weishaupt was a German aristocrat by the name of Baron Knigge, to whom fell the lot of supervising the approaches that were made to the Masonic lodges. All the while the Illuminati tried to convince the authorities that their only aim was with good deeds based on the life of Jesus Christ.

Unfortunately for the Illuminati, an 'act of God', so to speak, changed the course of events. In 1784, in Bavaria, a member of the Illuminati was struck by lightning and when the police examined his body they found letters from Weishaupt sewn into the lining of his coat. Immediate panic seized some of the other members with the result that four of them, led by a high-ranking member of the Illuminati named Utschneider, gave themselves up to the authorities and divulged the true purpose and intention of the organization.

Weishaupt had to flee for his life and finally found sanctuary in the town of Gotha in Saxony. There his problems increased. He had already been experiencing difficulties in keeping his ego-centred partners in line and often despaired of their lax morals and bad behaviour. His case was not helped by a scandal involving his own sister-in-law, whom he had made pregnant and for whom he had tried to elicit an unlawful abortion.

Adam Weishaupt died in Gotha in 1830 and although rumours have persisted from that time to the present that the Illuminati have continued to play a profound part in establishing what today's more fanatical right-wing groups especially refer to as the 'New World Order', there is little or no tangible proof for this belief.

At the same time, however, to suggest, as do some authors, that the Illuminati were a dead-end in terms of the development of Europe during the 18th and 19th century is to fail to understand the tremendous legacy that Weishaupt and his followers left behind them.

Although Weishaupt's own conception for the Illuminati never came to fruition in the way he intended, what cannot be doubted is the part his organization played in what was taking place in Europe at the time – for example the furtherance of the sort of ideas that fed into the French

Revolution. Nor can it be denied that the Illuminati remain an organization of significant interest to many people. Simply type the word 'Illuminati' into any internet search engine and over two and a half million responses will be at your disposal. Many of these relate to right-wing American Christian groups which claim that the Illuminati never died with Weishaupt and that the organization still exists – most notably as a secret, sinister extension of Freemasonry.

The simple truth seems to be that the Order of the Illuminati as conceived by Weishaupt did not long survive the death of its founder. It appears to have been an intellectual response to events taking place at the time it was created, but the very mechanisms by which it was supposed to operate made it virtually unworkable from the start. Of course it is in the interest of some to claim that the Illuminati is alive and well and that its desire to destroy society as we know it remains intact – but if this is indeed the case our exhaustive searches have failed to supply any tangible proof of it.

The existence of the Order of Illuminati as a historical entity stands, in our opinion, aside from the evidence we have provided regarding the reality and influence of the Star Families. The Illuminati was short-lived, ill-conceived and though specific regarding its intentions it was vague in terms of addressing them. Weishaupt's Order smacks of a form of anarchy, in which the Star Families would not have been remotely interested. Both agencies may have ultimately sought personal freedom for the individual, but the means by which this would be achieved were radically different in each case. We can never know whether Star Family members were among those participating in the Illuminati, but to us it seems somewhat unlikely.

Eliphas Lévi

Nor is there any proof whatsoever that either Adam Weishaupt or his Illuminati ever dabbled in the 'black arts'. Similar accusations of Satanism are regularly hurled at Freemasonry, and the Illuminati are invariably cited as proof of its existence within the Craft. This is in great part thanks to one individual. His name was Eliphas Lévi.

Born in 1810 in Paris, Lévi – whose real name was Alphonse Louis

Constant – came from humble origins but from a very early age showed himself to be clever and astute. Because of his intelligence, Constant managed to gain a place at a Paris seminary, with the intention of gaining a formal education and eventually becoming a Roman Catholic priest. Perhaps unfortunately for all concerned, the seminary was that of St Sulpice.

Of all French 19th-century seminaries, and there were many, St Sulpice had the strangest reputation. During the time Constant studied there it had become a hotbed of alternative thought and a place where esoteric and occult study seem to have gone hand in hand with orthodox Catholic belief. Some of the most famous individuals in the French esoteric tradition were directly associated with St Sulpice, and names such as that of the great opera singer Emma Calvé and the composer Claude Debussy made certain that the unorthodox approach and teaching of St Sulpice would be discussed in the most fashionable Paris salons, where the occult was proving to be of particular interest.

Immersed as he was in the undercurrents of the St Sulpice seminary, the assiduous Constant soon became deeply involved in occult thinking and practices. In truth he did not make a very good priest. In 1846, soon after being ordained, he met and married Neomie Cadot, who at the time was 17 years old. The marriage was soon annulled and Constant, by now dismissed from the Church, began to earn a good living in journalism.

But his esoteric training soon led him into less orthodox areas of publishing. Now calling himself Eliphas Lévi, in 1861 Constant published *The Dogma and Ritual of High Magic*. This was soon followed by *A History of Magic*, *Transcendental Magic* and *The Key of Great Mysteries*. The contribution Lévi made to blackening the name of Freemasonry came about indirectly, because he never specifically made a connection between Freemasonry and Satanism. What he did do was apparently to explain the significance of the pentacle, or five-pointed star, which had long been an important symbol to Freemasons.

Lévi claimed that when the pentacle appeared in its inverted form, i.e. with a point downward, it represented a potent satanic symbol. He claimed it was associated with a goat, an animal often equated with the devil, and images portraying the association soon became common.

It mattered little that the pentacle had regularly been used as a Christian symbol because a society thirsty for the sort of 'revelations' that Lévi claimed to be making took the image onboard. It was not long before anti-Masonic agencies, especially those associated with the Catholic Church, pointed out that the pentacle was prominent in Freemasonry and to reach the dubious conclusion that all Freemasons must therefore be Satanists.

The situation was not helped by a man called Albert Pike who, rather ironically, has gone down in history as a leading American Freemason.

Albert Pike

Born in Massachusetts in 1809, Pike was a contemporary of Eliphas Lévi. Like him, Pike had little schooling but showed himself to be as intelligent as he was imaginative. He eventually learned Sanskrit, Hebrew, Greek, Latin and French, became an avid traveller and ultimately settled in Arkansas, where his most famous career, as a Masonic writer, commenced.

He joined a Masonic lodge and in 1859 was elected Sovereign Grand Commander of the Scottish Rite of Freemasonry's Southern Jurisdiction,[6] and remained in the post until his death, 32 years later. During this period he did considerable and irreparable harm to Freemasonry.

Pike took it upon himself to develop many of the rituals of the order, despite the fact that he had not the faintest idea of what Freemasonry was truly about. For him it was a sort of intellectual game that he could twist and use as he saw fit. But the whole idea of Freemasonry is that no single person has the power to change ritual, and if everyone took Pike's approach, the Craft would become as diverse and as confused as the many denominations of Christianity.

Pike also inadvertently fed the imaginations of anti-Masons. In 1871 he published a book called *Morals and Dogma of the Ancient and Accepted Scottish Rite of Freemasonry*. Those who attack Freemasonry as an evil secret society state that Pike admitted that Freemasonry is a 'religion', and that its ideology is of 'Lucifer'. They base this assertion largely on the following extracts from Pike's work:

> 'Every Masonic Lodge is a Temple of religion; and its teachings are instruction in religion.'
> 'The true name of Satan, the Kabalists say, is that of Yahveh

reversed; for Satan is not a black god... Lucifer, the Light-
bearer! Strange and mysterious name to give to the Spirit of
Darkness! Lucifer, the Son of the Morning! Is it he who bears
the Light, and with its splendours intolerable blinds feeble,
sensual, or selfish Souls? Doubt it not!'

Pike believed that there were two powers at work in the universe. He
refused to refer to them as God and the Devil but rather as 'Lucifer' and
'Adonay'. Both these names refer to the planet Venus. Lucifer (the bearer
or bringer of light), is an ancient name given to Venus when it appears as
a morning star and Adonay is Venus in its manifestation as an evening
star. Pike saw Lucifer and Adonay as opposing but equally powerful
forces – neither was good and neither was evil.

However, the name Lucifer had already (incorrectly) become attached
to the Devil, and so of course Christians immediately jumped to their own
conclusions. They assumed that because of the Lucifer connection Pike,
and therefore all Freemasons, were practising Satanists who must therefore
be directly opposed to everything good within Christianity. The responsibility for this belief, which persists so firmly in some quarters today that
no amount of reasoning can shift it, must be laid firmly at the door of
Albert Pike.

Pike's 'revelations' about Lucifer and Adonay – which in any case are
not borne out by any Freemasonic practice we are aware of – merely
added to the ammunition of a Catholic Church that was already diametrically opposed to Freemasonry and everything for which it stood. Pike
did no favours to Freemasonry by making a number of apparently anti-
Catholic pronouncements, which were immediately seen by Catholic
sources as representative of Freemasonry in general.

Pike's personal views and those of Eliphas Lévi are still regularly cited
as 'proof' that Freemasons are not only anti-Christian but that they also
have a secret agenda to destroy all 'true' faith and replace it with a satan-
ically-motivated 'New World Order'. Freemasons arguing to the contrary
regularly find themselves in a lose-lose situation – their protestations are
either ignored or denounced by the conspiracy theorists as a slippery
cover for 'the truth' ('well, they would deny it, wouldn't they?'). The myth
of the 'demonic Freemason' has become so deeply enmeshed in the

common psyche of society that the Craft is still viewed with suspicion – and not only among those near-paranoid far-right groups, particularly in the US, who rant on about Masons and the 'New World Order'. Today, politicians in many Western countries are at great pains not only to disassociate themselves from Freemasonry, but have even legislated against Freemasons holding high office without first openly declaring their Masonic membership.

Even as a self-help group, Freemasonry has now been effectively neutered, because the slightest rumour that anyone in public life has been in any way influenced by his Masonic membership is likely to see the individual marginalized and passed over for promotion. This is particularly the case in the United Kingdom with regard to politicians, civil servants, academics, police officers or members of the judiciary. Meanwhile ministers of the Church of England or Nonconformist Christian denominations, amongst whom Freemasonic membership was once the norm, now embrace the Craft at their peril.

From the perspective of our own long years of research the present castigation of Freemasonry is, in any case, like closing the stable door after the horse has bolted. In our final chapter we will seek to demonstrate that the Star Families have already gained their main aims and that Freemasonry was simply one temporary weapon in the Star Family armoury. What is more, the present influence of Solomon's power brokers should not be expected to lie within an organization such as Freemasonry which, however elevated its intentions, is now merely a shadow of what it was even in Victorian times.

CHAPTER 13

The End of the Beginning

We have argued in the preceding chapters that institutions such as the Tironensians, Cistercians, Knights Templar and the Champagne Fairs, together with the more modern Freemasons, should not be viewed in isolation. Just as surely as the similarities in the New Testament gospels of Matthew, Mark and Luke have led to the conclusion that each, in its own way, is based on a 'lost' source – a collection of sayings and deeds of Jesus known to scholars as 'Q' (from *Quelle*, German for 'source") – we can clearly see that behind the Cistercians, Templars and the rest is a powerful agency that is related to all of them, but which also stands aloof.

King Solomon had set up his priestly elite with the long-term mission to create a world fit for Yahweh to rule. For Solomon and his contemporaries, the interaction between the two worlds of humankind and of the gods was on a far more complex level than most religions would view it today.

The only major modern religion to maintain a level of complexity comparable to Solomon's mindset is also the one with the most ancient roots: Hinduism. Its origins are lost in time but it still recognizes the existence of a single, great cosmic spirit (Brahman), which is worshipped via many manifestations such as Vishnu, Shiva and Shakti. In whatever form it is followed, Hinduism remains a monotheistic religion with many gods, a basically tolerant creed that acknowledges that all routes to the great cosmic power are valid.

The holiest religious text of Hinduism is the *Rig Veda*, which is also the oldest collection of human ideas, with the possible exception of the Sumerian Epic of Gilgamesh. It includes the following words: 'Truth is one; the Brahmins call it by many names.'[1]

We believe that King Solomon's perception would have been similar. Yahweh was his national god – his focus – but beyond Yahweh was the great cosmic force whose only earthly manifestation was the Divine Shekinah. The gods of other nations were to be respected, but all were inferior to the ultimate energy that lay behind both heaven and earth.

Unlike the followers of all later religions, the Star Families – Solomon's power brokers – never lost this understanding.

The Star Family Programme

The evidence indicates that the Star Family agenda was never to introduce any kind of 'Jewish state religion' for the world to follow. Their vision of God was far more complex than that of Christianity, Islam or rabbinical Judaism (a very different expression of Jewish thinking to their own). They considered all of these theological options to be valid but entirely secondary to the main principle. What mattered was creating a world where people loved God under any name they chose, and behaved in a manner that was in tune with the spirit of the Shekinah. This meant a well-ordered and prosperous society, free from poverty, depravity, or ill will of any kind.

And to achieve this meant first of all putting in place a political structure.

The Star Families had had no option but to use Christianity as their mechanism since, following the collapse of secular imperial Rome, there was no comparable network of power that covered virtually the whole of Western Europe. And this may not have been as cynical a ploy as it sounds, for there can be little doubt that many Star Family members did indeed become Christians in the fullest sense. Men like St Bernard of Clairvaux cannot have been a living a lie. He, like many other leading Christians from the ranks of the Star Families, no doubt found the Christian tradition to be an excellent means of embracing the complex relationship between humankind and Creator. It was simply that he understood far more than he ever divulged. He understood the importance of John the Baptist to 'true' pre-Pauline Christianity and, more importantly, the Shekinah and the female aspects of higher godhead – and he guided the Roman Church to a more sophisticated future based on these concepts without anyone realizing what he was doing.

Today, the Roman Catholic Church has become a mature religion with layers of sensitivity that justifiably make it a worldwide force in spiritual matters. And that is, in no small part, due to the efforts of Bernard and the Star Families.

We suspect that as time went on, the Star Families will have remodelled their approach many times and people of other religions, even agnostics, may have been amongst their number. Most are likely to have remained followers of John the Baptist but, whatever the beliefs of the individual, the Church had always provided their base of operations.

The single-minded concept of Christianity initiated by the Roman emperor Constantine I at Nicaea (*see* Chapter 3) had given Western Europe a single route to God. Over time, the Star Families realized that the very might of their enemy was their greatest weapon – they could enter the labyrinthine Europe-wide structure of the Roman Church and slowly introduce to it their ideas and plans, all under the banner of a Pauline Christ.

However, the later rise of Protestantism (*see* Chapter 9), followed by a proliferation of non-Catholic Christian denominations, meant that there was no longer a single means by which Solomon's power brokers might achieve their end.

They realized that the way forward lay in new, secular forms. We should not be surprised at this. The groundwork for Europe-wide secular networks had previously been laid by the creation of international trade by the wool-producing Cistercians and the establishment of banking by the Templars. And, importantly, the vice-like grip on all thinking by the Church had been relaxed thanks to the efforts of moderating thinkers such as Bernard of Clairvaux. There can be no doubt that the power Brokers' interpretation of their own mission evolved over the centuries and millennia, as new thinkers revisited the definition of the Solomonic 'New World Order' (we should like to make it clear that we use this term in the sense of a world based on the values of the Star Families, not the sense in which it is often used by extremist groups, as described in Chapter 12). Their values held true but their ideas on how to achieve it had to respond to events that could not always be controlled.

The new, secular cover for the Star Family mission was Freemasonry. The rituals that gave rise to it were ancient and based in a belief in the power of the Shekinah that had held good since the time of King Solomon and possibly thousands of years before him. The Templars had propagated rites associated with operative stonemasonry during the time of the Crusades, and other parts of the later Freemasonic ritual had been instigated in Scotland by Earl William Sinclair as a means of transmitting the secrets of the Solomonic priesthood and those of the Jerusalem Temple, now rebuilt in the form of Rosslyn (*see* Chapters 8 and 9).

The Reformation had required a major change in strategy and now those rituals, originally meant for the few, became the basis of a whole new broad-based fraternity. It was a revolutionary idea that was to catapult humankind forward socially, intellectually and, most importantly, democratically.

For more than three centuries after the reign of King James I, whose accession was a boost to Freemasonry in England and subsequently its American colonies, Freemasonry was the primary conduit for the will of the Star Families. As the 'Antients' and 'Moderns' were conducting their rather unbrotherly feud in England during the later half of the 18th century, elsewhere the Craft was the driving force behind movements in America and France that brought a revolution in social thinking. In America the people built a new republic from scratch, while in France the ordinary people snatched power from the king and the entrenched aristocracy. In both of these republics Christianity remained an important component of social life, but a clear divide was drawn between Church and state. The secular society had arrived, bringing with it a newfound sense of equality among citizens.

Freemason Rudyard Kipling expressed this equality in his poetry, stressing how the stations of outside life are forgotten inside the Freemasonic lodge:

> But once in so often, the messenger brings
> Solomon's mandate: 'Forget these things!
> Brother to Beggars and Fellow to Kings,
> Companion of Princes – forget these things!
> Fellow-Craftsmen, forget these things!'[2]

The New English Freemasonry

English Freemasonry, unlike the Craft in America and France, was to prove on the whole a fruitless breeding-ground for Star Family ideas and ideals. Whilst it continued to promote freedom and science, English Freemasonry in the 18th century had radically to alter its rituals and practices to accommodate the political necessities of the Protestant Hanoverian kings. This meant that all vestiges of true Freemasonry, and most especially its Star Family imperatives, were lost to most English Freemasons by the year 1800.

But they certainly were not lost to everyone. An example of this new sort of English Freemason appears as a character who is described in detail by the popular 19th-century novelist Anthony Trollope, that great fly-on-the-wall of middle-class Victorian life. He was particularly astute when dealing with the Church of England and its relationship to the State.

Anthony Trollope was born in 1815, the son of a genteel but impoverished barrister, and was educated at Harrow and Winchester schools. In 1834 his father Thomas moved the whole family to Bruges in Belgium in order to avoid being arrested for debt. Anthony soon returned to England and secured a job with the British Post Office, where he would remain for the rest of his working life (and where he invented the post box).

Transferred to Ireland in 1841, Trollope became a Freemason almost as soon as he arrived. He was initiated on 8 November 1841, in Banagher Lodge no. 306 and was raised in the same lodge on 31 December of the same year.

Just how deep Trollope's Masonic roots extended is not known because he kept this part of his life private, but he could not avoid it emerging in his novels and in the way he treated some of the characters he created. Like all novelists some of his characters contain autobiographical elements and this certainly seems to be the case with a character Trollope named Dr John Thorne. Thorne appears in the novel *Barchester Towers*, published in 1857. Trollope seems to imply that Thorne was a Freemason and what he has to say about him is compelling:

> He, however, [Dr Thorne] and others around him, who still maintained the same staunch principles of protection – men like himself, who were too true to flinch at the cry of a mob – had their own way of consoling themselves. They were, and felt themselves to be, the only true depositories left of certain Eleusinian Mysteries, of certain deep and wondrous services of worship by which alone the Gods could be rightly approached.

Here Trollope refers to a group of people who possess the knowledge of a truly ancient route to God. He goes on to say that this hereditary group passes on its knowledge in secrecy:

> To them and them only was it now given to know these things, and to perpetuate them, if that might still be done, by the careful and secret education of their children.

And Trollope says that these people appeared to be normal Christians to the outside world but practised their own beliefs in private:

> We have read how private and peculiar forms of worship have been carried on from age to age in families, which to the outer world have apparently adhered to the services of some ordinary church. And so it was by degrees with Mr Thorne. He learned at length to listen calmly while protection was talked of as a thing dead, although he knew within himself that it was still quick with a mystic life. Nor was he without a certain pleasure that such knowledge, though given to him, should be debarred from the multitude.

Bearing in mind the fact that Thorne was a fictional creation and also accepting the author's own family background and Masonic allegiance, it seems more than probable that in *Barchester Towers*, Trollope is speaking of matters that related directly to himself.

The name 'Trollope' is Norman in origin and the family was originally a junior branch of another Norman family, that of le Loup (Wolf), latinized as Lupus. The Lupus family were directly descended from Hugh Lupus (Hugues le Loup), one of the staunchest followers of William the Conqueror at the time of his invasion of England in 1066. The Lupus family became earls of Chester in 1071 and as part of the Conqueror's inner circle were almost certainly Star Family members. Very telling in this regard is the motto of the Trollope family, which translated from Latin means 'I hear but I say nothing'.

However, it is clear that what Trollope is describing in the case of Dr Thorne is something much deeper and more ancient than simple Freemasonry. Almost everything in this extract from *Barchester Towers* smacks at a description of Star Family beliefs and the way these were passed down a family line, whilst being, as Trollope puts it, 'debarred from the multitude'.

Star Families and the Industrial Age

A once-secret group of scientific thinkers, known to its members as 'The Invisible College' had transformed itself into the Royal Society back in 1660 (*see* page 195). This organization was the first in the world to throw off the yoke of religious constraint and wholeheartedly embrace the objective investigation of the possibilities of science. And these men were mostly, if not all, Freemasons, acting in accordance with Star Family ideals. For these men, the more they discovered about the universe and its wonders, the greater their awe for the great cosmic force, the supreme godhead, represented in Star Family lore by the Shekinah and standing above any narrow human religious dogma. The Star Families had let investigation and imagination free in the Western world and by the close of the 18th century change was everywhere.

At the time that the Americans and French were establishing new republics, new technology and labour structures were fast giving rise to what is called the Industrial Revolution. This watershed for civilization began in Britain and spread quickly throughout the Western world. An economy based, since history began, on small-scale handiwork was replaced by one dominated by machinery that produced textiles, food and goods of every kind in great mills and factories. The resulting growth became exponential because machines were designed that could produce better machines.

In Britain especially, transport developed alongside industry, first with a network of great canals to carry coal and raw materials, then with improved roads, and finally railways. The world had not changed so dramatically since Neolithic times, when the development of agriculture had transformed society by providing regular food supplies, and most importantly, allowing societies to support a class of people with time for creativity, investigation and invention.

This time, though, the changes were astonishingly rapid. In little more than 150 years, between 1750 and 1900, Western Europe had been transformed by a seemingly unstoppable momentum of technological progress. The most powerful people were no longer those who owned or ruled the land but those who controlled the means of production.

At the turn of the 20th century, a famous Freemason by the name of Henry Ford stated:

There is but one rule for the industrialist, and that is: Make the highest quality goods possible at the lowest cost possible, paying the highest wages possible.

Ford installed the world's first moving assembly line in his Highland Park, Michigan, factory on 1 December 1913, and immediately reduced the time taken to produce his Model T motor car from over 12 hours to just 93 minutes. The ability to mass-produce enormous quantities of inexpensive products led, by the mid 20th century, to the age of 'consumerism' in the West, when the sort of Dickensian poverty that had characterized large segments of society in previous eras was increasingly rare. This too was in keeping with Star Family ideals.

The Star Families and the East

This survey has focused on Star Family influence in Western Europe and America. But what about the East? It appears that in the period following the division and collapse of the Roman Empire, the Star Families had originally ignored Byzantium (the eastern remnant of the Roman Empire) and the other lands of the Eastern Church. Perhaps the challenge of infiltrating an Orthodox Church hierarchy that was still firmly under imperial control was too great, or else their plan was to take control of the politically fragmented West first and then absorb the East.

In the end, Byzantium was to become part of the Islamic sphere of control, culminating in the fall of Constantinople in 1453. The mantle of heirs to Byzantium and Eastern Rome was assumed by the Orthodox rulers of the burgeoning Russian empire.

Being outside the Catholic sphere, Russia never enjoyed the benefits brought to the West by the Cistercians and the Templars and other agents of the Star Families. Until the 19th century, indeed, its social and economic structures were basically feudal and medieval. The Catholic Church could never have given the Star Families a route into Russia, while the Russian Orthodox Church was strictly controlled by the tsars. But Freemasonry gave the Star Families an excellent potential means to influence the course of Russian history.

The earliest reliable information about Russian Freemasonry dates from 1731 when the Grand Lodge of England appointed Captain John Phillips as the provincial Grand Master of Russia, empowering him to establish lodges in Russia – under the control of London.

Little is known about this Englishman who apparently first took Freemasonry to Russia. But the next Grand Master of Russia is a different matter, because there is little doubt that he was a Star Family member, with a mission to infiltrate the working of the Russian aristocracy.

The Hon. James Keith, who was appointed in 1741, was a member of a Norman family who c. 1150 had been granted the lands of 'Keth' by King David I of Scots. James Keith's ancestor, Sir Robert de Keth, had led the Scots cavalry at the battle of Bannockburn in 1314 at which, it is frequently claimed, the Knights Templar turned the tide of battle in favour of the Scots (*see* page 133). The heads of the Keith family were made hereditary Great Marischals of Scotland by King Robert the Bruce, and as leaders of the Scots cavalry, the Keiths were involved in most of the major Scottish battles over the centuries.

James Keith's father, the ninth Earl Keith, had led the Jacobite cavalry at the battle of Sheriffmuir in 1715 and Keiths had also supported the 1745 Jacobite uprising. Like the earls of Roslin (Rosslyn), the Keith family forfeited their lands, castles and titles as a result of their 'disloyalty' to the new Hanoverian monarchy.

Keith had gone to work for Tsar Peter II of Russia with a letter of commendation from the king of Spain. The tsar gave him command of a regiment of imperial guards. The Scot went on to achieve the rank of general of infantry and a reputation as one of the ablest officers in the Russian army as well as a capable, and liberal, civil administrator.

The motto of the Keith family is *Veritas vincit* or 'Truth conquers'. We will recall that the only words carved into the fabric of Rosslyn Chapel end with the Latin words *veritas omnia vincit* – 'Truth conquers all' (*see* page 166). Given that this is a scriptural quotation associated with the rebuilding of the Jerusalem Temple, there can be little doubt of James Keith's Star Family credentials.

While the earliest Masonic lodges in Russia had been formed by foreigners, it is recorded that under James Keith, Masonry started to move into Russian society, with a strong intake of young military officers from the country's leading families. Keith was undoubtedly beginning a process of gaining influence over the next generation of the social elite. The Star Families were employing Freemasonry as a perfect means of bringing about change.

However, Russia has never been an easy place in which to wield influence. Imperial Russia remained a land of peasants, accounting for more than 80 per cent of the population. There were two main categories of peasants, those living on imperial lands and those living on the land of private landowners. The latter were serfs. As well as having obligations to the state, they also were obliged to their landowner, who governed their lives. Serfs were forbidden to leave the property where they were born and were required to make regular payments to the landowner of labour and produce – usually 50 per cent of their time and produce. By the mid-19th century around half of all Russians were serfs.

Land and resources were shared within communes and the fields were divided among the families with a complex of strip plots, distributed according to the quality of the soil. Of course, the land was not owned by the communes but by the landowner class known as *dvoryanstvo*.

Serfdom was eventually abolished in 1861 but on terms advantageous to the landlords. The pressure for further reform grew but the smaller landowners made sure it did not happen. Some social and economic changes had begun in the 1860s as the country attempted to embrace market-driven capitalism. While these reforms had liberalized economic, social and cultural structures to an extent, attempts to reform the political system were blocked.

By 1900, the lives of the majority of Russians had not changed significantly for a thousand years. It was a highly volatile situation, and in 1905 an empire-wide uprising of both leftist and general violence occurred. The government regained control with difficulty, and Tsar Nicholas II reluctantly created a form of constitution, with a parliament (Duma) and prime minister. The tsar dismissed the Duma three times until a reactionary and right-wing majority was secured. The tsar's prime minister, Count Pyotr Arkadyevich Stolypin (1862–1911), followed a two-handed approach, determined that change should come from the top and not through political rebellion. Under Stolypin, leftist unrest was firmly, even brutally, suppressed. But at the same time, Stolypin introduced agrarian reforms from 1906–11 that transformed Russia from a land of strip fields to consolidated farms, boosting productivity enormously. It is likely that we can see Freemasonic and Star Family influence manifesting itself through the strenuous efforts of Stolypin and other pragmatic Russian aristocrats of the period who strove to drag the empire out of the sort of feudalism that had once endured in much of Western Europe.

But Stolypin's efforts proved fruitless. He was assassinated in 1911 and before his reforms could be continued Russia was engulfed in the chaos of the First World War.

The Russian Revolution

War was the last thing that the politically and socially volatile and economically weak Tsarist state needed. The consequences were predictably disastrous. In 1917, with the country on the verge of collapse and troops in open rebellion against their officers, the Russian Revolution began in earnest.

In March of that year Nicholas II abdicated and a moderate leftist provisional government was in place. But by October this had been overthrown by the radical Marxist Bolshevik party and the workers' soviets (councils), led by Vladimir Lenin. There was also a broadly based movement in the rural areas as peasants seized the land for themselves. These events eventually led to the establishment of the Union of Soviet Socialist Republics in 1922.

Stolypin and men like him had firmly believed that Russia could be dragged out of its feudal state by peaceful and constitutional means. But once revolution took hold in Russia, as in the case of the French over a century earlier, it took on a momentum of its own. Freemasonry was still present and many of Lenin's generals and fellow revolutionaries were Freemasons. But these were very different from the aristocratic Masons fostered by Keith, and how much real Star Family influence was present after the revolution is doubtful, for Soviet Russia turned into something far removed from the state envisaged by Star Family ideals.

The experiment with communism spanned eight decades and, while raising many from abject poverty, it also cost many millions of Russian lives, particularly under Stalin. Had Stalin lived long into the nuclear age it could also have led to the total destruction of our planet and it is hard to believe that such a political, economic and social diversion for Russia could have been planned by anyone. Nevertheless, we can see at the start of the 21st century that, no matter how tentatively, Russia is beginning to take its place amongst the democratic nations of the world and in such an extreme case as Russia represented, perhaps it could only do so after the total destruction of its feudal past that communism represented.

The Age of the Superpowers

At the end of the Second World War much of Europe and great parts of Asia lay in tatters. Having shared the victory over Nazi Germany and Imperialist Japan, the US and the USSR now eyed one another suspiciously over the shattered states of Europe. The age of the superpowers had begun. These two global powers, each with its own very different ideology and sphere of influence, were defined by their ownership of atomic weaponry that at its peak could destroy not just each other, but the world, ten times over. This was the Cold War, when at times only the fear of global destruction restrained the superpowers from conflict.

Military strength aside, the most important priority after the war was rebuilding the shattered economies of Europe. If countries could be bound by closer trade and economic ties, their eventual interdependence would make any notion of war unacceptable, and also make it easier to keep them under either Western or Soviet political influence. In the East, this idea saw the emergence of Comecon, the tightly-bound trading community of communist states, designed to keep Moscow's satellites firmly in line. Outside the Soviet sphere, the US instigated the Marshall Plan.

The Marshall Plan and the Common Market

The Marshall Plan was created by US secretary of state and former army general George C Marshall in 1947. Apart from their personal vision regarding the rebuilding of a world shattered by war, President Harry S Truman and Marshall had something else in common – they were both enthusiastic and long-serving Freemasons.

Truman probably ranks as the most elevated Freemason ever to hold the American presidency. He had been initiated into the Craft in February 1909 and went on to hold a string of illustrious titles, eventually becoming a 'Sovereign Grand Inspector General' of the 33rd degree, the highest degree in Freemasonry. (Although there are errant branches of Freemasonry that profess degrees higher than the 33rd degree, this is generally accepted as being the highest accolade a Freemason can attain.) In 1959 he achieved an honour for his 50 years as a Freemason

Marshall was slightly more reserved about his Masonic membership and had been initially created a Mason in Washington, DC. He is remembered by his brethren not only for his dedication to the US but also because he may rank as one of very few Freemasons awarded the Nobel Prize for peace, which came to him in 1953. This is particularly noteworthy for a man who spent most of his life as a soldier.

The Marshall Plan offered billions of dollars to rebuild Western Europe but was so devised that in order to benefit from the plan, European states would have to co-operate, often with their former enemies. George Marshall fought avidly to get the plan accepted. This is part of a speech he gave at Harvard University in June 1947:

> It is logical that the United States should do whatever it is able to do to assist in the return of normal economic health in the world, without which there can be no political stability and no assured peace. Our policy is directed not against any country or doctrine but against hunger, poverty, desperation, and chaos. Its purpose should be the revival of a working economy in the world so as to permit the emergence of political and social conditions in which free institutions can exist.

Were George Marshall, President Truman, or even President Franklin D Roosevelt, whom Truman had served as Vice President, Star Family representatives, or were their actions simply coloured by their Freemasonic membership? It is impossible to say, though Roosevelt's human vision and actions, even before the Second World War, might indicate that he was working to a greater imperative than even that offered by the Craft. The Roosevelts were an old New York Dutch family that produced two visionary presidents, Theodore (1901–09) and FDR, both noted for their exceptional reforming programmes.

The European Common Market

At the start of the 21st century, an economically and, increasingly, politically united Europe bears testimony to the success of both the Marshall Plan and its underlying ethos. In 1950, with the plan well under way in the West, three former wartime protagonists, France, Italy and West Germany, joined forces with the smaller 'Benelux' states (Belgium, Netherlands, Luxembourg) to form the European Coal and Steel Community. From this small but significant beginning, the seeds of the European Common Market and ultimately the European Union were born.

In 1957 the Treaty of Rome founded the European Economic Community. The member states opted for an open market in which in trade could be carried out across their borders without restriction. In 1973, three more states (Britain, Denmark and Ireland) extended this 'Common Market' to nine members, and today, now officially called the European Union, the organization stands on the verge of including almost every European state west of Russia. Even Switzerland, which for centuries has assiduously resisted international alliances of any kind, is tempted to join.

As we will see, this process, beginning with cross-border trade agreements and culminating in a regional bloc with all the structures of a single confederal state, did not happen by chance. It was a clear part of the Star Family agenda for the future of the world (*see below*, page 283).

The Star Families and Freemasonry Today

With the establishment of an integrated Europe, the question is have Solomon's power brokers – the Star Families – achieved their ultimate goal? We do not think so. But we suspect that Star Family plans are about to enter a final phase.

Certainly Freemasonry, which began as a convenient setting for the expression of Star Family ideals, is a spent force in most regions of the world. At the start of the 21st century, membership of the Craft is in global freefall. Fears on both sides of the Atlantic that Masons are exclusive and nepotistic, always seeking to give fellow Masons a 'leg up' in business, the professions, or government, have led to an insistence in certain professions that Masonic membership be made public. This is especially true in the case of the police and the judiciary. The supposed secrecy of Freemasonry had undoubtedly fuelled such allegations and has led to a series of modern myths of Freemasons helping each other, even in defiance of the law.

As we have indicated, not only is it no longer professionally useful to be a Freemason, it is very likely to be detrimental to career prospects. Certainly, in the British police membership is allowed but it is a permanent barrier to promotion.

We have noted (*see* Chapter 12) that some conspiracy theorists claim to believe that our planet is being directed towards a 'New World Order' – which they define as a global one-party state in which nationalism will become a thing of the past and in which all people will be subject to the same world government. Its leaders, we are told, will no longer be elected democratically but will be self-elected from amongst a small, secretive oligarchy.

Who exactly lies behind this mother of all conspiracies seems to depend on the religious and political affiliations of those proposing it. To some it is a plot fomented by mainly economic agencies, for example rich banking families, oil companies or drug companies. Inevitably in the conspiracy-theory world, anti-Semitism also raises its ugly head when we are told of secret Jewish plans to control the world. Some people even suggest, rather bizarrely, that the British royal family leads the conspiracy. Unsurprisingly, Freemasons are especially popular targets for accusations of complicity in the New World Order. At the other end of the spectrum, there are also those who suggest that the New World Order will not be remotely sinister and will be created for the good of humanity.

We find it amusing that the world is split into two groups: those who think that they are being conspired against and those who deny the whole concept of conspiracies. Most conspiracy theorists are focused on a specific event, such as those who believe that the Moon landings were faked or that Princess Diana was murdered. Such people tend to get the idea first and then seek out the evidence that appears to support their notion. No amount of counter-argument or evidence to the contrary is likely to modify their opinions.

At the other extreme are the people who will dismiss *any* idea that behind certain events there might lie a conspiracy of sorts. This is surely unwise. A conspiracy is an entirely normal human phenomenon. It need be nothing more than two or more people acting discreetly together to gain advantage of some kind. The phrase 'it's just a conspiracy theory' is now used unthinkingly to dismiss any unorthodox or untraditional explanation.

It is probably true that most people believe in the 'random accident' theory of history, where good and bad things come about largely by sheer happenstance. History is seen as a series of random events over which, in the long run, humans have little control.

To a great extent we have to agree. However, we also believe that there is evidence of a hand – albeit a shaky one – attempting to steer the tiller of social, political and economic development in the Western world for a very long time. This is the hand of those whom for convenience we have called the Star Families, whose ancient ancestors were commissioned by

Solomon to create a world living in harmony. Solomon's power brokers may not have succeeded in becoming masters of human destiny, but this is not to deny that such has been their aim. Moreover, they have probably had more influence over the course of historical events than any other single group in history.

Solomon's power brokers have lurched from disaster to success and back again many times over. The peaks of their success and influence came in the 12th and 13th centuries and again in the 18th to 20th centuries. They may not have controlled history, but they at least strongly contributed to many particular historical developments and trends, from the European wool economy of the Middle Ages to the American and French Revolutions.

But are the Star Families still influencing events today?

Our view is that they probably are – possibly at the highest levels. In some respects human society has never been harder to direct than now, but in the world today there is, once again, a single power-base to infiltrate. In the past the key international power structure was based on the Catholic Church. The Vatican is no longer of great importance politically – but the White House is.

It seems to us that the often reactive and short-termist nature of US foreign policy (as in Panama, Somalia and Iraq), driven as it is by ambitious elected individuals, belies the existence of powerful people who grasp the longer-term 'big picture'. These people will be connected to, but outside, the people's elected representatives. It stands to reason that it would be impossible to work towards a 'grand scenario' if short-term, elected individuals were really allowed to make important decisions. Many people, in the US and elsewhere, express surprise at the poor calibre of the men elected to lead this superpower.

Whilst the leaders of the infant United States were intellectuals and visionaries of the highest standing, recent incumbents of the White House seem to many to be little more than 'big smile and handshake' front-men. They appear like the charming front-of-house people who 'meet and greet' guests in a restaurant whilst unseen cooks perform the real wizardry. The days of the old families such as the Roosevelts, the Adamses and the Tafts seem to be over and it is possible that Star Family influence is now more likely to work as a 'power behind the throne' rather than via presidents and prime ministers. Perhaps we should search for the Star Families amongst high-ranking civil servants, bankers and financiers because genuine power lies in such hands, rather than in that of leading politicians.

The Star Families and the Catholic Church

But what of the former masters of the Old World – the Vatican? Does the Roman Catholic Church still have a major influence on world events and could it still be a significant vehicle for the Star Families? Apparently not, in these days of increasing secularization and with a dramatic fall in the number of practising Christians – though perhaps we should be somewhat careful in making such a carte blanche statement.

In April 1998, shortly after *The Hiram Key* became a bestseller in Italy, Chris Knight was in the Italian city of Perugia as the principal speaker of the annual conference of the Italian Grand Lodge of the Ancient and Primitive Masonic Rite of Memphis and Misraim. This is an international branch of Freemasonry, which was an amalgamation of two traditions brought together by Grand Master Giuseppe Garibaldi – the man who also helped create the modern state of Italy. The earliest record of the Rite of Misraim dates back to 1738, but the ritual claims great antiquity involving the Templars and elements of ancient Egyptian knowledge.

When the Rite (lodge) published the list of speakers, the Grand Master, Professor Giancarlo Seri, was telephoned by a senior figure from the Vatican. The person asked if it was true that Christopher Knight was to speak at their conference, and when this was confirmed he asked if it was possible to send an observer. The Grand Master agreed to the request and asked the caller if he had read *The Hiram Key* and if so, what he thought of it. The reply came, 'It is a very interesting book – but there are some things which should not be said in public.'

Over the course of the three-day visit, Professor Seri told Chris that many cardinals and a number of popes have been Freemasons. He said that the then pope, John Paul II, was not a Freemason but his predecessor was. Giancarlo is a 97th degree Freemason – the highest level with Memphis and Misraim. He explained that, remarkably, the Vatican acknowledges his Masonic rank by according him the equivalent status of a bishop.

We have argued that there has been a long-standing policy of entryism into the Roman Church by the Star Families. We have also suggested that after the Reformation, Freemasonry became the principal route for social reform by this group. Now that Giancarlo Seri has told us that he believes that Freemasonry exists in the Vatican, the question arises as to whether there could still be a power base of Freemasonry within the Roman Church? One man is certainly worthy of close inspection. His name is Annibale Bugnini.

Bugnini was 24 years old when he was ordained into the Congregation of the Mission (known as the Vincentians) in 1936. From 1947 he began to be involved in the field of specialized liturgical studies, becoming the director of *Ephemerides Liturgicae*, one of Italy's best-known liturgical publications. The following year Father Bugnini was appointed secretary to Pope Pius XII's Commission for Liturgical Reform and was soon made Professor of Liturgy in the pontifical institution known as the Propaganda Fide (I) (Propagation of the Faith) University, and by1957 he was Professor of Sacred Liturgy in the Lateran University.

In 1960 Pope John XXIII appointed Bugnini to the post of Secretary to the Preparatory Commission on the Liturgy for the Second Vatican Council (Vatican II) – a position which enabled him to exert considerable influence upon the destiny of the Church. He was closely involved with the drafting of the preparatory *schema* (plural *schemata*), the draft document that was to be placed before the Council Fathers for discussion.

The Bugnini Schema, as it was called, was accepted by a plenary session of the Liturgical Preparatory Commission in a vote on 13 January 1962. But Cardinal Gaetano Cicognani, the president of the commission and the Vatican secretary of state, refused to sign it when he realized how far-reaching its proposed reforms were.

Bugnini knew that unless the cardinal could be persuaded to sign the schema, it would be blocked. He quickly arranged for approaches to be made to the pope, who was persuaded to instruct Cardinal Cicognani not to return until the schema had been signed. The old cardinal was reportedly in tears as he waved the document in the air and said: 'They want me to sign this but I don't know if I want to.' Then he laid the document on his desk, picked up a pen, and signed it. Four days later he was dead.

However, Bugnini's victory was short-lived. Pope John suddenly ordered

Father Bugnini's dismissal from his chair at the Lateran University, his secretaryship of the Liturgical Commission and from all the other senior positions he held. The reasons for this action have never been made public but they must have been very serious indeed to cause this tolerant pontiff to act in so public and drastic a manner against a priest who had held such an influential position in the preparation for the Vatican Council.

But that was not the end of the matter. A small but influential group of figures within the Church emerged to support Bugnini's Schema. Father Edward Schillebeeckx, the Belgian Professor of Dogmatics at the Catholic University of Nijmegen, described it as 'an admirable piece of work'. It was eventually passed without substantial alteration, receiving the almost unanimous approval of the Council Fathers on 7 December 1962, and became Vatican II's 'Constitution on the Sacred Liturgy'.

But the Constitution contained no more than general guidelines. To achieve total victory, Father Bugnini and his supporters needed to obtain the power to interpret and implement it.

Pope John XXIII died in June 1963, and then on St John's day – the summer solstice – of that year a new pope was chosen. Giovanni Montini, from a noble family well known for their Masonic associations, became Pope Paul VI.

Seven months later Father Bugnini was appointed to the crucially important position of Secretary of the Concilium. Why the new Pope Paul VI chose to promote Bugnini to this high office after he had been prevented from achieving it by Pope John XXIII is unknown.

Father Bugnini's influence was greatly increased when he was appointed to another high office, that of Secretary of the Sacred Congregation for Divine Worship. He was now in the most influential position possible to consolidate his planned changes. Other heads of commissions, congregations, and the Concilium came and went – but Father Bugnini always remained in office.

In 1974 Archbishop Bugnini explained that his reforms had four stages. Firstly, the switch from the use of Latin in the liturgy to the local language of worshippers; secondly, the reform of the liturgical books; thirdly, the translation of the liturgical books; and fourthly, the adaptation or 'incarnation' of the Roman form of the liturgy into the usages and mentality of each individual church. This process amounted to the complete elimination of any remaining vestiges of the old Latin Roman rite.

But then, at the very moment of his triumph, Bugnini – by now an archbishop – was again dismissed. At first the outside world could not understand what had happened. Then, in April 1976, Tito Casini, Italy's leading Catholic writer, publicly accused Bugnini of being a Freemason.

The evidence that Bugnini was a Freemason was presented directly to Pope Paul VI, who was most probably a Freemason himself. But the pope was warned that if action was not taken at once, the matter would be made public.[3] Pope Paul had no choice; Archbishop Bugnini was removed from office and his entire Congregation was dissolved.

Could it be that Freemasons have, in such recent times, changed the Roman Catholic Church beyond recognition? It appears so. What is more, the all-encompassing changes in Roman Catholic worship smack of a Star Family determination to 'ally' Christian denominations and then to further connect them to other belief patterns that are not of the Judeo-Christian family.

One senior Vatican official, Cardinal Ratzinger, the head of the Congregation for the Doctrine of the Faith (the successor to the Inquisition), said: 'I am convinced that the crisis in the Church that we are experiencing is to a large extent due to the disintegration of the liturgy.' Ratzinger blamed Freemasonry, and never forgave it. In November 1983 he declared:

> The Church's negative judgment in regard to Masonic associ-
> ations remains unchanged since their principles have always
> been considered irreconcilable with the doctrine of the
> Church and therefore membership in them remains
> forbidden. Catholics who enrol in Masonic associations are in
> a state of grave sin and may not receive Holy Communion.
> Local ecclesiastical authorities do not have the faculty to
> pronounce a judgment on the nature of Masonic associations
> which may include a diminution of the above-mentioned
> judgment.

Cardinal Ratzinger is, of course, now Pope Benedict XVI.

The Death of a Pope

On 26 August 1978, the 65-year-old Cardinal Albino Luciani became Pope John Paul I in succession to Paul VI. It was to be a papacy of just 33 days and the circumstances of his death gave rise to a number of conspiracy theories involving Freemasons.

Prior to his elevation to the throne of St Peter, Luciani had been considered a conservative. For example, he had been a public defender of Pope Paul VI's encyclical on sexual mores which restated the Catholic Church's opposition to artificial birth control. But once in office, the new pope began to express reservations and caused considerable worry within the Vatican when he met with representatives of the United Nations to discuss the issue of overpopulation in the Third World.

Some in the liberal wing of the Church expressed the hope that the new pontiff would reverse the ruling on contraception. However, in a private conversation with Chris Knight, a Vatican official claimed that the purpose of the Roman Catholic Church's continued opposition to contraception is to maintain population numbers in the 'Christian' world in case of a future great war against Islam. Such long-term plans would be undone if the Church ever allowed contraception, because once implemented it would be virtually impossible to put in place again.

But John Paul I died without issuing any such reversal of doctrine. His successor's continued support for the ban on artificial birth control has led some to suggest that John Paul I was indeed murdered to prevent him taking this action. And the circumstances of his death do look rather suspicious.

The cause of death as officially reported by the Vatican was 'possibly associated with a myocardial infarction'. This adds nothing, as this is a heart attack – the most common cause of death in the world. Without under-standing what *caused* the assumed heart attack it is impossible to know whether it was due to a natural or an unnatural cause. We will never know because no autopsy was performed. The Vatican insisted that a papal autopsy was prohibited under Vatican law – yet it is known that an autopsy was carried out on the remains of Pope Pius VIII.

A number of close friends of the deceased pope claim that they were ordered out of the way whilst some kind of inspection was made of the corpse, perhaps, some suggest, a full autopsy. If so, then the fact that no results were subsequently released might suggest that some evidence had been found that John Paul's death was not due to natural causes, but due either to murder or perhaps an accidental overdose of medication to which the Vatican might not wish to admit.

The Vatican's handling of several other events surrounding the death provoked further suspicion. It claimed that a papal secretary had discovered the dead pope, whereas it was a nun bringing him coffee who made the initial discovery. Furthermore it claimed he had been reading Thomas à Kempis' *Imitation of Christ,* yet the pope's copy of that book was in Venice at the time. The Vatican certainly lied about the time of death, and conflicting stories were told as to his health. There were suggestions that his ill health was due to heavy smoking – yet he had never been a smoker.

The Vatican Bank Connection

The British crime investigator and author David Yallop claims that he was invited to examine the circumstances of John Paul I's death 'at the request of certain individuals resident in the Vatican City who were disturbed by a cover-up'. He carried out a three-year investigation before publishing his findings,[4] in which he argued that the pope was in 'potential danger' because of alleged corruption in the Istituto per le Opere Religiose (commonly known as the Vatican Bank), which owned many shares in another bank, the Banco Ambrosiano.

Yallop identified a crime involving two senior executives of Banco Ambrosiano, namely Archbishop Paul Marcinkus, the chairman of the Vatican Bank, and Banco Ambrosiano chairman Roberto Calvi – who was later found hanged under Blackfriars Bridge in London. Yallop also brought the spotlight to bear on a Freemasonic lodge called Propaganda Due (P2) that allegedly operated inside the Vatican.

The Banco Ambrosiano had been founded in 1896 as a Catholic bank to counterbalance Italy's 'lay' banks, and it soon became known as the 'priests' bank'. Roberto Calvi was appointed chairman in 1975 and expanded the bank's interests by creating a number of offshore companies in the Bahamas and South America, and becoming involved in a number of business ventures. Calvi also became involved with the Vatican Bank and was close to Marcinkus. The complex network of overseas banks and companies set up by Calvi allowed him to move money out of Italy, to inflate share prices, and to secure massive unsecured loans.

The P2 Masonic lodge had been founded in 1877, under the authority of the Grand Orient of Italy, as a lodge primarily for the benefit of Freemasons visiting the Vatican. In the mid-1960s it only had some 14 permanent members, but when Licio Gelli became Worshipful Master of the lodge in the 1960s he rapidly expanded its membership to over 1,000 Masons drawn from Italy's business and governmental elite. Such sudden and rapid expansion was unusual and the Grand Orient of Italy, suspecting some illegal activity, withdrew the lodge's charter in 1976, banning Gelli from having any further involvement with Freemasonry.

However, P2 continued in an unofficial capacity and it was raided by the police in 1981, when they found incriminating evidence against Calvi, who was then arrested, tried and sentenced to four years in jail. However, he was released pending an appeal, and kept his position at the bank.

The police raid uncovered a membership list of the P2 lodge with over 900 names on it. The Freemasons involved included many leading politicians, and a number of senior military officers. Notably, the list included Silvio Berlusconi, who would later become Italian prime minister and Victor Emmanuel, Prince of Naples and the head of Italy's former ruling dynasty, the house of Savoy – which we firmly believe to be a Star Family.

Another document found by the police was entitled *Piano di Rinascita Democratica* ('Democratic Rebirth Plan') which was a declaration of the lodge's grand plan of forming a new political and economic elite to lead Italy towards a more authoritarian form of democracy. This led to the fall of the Italian government and the sacking of all senior figures in the secret services, because rightly or wrongly they became associated with the plan.

In 1982, while Calvi was still free, pending appeal, it was discovered that the Banco Ambrosiano could not account for over 1.25 billion dollars. Calvi fled to London. His personal secretary committed suicide by jumping from her office window. When Calvi was found hanging from Blackfriars Bridge on 18 June the circumstances did not suggest suicide, although that was the verdict of the British inquest. The Banco Ambrosiano soon collapsed, and the Vatican eventually agreed to pay out a substantial sum to its creditors but without accepting liability.

These are muddy waters indeed. But it seems that Freemasonry and the Vatican have been bedfellows for many years despite their apparent dichotomy of purpose. Both are secretive in their own way and both have, or do, seek to influence the future of humankind. In a conversation with a Roman Catholic priest, we argued that it was doubtful that many cardinals actually believe in the myth of Christ – or even in the existence of an interactive God. We were stunned to receive the reply that that was probably a fair assessment and that the Vatican's mission was today more political than theological.

It seems to us self-evident that there are two distinctly different factions at work within the Vatican. Whilst on the one hand these might be viewed as nothing more than the expected liberals and conservatives, our historical hindsight demonstrates a possible battle inside the ruling elite of Catholicism that has been taking place since medieval times. There is no doubt that Star Family members have, at times, enjoyed elevated positions inside the Vatican, and that several popes have clearly been Star Family members. The events surrounding recent dramatic changes in Catholic forms of worship, the death of Pope John Paul I and the whole Calvi incident might well indicate that Star Family presence is still strong behind those ancient and sacred walls.

A Developing World

Governments and global organizations seek to direct the future for us all. And either because of, or in spite of them, life is getting better for most people in the Western world and a little more hopeful for those in third world countries.

Hard though it is to achieve global agreement, people and governments are striving to find common policies to counteract the injustices of the past, not only against our fellow human beings but also against the very planet on which we live. In the West, at least, individual responsibility for matters that once devolved entirely onto the elite ruling factions, has now shifted, giving us all some sort of say in our own destinies and those of our fellows. In times of crisis, ordinary people in the West now rush to help feed the hungry and to cure the sick in far-off places to which they have no direct, personal connection. Of course there are many occasions on which we still observe people and states acting out of self-interest, greed, hypocrisy and double-dealing can be seen to be a prime motivation, but the mere fact that we realize this to be the case means that we can do better and can continue to strive to make the world a fairer and more equitable place. As the Dalai Lama has said, the fact that 'the news' is nearly always bad news, means that good news, or even ordinary news, is far too commonplace to be worth reporting.

By any definition we are still far from establishing the New Jerusalem held in the hearts and minds of visionaries over the last 3,000 years. But the concept stays alive in our minds and while there is a long, long way to go we must remember the old Chinese proverb: every journey starts with the first step.

The Bilderberg Group

Perhaps the Star Families are still strong in the upper echelons of Freemasonry, but we doubt it. As we have suggested, the Craft has run its course for them. It is possible, however, that Star Family influence has been involved with the development of the 'Bilderberg Group', an unofficial annual invitation-only conference of around 100 influential people in the fields of business, academia, media and politics. This elite assembly has met annually since 1954, for most of that time in secret, at exclusive resorts throughout the world, normally in Europe, although sometimes in the US or Canada.

The original intention of the Bilderberg Group was to further the understanding between Western Europe and North America. Each year, a 'steering committee' devises the select invitation list with a maximum of 100 names. The location of their annual meeting is no longer secret, and the agenda and list of participants are openly available to the public. But, to encourage complete openness among the participants, the topics of the meetings are kept secret and those attending pledge not to divulge what was discussed.

Recent or current Bilderberg members include: former President Bill Clinton, Tony Blair, Angela Merkel (chancellor of Germany), Paul Martin (ex-Canadian prime minister), Stephen Harper (Canadian prime minister), Romano Prodi (Italian prime minister and former president of the European Commission), Henry Kissinger (ex-US secretary of state),

Richard Perle (ex-US secretary of defense) and Donald Rumsfeld (US secretary of defense).

We strongly believe that the Star Families are present because the Bilderberg Group appears to demonstrate a sense of direction that is beyond any one obvious agency. The Bilderberg Group itself may have little power to alter anything substantial in the world but its combined membership contains individuals who are either prime movers within Western society or who have significant influence on decision-making at high levels. Specifically, powerful members of the Bilderberg Group, such as Clinton or Blair, may not actually be Star Family members themselves, but might well be influenced by Bilderberg members who are.

The Israel Issue

One other important question needs to be examined before we conclude our survey. Why does the US support the state of Israel when it gets nothing in return except for the increasing frustration of the Muslim world, which in some radical Islamic quarters is now expressed as terrorism? The disaster of 9/11 would probably not have happened if the Americans had not given money, arms and political support to Israel over many decades, while apparently showing considerably less enthusiasm for resolving the grievances of the Palestinians.

For years, observers around the world have been perplexed as to why Washington has maintained its large-scale military, financial, and diplomatic support for Israel. Well over $3 billion in military and economic aid is sent annually to Israel and is rarely questioned in Congress by liberals who normally challenge US aid to governments that engage in widespread violations of human rights, or by conservatives who generally oppose foreign aid of any kind. Whilst all Western countries agree that Israel has a right to exist in peace and maintain security, no other country provides arms or diplomatic support to the degree of the US. The White House often finds itself alone in its wholehearted support of Israel at the United Nations and in other international forums when objections are raised over what are seen as Israeli violations of international law.

Although US backing of successive Israeli governments, like most foreign policy decisions, is often rationalized on moral grounds, there is little evidence that moral imperatives play more of a determining role in guiding US policy in the Middle East than in any other part of the world. Most Americans do share a moral commitment to Israel's survival as a state, but this would not account for the level of financial, military, and diplomatic support provided by their government. American aid to Israel goes well beyond protecting Israel's security needs within its internationally recognized borders. US assistance includes support for policies in occupied territories that often violate established legal and ethical standards of international behaviour.

One simple explanation often put forward is that this single-minded US support for Israel is driven by rich American Jews who put pressure on successive governments to maintain and increase such support for their spiritual homeland. But this seems a very improbable answer. We suspect that there is as much anti-Semitism in Washington as there is support for the 'Jewish cause' – and most politicians will surely be ambivalent on the issue. Surely, the price of US support is far too high to be due to a lobbying of a minority group, even one as influential as the 'Jewish business community'.

If the so-called 'Jewish lobby' had been the cause of US backing for Israel, one would expect such support to have been there from the founding of the Jewish state in 1948. However, US military and economic aid did not begin until after the 1967 war. The fact is that US military assistance to Israel only arrived in earnest after Israel had proved itself to be by far the dominant force in the region surrounding Jerusalem – the ancient Holy Land. The Israelis had shown that they could defend themselves against the surrounding states, whether the latter acted singly or together, and that they were clearly going to be the long-term rulers of Jerusalem.

It seems to us that Washington has been more interested in backing whoever controls the ancient Holy Land than it is in supporting the modern Jewish state in particular. The pattern of US aid to Israel tells its own story. Immediately after Israel's decisive victory in the 1967 war, US aid increased by *450 per cent*.

Then, following the 1970–71 civil war in Jordan, when Israel's potential to curb revolutionary movements outside its borders became apparent, US aid increased further by a staggering 700 per cent. And again, after Israel successfully repelled the Arab armies that launched a surprise attack in the 1973 Yom Kippur war, US military aid went up by yet another 800 per cent.

The more that the Israeli government proved that it dominated the region, the greater US aid became. In 1983, when the US and Israel signed memoranda of understanding on strategic co-operation and military planning and then conducted their first joint naval and air force exercises, Israel was given an additional $1.5 billion in economic aid and $500,000 towards the development of a new jet fighter.

This support for what appears to be the winning horse in the race to control the Holy Land continues unabated at the present time. And that is in spite of the cautionary words of high-profile conservatives in the George W Bush administration (including former secretary of state Colin Powell) that an apparently unconditional backing of Israel's government would make it more difficult to get the full co-operation of Arab governments in the campaign against the al-Qaeda network.

Another factor that has to be acknowledged is that the Christian right in the US, representing tens of millions of voters for the Republican Party, has given widespread support for Israel. Their viewpoint seems to be based on a messianic theology that sees the return of Jews to the Holy Land as a precursor for the second coming of the Messiah. The battle between Israel and its Arab neighbours is, in their eyes, simply a continuation of the battle between the Israelites and the Philistines – a precursor to the coming of a messianic new age: the dawn of a New World Order.

And maybe this is nearer to the real motivation of the US than one might expect.

We find it strange that the only unquestioning support for President George W Bush's 2003 invasion of Iraq came from British Prime Minister Tony Blair. It was as though the two men had some evidence that was being withheld from the public and all other national leaders – even within NATO. And once again, when Israel invaded Lebanon in 2006, these two influential Western leaders were, to begin with, virtually alone in making no attempt to establish a ceasefire, despite worldwide calls for one.

But both men are Christians. The president is a Methodist and Tony Blair an Anglican but with widely reported Roman Catholic sympathies (his wife, a prominent lawyer, is a Catholic and he has attended mass). Could they *really* know something very secret that affects Israel? Could there be some bigger plan being played out that involves, or has been instigated by, the Star Families?

The End Game: A World United

Our combined dozens of years of research have involved looking at large amounts of complex information. Using forensic techniques, we have been able to identify clear patterns in history that, as we have shown, reveal the presence of a group we have called collectively the 'Star Families'. When the circumstances of the past are looked at holistically, rather than in an artificially pigeonholed manner, it becomes absurd to deny that events such as those that occurred in Europe and the Holy Land in the 12th century are unconnected.

However, it is much harder to see one's own time with such clarity because some revealing key events may not yet have happened. It is therefore necessary for us to speculate a little. Our researches have led us to understand, and even empathize with, the values and objectives of this unseen group of power brokers founded in the time of King Solomon. So, in speculating about the present and future, we are able to ask ourselves: what would we do if we were them?

The greatest objective of the Star Families is to unify – to create a single world over which God can rule. They wish to bring down international barriers and unify man's relationship with God without interfering with any person's right to follow his or her own religious preferences. They want a tolerant and prosperous global society where trade is fair and wealth and justice are distributed with equity.

Equitable trade and shared prosperity, they believe, are a far better means of preventing war than accumulated weapons and threats of destruction. So, if we were the leaders of the Star Families today, we would look to create economically interdependent blocs of states that can evolve both in breadth and depth.

For example, we would seek to convert a recently warring group of neighbouring countries into a trading bloc. This would grow in depth by increasingly aligning social structures such as trade legislation, criminal law, foreign policy and taxation. At the same time we would seek to increase the breadth of the bloc by attracting surrounding countries until a whole region or continent comes to see itself as a single entity – one people united.

Earlier we looked at the creation of the European Economic Community in the wake of the Marshal Plan (*see* page 267). Today, in a single generation, the European Economic Community has become a quasi-confederation of 27 countries with a shared future under the banner of the European Union. Eight of the admissions are states that were previously part of the Warsaw pact – recent enemies of the West and satellite nations of the Soviet Union, and 12 of those countries already have a shared currency in the form of the euro. Croatia, Macedonia and the Muslim state of Turkey are also poised to join the European Union. How long before even Russia applies for membership?

It is interesting to note that the euro was introduced with a value of almost exactly one US dollar. This can scarcely have been mere chance: such a step would be obvious to anyone, or any group, contemplating a potential world currency. As Paul Volcker, the former chair of the US Federal Reserve, said: 'A global economy requires a global currency.'

How many years will it be before the United States of America and the United States of Europe converge their currencies? Not too many, we suspect.

And when Canada and Mexico, the partners of the US in the new North American Free Trade Area, are eventually subsumed into the US and adopt the US dollar, as they surely will, will their citizens be offered an exchange rate of $1 to the peso and the Canadian dollar? Just as West Germany bravely offered one deutschmark for every near-worthless East German mark when the two Germanies were once more united?

Looking ahead one further generation the unified world will need a global capital. If we were Solomon's power brokers there would be only one choice: Jerusalem.

The city is at a crossroads politically and socially as well as physically. At the centre of the earth on any old map sits the city of Jerusalem. Even today it stands at the centre of Europe to the north, Africa to the south, Asia to the east and the Americas to the west. As a holy city for Judaism, Christianity and Islam it offers a unique, neutral location for a true New World Order.

We believe it probable that once the Israeli state has achieved a relatively stable relationship with its neighbours, someone in high office will discreetly propose that Jerusalem should become the new headquarters of the United Nations, a politically neutral ground belonging to no single country. That person is likely to be the secretary-general of the United Nations. He or she may speak the words but it will not be their idea. It will come from deep within the Star Families.

From there, with the convergence of nations and currencies, it will be a natural step to convert Jerusalem into the global capital of a United Earth.

King Solomon's vision will have been achieved, but in a way far beyond what he envisaged. The most enigmatic, and at times the saddest, city that has always been the navel of the planet will have attained its ultimate goal:

The harmonious union of humankind.

The Rosslyn Question

We have told the story of how we believe a small group of families have influenced the course of Western civilization since they spilled out into the world after the fall of Jerusalem in AD70. The evidence we have put forward is, we believe, too strong to be dismissed as a series of very odd coincidences.

Our research methodology is unusual in this day and age because it is holistic rather than specialist. We synthesize across boundaries between specialisms in a manner that modern academics would be unlikely to do. We are more 'historical detectives' than cataloguers of past events, such as one might find in the history department of a modern university. Yet there is no significant element of our evidence that is not either derived from those academically highly respectable sources or else is easily testable by scholars.

The investigation we have conducted has been long and hard and we are confident that we have clearly identified the same 'fingerprints' reappearing on key events over the last 2,000 years. There will be no shortage of people who will dismiss what we have to say, simply because it is not what they wish to believe. They will insist that the past is just a set of individual events that cannot be connected. But surely life is all about connections, influences, reactions, and sometimes conspiracies.

If the past is to be understood, each pivotal event has to be viewed in the broadest possible context to spot any underlying pattern. As one eminent scholar said to us, 'I can't say if you are right or not but you have joined up the dots of history better than anyone before.'

So, are we right?

We believe we have a persuasive case that provides the most cogent explanation for the way the world is today. There simply is no other theory that makes sense of all of the available evidence. Yet there is a potential proof that could, and should, be investigated.

And that is the tiny Scottish building known today as Rosslyn Chapel.

Over the years Chris Knight has taken a number of world-class experts to Rosslyn, and they have all shared our conviction that this is a very special structure. Those who understand ancient Jerusalem, its people and their Temple of Yahweh have immediately recognized the undoubted connection. Those who understand stone confirm it is made from the same seam of rock as Jerusalem's Temple.

The standard explanation – that Rosslyn is the lady chapel of an intended but never built collegiate church – is unquestionably wrong. The possibility of this theory being correct is precisely zero because, as Dr Miller of Cambridge University has pointed out (*see* Chapter 8), the west wall is not tied into the fabric of the main building and any attempt to build further would have resulted in the collapse of the entire structure.

Proponents of the collegiate theory will point to the 'foundations' for the collegiate church, which are said to exist on the surrounding hilltop. But in drawing attention to this evidence, they are strengthening our case. As we have explained, these foundations cannot possibly be what they seem, it confirms that Earl William Sinclair and his associates were deliberately setting out to fool people. They were obviously building something *unauthorized* that had to be kept secret from the world in general and the Church in particular.

Given that all the experts on ancient Judaism taken to Rosslyn (such as Philip Davies and James Charlesworth) confirm that it is not only Jewish in feel but specifically Herodian in its design, then surely our association of Rosslyn with the Jerusalem Temple has to be correct. And as the only words carved into the building are words that were central to the rebuilding of Zerubbabel's Temple in Jerusalem, we feel the case is beyond reasoned debate.

John Richie, who has lived all his life in the village in which Rosslyn sits, was originally a supporter of the standard explanation of the so-called chapel. Until, that is, he looked very closely at the subject himself and became an unexpected convert to the explanation expounded in this book. He and Alan Butler have recently brought new evidence to the fore as to why it is 'dedicated' to St Matthew, as we explain in Chapter Eight.[1]

In April 1996, on the occasion of the launch of Chris' book *The Hiram Key* at Rosslyn in April 1996, one of the four trustees of the building publicly stated that they would support an archaeological dig. The Dead Sea Scrolls scholar and archaeologist, Professor James Charlesworth, shared our belief that Essene scrolls were hidden below Rosslyn, and subsequently put forward a proposal for an investigation.

It did not happen.

But, with the weight of new evidence now available, we believe it is now unreasonable to continue to block such an important archaeological quest. Rosslyn must be properly examined.

We therefore call on all those involved with Rosslyn, particularly Historic Scotland, to enter into a public debate and be seen to evaluate the evidence with equity and justice. The obfuscation and deliberately disingenuous standard storyline must be set aside so that the real facts can be considered.

The world is now ready to face the reality of our past – and better understand our future. Those ancient and once very secret Jewish documents must be recovered.

Notes

Chapter 1

[1] According to the 1st-century historian, Josephus (*Antiquities of the Jews*, 2:10) Moses became a general of the Egyptian army fighting in a major war against the Ethiopians. In his book *The Works of Josephus*, William Whiston suggests that whilst the Bible itself does not specifically record that Moses was an Egyptian general, Acts 7:22 probably confirms this history.

[2] Deuteronomy 2:31–35

[3] Knight, C and Lomas, R: *Uriel's Machine*, Century, 1999

[4] The authors apologize to any Hindu readers who might find our well-intentioned explanation rather simplistic.

[5] The devil only really became a truly separate concept when the Christian Church transferred the responsibility for all evil to the fallen angel of light called Lucifer, and later also known as Satan (a word that originally meant 'adversary' in the Dead Sea Scrolls). Lucifer was the ancient name of Venus and the Church's action in blaming all bad things on Lucifer, the bringer of light and knowledge, was an attempt to besmirch ancient beliefs surrounding the veneration of Venus that did not fit in with their own interpretation of the story of Jesus. They were successful in this plan, as truth has indeed been turned on its head.

[6] Knight C and Lomas R: *The Book of Hiram*, Century, 2003

Chapter 2

[1] Daraul, A: *Secret Societies*, Tandem, 1969

[2] Schonfield, H: *The Essene Odyssey*, Element, 1984

[3] Josephus wrote in *Jewish Antiquities* (Book 18, Chapter 5, Paragraph 2): 'Now some of the Jews thought that the destruction of Herod's army came from God, and that very justly, as a punishment of what he did

against John, that was called the Baptist: for Herod slew him, who was a good man, and commanded the Jews to exercise virtue, both as to righteousness towards one another, and piety towards God, and so to come to baptism; for that the washing [with water] would be acceptable to him, if they made use of it, not [for] the putting away [or the remission] of some sins [only], but for the purification of the body; supposing still that the soul was thoroughly purified beforehand by righteousness. Now when [many] others came in crowds about him, for they were very greatly moved [or pleased] by hearing his words, Herod, who feared lest the great influence John had over the people might put it into his power and inclination to raise a rebellion (for they seemed ready to do any thing he should advise) thought it best, by putting him to death, to prevent any mischief he might cause, and not bring himself into difficulties, by sparing a man who might make him repent of it when it would be too late. Accordingly he was sent a prisoner, out of Herod's suspicious temper, to Machaerus, the castle I mentioned before, and was there put to death.'

4 1QM 11:16

5 Josephus: *Jewish War*, 2:8:10

6 Luke 7:22-23 and Matthew 11:4-5

7 Eisenman, R: *James, the Brother of Jesus,* Watkins Publishing, 2002

8 1Qs 1: 13–15 (Dead Sea Scrolls)

9 1Qs 12: 5

10 Galatians 1:15–16.

11 1 Corinthians 9: 2–25.

12 Brandon G F: *The fall of Jerusalem and the Christian Church,* S.P.C.K 1951

13 Furneaux R: *The Other Side of the Story*, Cassell, 1953

14 This and the preceding quotation are both from *The Jewish War*

Chapter 4

1 For a fuller discussion *see* Knight, C and Lomas, R: *The Book of Hiram,* Century, 2003

2 Fulk (or Fulcher) of Chartres, *Gesta Francorum Jerusalem Expugnantium*

3 Recorded by Orderic Vitals, a Star Family member and chronicler who later became a priest at Cluny in 1132.

Chapter 5

1 Kenyon, K M: *Digging up Jerusalem*, Benn, 1974

2 Allegro, J M: *The Treasure of the Copper Scroll,* Garden City, NY, Doubleday, 1960

[3] Allegro, J M: *The Dead Sea Scrolls and the Christian Myth*, Prometheus Books, 1984

[4] Herbert A S: *The Song of Solomon*, Peak's Commentary on the Bible, Nelson, 1963

[5] Castano, Engels, Haverkamp and Heberer: *The Jews of Europe in the Middle Ages*, Hatje Cantz, 2005

Chapter 6

[1] Bernier, F: *The Great Architects of Tiron, The Steps of Zion*, ULT, Arizona, 2005. The document in its entirety can be viewed at http://www.frontierpublishing.nl/fb_tiron.pdf

[2] Butler, A: *The Goddess, the Grail and the Lodge*, O Books, 2004; and *The Virgin and the Pentacle*, O Books, 2005

[3] Charpentier, L: *The Mysteries of Chartres Cathedral*, A B Academic Publishers, 1997

[4] Ochsendorf, J: 'Bridging the Void'. Reported in *New Scientist*, 10th June 2006

[5] See Chapter Ten.

[6] *New Cambridge Medieval History*, vol. 5, *c.*1198–*c.*1300, Cambridge University Press, 1999

[7] It is worth noting that the terms for 'pound' are still used colloquially in France (*livre*) and Germany (*Pfund*) for half a kilo (500g)

[8] See http://yale.edu/lawweb/avalon/jeffplan.htm

[9] For a full description see Knight, C, and Butler, A: *Civilization One*, Watkins, 2004

[10] Butler, A: *Sheep*, O Books, 2006

Chapter 7

[1] Butler, A, and Dafoe, S: *The Warriors and the Bankers*, Templar Publishing, Toronto, 1999

[2] It is interesting to note that the original name of the Templars was 'The Poor Fellow-soldiers of Christ and the Temple of Solomon'; they were never called 'The Poor Fellow-soldiers of *Jesus* Christ and the Temple of Solomon'.

Chapter 8

[1] 1 Kings 8:1–2.

[2] The mainstream Jewish calendar is lunar, so the start of any month cannot be tied down exactly to the Western solar calendar. Tishri falls in September or October, depending on the new Moon, since the first sighting of the Moon after its darkness heralds the start of a Jewish month. After the Babylonian exile most Jews adopted the Babylonian

lunar calendar and *Rosh HaShanah* (the New Year) moved to the autumn equinox from the spring equinox. But the Essenes retained the solar calendar. A letter found at Qumran decries the use of the lunar calendar that made the holy days fall on the wrong day of the week and month. In addition, the Qumran library included 18 copies of the Book of Jubilees, which describes the Essene solar calendar in detail. Indeed, it was the change in the calendar that caused the Essenes to separate themselves from the Jerusalem priesthood in the first place.

3 Cited in Wallace-Murphy, T: *An Illustrated Guide to Rosslyn Chapel*, The Friends of Rosslyn, 1993

4 Crawford, Barbara E: *William Sinclair, Earl of Orkney, and His Family: A Study in the Politics of Survival,* Edinburgh, 1985

5 See Knight, C: *The Hiram Key,* Arrow Books, 2006

6 Novelist Dan Brown seems to have been influenced by Chris's finding, because in *The Da Vinci Code* Brown describes Rosslyn Chapel as having a huge Seal of Solomon carved into the stone floor. It is not carved there, but it might as well have been.

7 See *The Hiram Key*

8 The books of Ezra and Nehemiah in the Catholic Bible were formerly known as the First and Second Books of Esdras (Esdras is a Greek form of Ezra). The non-canonical Book of Esdras was therefore called the Third Book of Esdras, but is now usually called the First Book of Esdras (1 Esdras) or just the Book of Esdras.

9 Confirmed by Tessa Ransford, Director of the Scottish Poetry Library.

Chapter 9

1 In *The Hiram Key*, Arrow Books, 2006

2 Information provided by Dr Jack Miller based on geological surveying information.

Chapter 10

1 Stevenson, D: *The Origins of Freemasonry: Scotland's Century 1590–1710,* Cambridge University Press, 1988

2 Note dated May 14, 1650, in the Public Records Office, London, State Papers A, Interregnum A

3 J Summerson: *Sir Christopher Wren, P.R.S.,* Notes and Records of the Royal Society of London

4 Gilbert, A: *The New Jerusalem,* Corgi, London, 2002

5 Lamentations 1:1

Chapter 11

1 Brown, R H: *Stellar Theology and Masonic Astronomy*, D Appleton and Co, New York, 1882

2 George Washington's Masonic apron may be seen in the Masonic Temple museum, Philadelphia.

3 For further details see Alan Butler's *The Virgin and the Pentacle*, O Books, 2005

4 David Ovason: *The Secret Zodiacs of Washington DC*, Arrow Books, 2000

Chapter 12

1 From the historical pages of the Grand Orient of France website http://www.godf.org/foreign/uk/index_uk.html

2 Freemasonry is consistent with, rather than an extension of, Christianity. Whilst many Freemasons are Christians the only prerequisite for membership is that an aspirant acknowledge the existence of a deity.

3 We take the word 'them' to mean Christianity of both sorts, Catholic and Protestant but it might equally mean the Catholic Church and the pope.

4 Crétineau-Joly, *The Roman Church and Revolution*, c.1860 Publisher unknown

5 Revelation 17:18 (King James Bible)

6 Shortly after becoming a Mason, at the outbreak of the American Civil War, Pike was commissioned as a brigadier-general and given a command in the Indian Territory where he trained three Confederate regiments of Indian cavalry. He was often seen wearing Indian regalia himself. Pike is the only Confederate military officer to be honoured with a statue in Washington, D.C.

Chapter 13

1 Rig Veda 1:164:46

2 Kipling, R: *Banquet Night*

3 Davies, M: *Liturgical Time Bombs In Vatican II*, Tan Books, 1998

4 Yallop D: *In God's Name*, Jonathan Cape, 1984

Postscript

1 Butler, A and Richie, J: *Rosslyn Revealed – A Library in Stone,* O Books, 2006

Time Line

BC

AD

1070	Hugues de Payen born
1071	Seljuk Turks take Jerusalem
1090	Bernard of Clairvaux born
1095	First Crusade starts
1099	Jerusalem taken by Crusaders; Godfrey of Bouillon elected chief
	Henri de St Clair takes the title Baron of Roslin (Rosslyn)
	Death of Pope Urban II
1100	Death of Godfrey de Bouillon, first king of Jerusalem
	Death of William II of England
	Baldwin I made king of Jerusalem
1104	Hugues de Payen travels to Jerusalem with Count Hugues of Champagne
1113	Bernard joins the Cistercian Order
1114	Hugues de Payen and Hugues of Champagne again visit Jerusalem
1115	Bernard becomes abbot of Clairvaux
1118	Nine knights under Hugues de Payen start to excavate the ruined Temple
1120	Fulk of Anjou takes oath to join Templars
1125	Hugues of Champagne takes oath in Jerusalem, making eleven Templars
1128	Council of Troyes grants rule to Templars
1136	Hugues de Payen dies
1140	Templars take scrolls from the Temple to Scotland
1285	Philip IV the Fair succeeds as French king, aged 17
1292/3	Jacques de Molay elected last Grand Master of the Templars
1307	Philip IV arrests all Knights Templar in France
1447	Documents from under the Jerusalem Temple now at Rosslyn
1598	First documented minutes of a Masonic lodge
1601	James VI of Scots becomes a Mason
1603	James VI becomes James I of England
1625	James I dies; Charles I becomes king
1641	Sir Robert Moray initiated into Freemasonry at Newcastle
1642	The English Civil War starts
1646	The end of the main phase of the English Civil War at Oxford
	Elias Ashmole initiated in Warrington Lodge

1649   Charles I executed; republic (the Commonwealth) established

1658   Oliver Cromwell dies

1660   Charles II restored as king of England

1688   'Glorious Revolution' in Britain: James II flees; William III and Mary II joint rulers

1714   First recorded minutes of the Grand Lodge of York

1715   First failed Jacobite uprising to restore the Stuart line

1717   Formation of Grand Lodge of London

1724   Formation of Irish Grand Lodge

1736   Formation of Scottish Grand Lodge

1745   Second Jacobite uprising

1801   The Supreme Council of the thirty-third degree for the United States of America is formed

1813   Formation of United Grand Lodge of England

1877   The 'Propaganda II' (P2) Masonic lodge founded in the Vatican

1947   Discovery of the Dead Sea Scrolls at Qumran

1951   Excavation of Qumran starts

1954   Bilderberg Group of world intellectuals and political elite formed

1955   The Copper Scroll opened and deciphered as an inventory of hidden treasures

1976   Reformer of the Catholic mass, Archbishop Bugnini, accused of being a Freemason

1978   Pope John Paul I dies 33 days after taking office

1982   Roberto Calvi found hanging from Blackfriars Bridge

1991   First public access to full collection of the Dead Sea Scrolls

Bibliography

Note: Extracts from the Bible are taken from the Authorised (King James) Version of 1611.

Allegro, J M: *The Dead Sea Scrolls and the Christian Myth.* Prometheus Books, 1984

Allegro, J M: *The Treasure of the Copper Scroll.* Garden City, New York, Doubleday, 1960

Bernier, F: *The Great architects of Tiron. The Steps of Zion.* ULT, Arizona, 2005

Brandon, G F: *The Fall of Jerusalem and the Christian Church.* London, SPCK, 1951

Brown, R H: *Stellar Theology and Masonic Astronomy.* New York, D. Appleton & Co., 1882

Butler, A and Defoe, S: *The Warriors and the Bankers.* Templar Publishing, Toronto, 1999

Butler, A: *Sheep.* O Books, 2006

Butler, A: *The Goddess, the Grail and the Lodge.* O Books, 2004

Butler, A: *The Virgin and the Pentacle.* O Books, 2005

Castano, Engels, Havercamp and Heberer: *The Jews of Europe in the Middle Ages.* Hatje Cantz, 2005

Charpentier, L: *The Mysteries of Chartres Cathedral.* AB Academic Publishers, 1997

Crawford, Barbara E: *William Sinclair, Earl of Orkney, and his Family: A Study in the Politics of Survival.* Edinburgh, 1985

Crétineau-Joli: *The Roman Church and Revolution.* Publisher unknown. *c.*1860

Daraul, A: *A History of Secret Societies.* Tandem, 1969

Davies, M: *Liturgical Time Bombs in Vatican ll.* Tan Books, 1998

Eisenman, R H: *James, the Brother of Jesus.* London, Watkins, 2002

Furneaux, R: *The Other Side of the Story.* London, Cassell, 1953

Gilbert, A: *The New Jerusalem.* London, Corgi, 2002

Herbert, A S: *Peak's Commentary on the Bible: The Song of Solomon.* London, Nelson, 1963

Kenyon, K M: *Digging up Jerusalem.* London, Benn, 1974

Kipling, R: *Banquet Night*

Knight, C and Butler A: *Civilization One.* London, Watkins, 2004

Knight, C and Lomas, R: *The Book of Hiram.* London, Century, 2003

Knight, C and Lomas, R: *Uriel's Machine.* London, Century, 1999

Knight, C and Lomas, R: *The Hiram Key.* London, Arrow Books, 2006

Miller J Dr: 'Geological surveying information' *New Cambridge Medieval History, Vol 5.* Cambridge University Press, 1999

Ochsendorf, J: *Bridging the Voice.* Reported in *New Scientist,* June 10, 2006

Ovason, D: *The Secret Zodiacs of Washington DC.* London, Arrow Books, 2000

Schonfield, H: *The Essene Odyssey.* Shaftesbury, England, Element,1984

Stevenson, D: *The Origins of Freemasonry: Scotland's Century 1590–1710.* Cambridge University Press, 1988

Summerson, J: *Sir Christopher Wren PRS.* Notes and Records of the Royal Society of London

Wallace-Murphy, T: *An Illustrated Guide to Rosslyn Chapel.* Publisher and date unknown

Whiston, William: *The Works of Josephus.* Hendrickson Publishers, inc., 1987

Williamson, G A (trans): *Josephus and The Jewish War.* Harmondsworth, England, Penguin, 1981

Yallon, D: *In Gods Name.* London, Jonathan Cape, 1984

Index